CURTIS BROWN, L̲T̲D̲
13, King Street, Covent Garden, London.

Marie Fedorovna

EMPRESS OF RUSSIA

Marie Fedorovna

EMPRESS OF RUSSIA

E. E. P. TISDALL

Illustrated

THE JOHN DAY COMPANY
NEW YORK

Contents

Illustrations

All following page 128

Marie Fedorovna, Empress of Russia

Alexander II

Alexander III

Marie Fedorovna and her sister Alexandra

Imperial Romanoff family

The victims of Ekaterinburg

Nicholas II

Alexandra Fedorovna

The Dowager Empress in exile

TREE OF THE IMPERIAL ROMANOFFS

SHOWING LINES OF DESCENT IMPORTANT IN THIS STORY

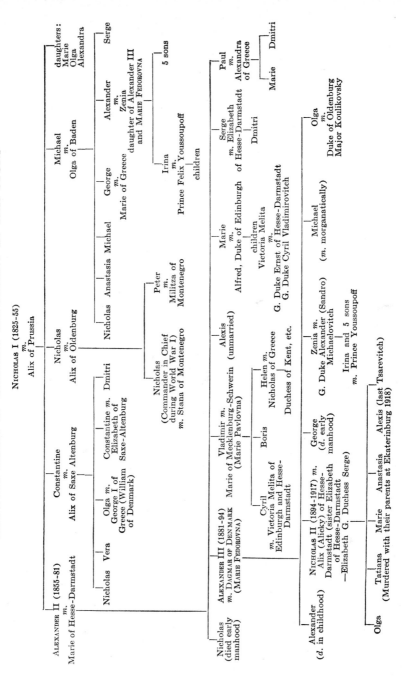

AN ALPHABETICAL WHO'S WHO

of members of the Romanoff family who play some part in this story, with relationships, parentage, etc. The reader may sometimes find this useful for reference as various family names recur.

Following the Russian custom, Romanoffs were commonly referred to not only by their Christian names but with the principal Christian name of their fathers added after this. Thus: Michael the son of G. Duke Michael was Michael Michaelovitch; Vladimir the son of Alexander II was Vladimir Alexandrovitch; Dmitri son of G. Duke Serge was Dmitri Sergovitch; Olga daughter of G. Duke Constantine was Olga Constantinovna (fem.); Tatiana daughter of Nicholas II was Tatiana Nicholaevna, etc.

Alexander II (Emancipator of the Serfs), born 1818, son of Nicholas I and Alix of Prussia. He married Marie of Hesse-Darmstadt (Marie Alexandrovna) in 1841 and succeeded to the throne in 1855. In 1880, shortly after Marie Alexandrovna's death, he married morganatically his mistress, Catherine Dolgorousky, whom he named Princess Yourievsky. Assassinated by Nihilists 1881.

Alexander III ("Sasha"), born 1845, second son of Alexander II and Marie of Hesse-Darmstadt (Marie Alexandrovna). He married DAGMAR of Denmark (MARIE FEDEROVNA) in 1866. Became Tsarevitch in 1865 on premature death of elder brother Nicholas, being affianced to DAGMAR of Denmark at his brother's deathbed. Succeeded to throne on assassination of his father in 1881. Died 1894. His son Nicholas II was the last Emperor.

10

Alexander Michaelovitch, G. Duke ("Sandro"), son of G. Duke Michael, the youngest brother of Alexander II. Born 1866. In 1894 he married G. Duchess Zenia, eldest daughter of MARIE FEDOROVNA, and was intimately connected with his cousin Nicholas, the last Emperor, during the early years of his reign. Five sons and one daughter.

Alexandra Fedorovna, Empress ("Alicky"), third daughter of G. Duke Louis of Hesse-Darmstadt and Prs. Alice of Great Britain. Born 1872, married Nicholas II, last Emperor, in 1894, murdered at Ekaterinburg 1918. Five children.

Alexis Alexandrovitch, G. Duke, fourth son of Alexander II and Marie of Hesse-Darmstadt (Marie Alexandrovna) and brother of Alexander III ("Sasha"). Alexis never married, followed a naval career but was chiefly noted for a life of amorous intrigues.

Alexis Nicholaevitch, last Tsarevitch of Imperial Russia, fifth and youngest child of Nicholas II and Alix ("Alicky") of Hesse-Darmstadt (Alexandra Fedorovna). Born 1904, suffered from hemophilia. His rights to throne disclaimed by Nicholas II upon abdication in 1917. Murdered at Ekaterinburg 1918.

Anastasia Nicholaevna, G. Duchess, fourth daughter of Nicholas II, last Emperor. Born 1901, murdered Ekaterinburg 1918.

Constantine Nicholaevitch, G. Duke, brother of Alexander II, suspected of Nihilist plots against throne, married Alix of Saxe-Altenburg. Great-grandfather of the Duchess of Kent through his daughter Olga, the first Queen of Greece.

Cyril Vladimirovitch, G. Duke, eldest son of G. Duke Vladimir (brother of Alexander III) and Marie Pavlovna. He married in 1906 Victoria Melita, daughter of Alfred Duke of Edinburgh and G. Duchess Marie of Russia, after her divorce from G. Duke Ernst of Hesse-Darmstadt. The international scandal caused Nicholas II to banish the couple from Russia for several years.

Dmitri Pavlovitch, G. Duke, only son of G. Duke Paul (brother of Alexander III) and Prs. Alexandra of Greece. His mother died at his birth and he and his sister were virtually adopted by Elizabeth G. Duchess Serge, who was childless. After the murder of G. Duke Serge in 1905, G. Duchess Elizabeth took the Veil and Dmitri and his sister became wards of the Emperor and Empress and lived with the Imperial Family.

Dmitri assisted Pr. Felix Youssoupoff in the murder of Rasputin in 1917, escaped from Russia after the Revolution to the British Forces in the Middle East. He married an American, d. 1942.

Elizabeth, Prs. of Hesse-Darmstadt and G. Duchess Serge ("Titinka"), daughter of G. Duke Louis and Prs. Alice of Great Britain. Married G. Duke Serge, brother of Alexander III, in 1884, and was instrumental in bringing about the marriage of her sister "Alicky" (Alexandra Fedorovna) with Nicholas II, the last Emperor. After the assassination of her husband in 1905 G. Duchess Elizabeth took the veil, founding the Order of Mary and Martha, the only working order of nuns in Russia. She was murdered by the Bolsheviks in 1918, and has since been acclaimed by many Russians as a saint. Her only son, Dmitri, became a ward of Nicholas II and grew up with the imperial family. He was one of the murderers of Rasputin.

George Michaelovitch, G. Duke, son of G. Duke Nicholas, the brother of Alexander II. George was brother of G. Duke Alexander ("Sandro"), who was son-in-law of MARIE FEDOROVNA.

Helen Vladimirovna, G. Duchess, only daughter of G. Duke Vladimir (brother of Alexander III) and Marie Pavlovna. She married Pr. Nicholas of Greece in 1901. The Duchess of Kent is her youngest daughter.

Irina Alexandrovna, Prs., daughter of G. Duke Alexander ("Sandro") and G. Duchess Zenia (eldest daughter of MARIE FEDOROVNA). Born in 1895, she married Pr. Felix Youssoupoff, heir of one of the richest and oldest Russian families, in 1914. Empress MARIE FEDOROVNA always spoke of Irina as her favorite grandchild.

Marie, Duchess of Edinburgh, only daughter of Alexander II and Marie Alexandrovna and sister of Alexander III. Born in 1855, she married Alfred, Duke of Edinburgh, second son of Q. Victoria, in 1874. Had two daughters; one, Victoria Melita, after being divorced from G. Duke Ernst of Hesse-Darmstadt, married G. Duke Cyril of Russia in 1906, and the other, Marie, became Queen of Rumania.

Marie Alexandrovna, Empress, Prs. of Hesse-Darmstadt. Married Alexander II (then Tsarevitch) in 1841. Six sons, one daughter. Died of cancer in 1880.

MARIE FEDOROVNA, Empress, Prs. Dagmar of Denmark ("Minnie"), second daughter of Christian IX and Louise of Hesse-Cassel. Her elder sister was Queen Alexandra of Great Britain; her brother Frederick became King of Denmark in 1906 and her second brother William ("Willy") was elected as George I of Greece. Thus she was at one time sister-in-law to two queens, Greece and Denmark, and to Edward VII of Great Britain. Born in 1847, she married Alexander III ("Sasha"), and was famous as Dowager Empress of Russia from 1894 to 1917. Died 1928.

Marie Nicholaevna, G. Duchess, third daughter of Nicholas II, last Emperor, and Alexandra Fedorovna ("Alicky"). Born in 1899, she was murdered by the Bolsheviks at Ekaterinburg 1918.

Marie Pavlovna, G. Duchess, Prs. of Mecklenburg-Schwerin. In 1872 she married G. Duke Vladimir, eldest brother of Alexander III. She was at one time suspected of being a spy of Bismarck, who had called her "the cleverest girl in Germany." She was celebrated as leader of imperial society and was both a close friend and a rival of MARIE FEDOROVNA. She was great-grandmother of the Duchess of Kent, her only daughter, Helen, marrying Pr. Nicholas of Greece. Cyril, her eldest son, married Victoria Melita, the divorced daughter of the Duke of Edinburgh, causing a scandal and family quarrel resulting in the temporary banishment of the couple.

Michael Alexandrovitch ("Mischa"), G. Duke, a son of Alexander III and MARIE FEDOROVNA. Born in 1878, he contracted a morganatic marriage with Mme. Woulfert in 1913 and was banished. Recalled when World War I broke out, he greatly distinguished himself leading the Cossacks. Offered the throne in place of Nicholas II when the 1917 Revolution broke out, he refused it, thereby leaving the gap which the Bolsheviks filled. He was murdered in 1918.

Michael Michaelovitch, G. Duke, son of G. Duke Michael, the youngest brother of Alexander II. Michael Michaelovitch was a brother of G. Duke Alexander ("Sandro"), who was son-in-law of MARIE FEDOROVNA.

Michael Nicholaevitch, G. Duke, was the youngest brother of Alexander II. He married Olga of Baden and had five sons and one daughter. He was a popular Viceroy of the Caucasus for many years. He was an intimate friend of MARIE FEDOROVNA, and his son Alexander ("Sandro") married her daughter Zenia.

Militiza, Prs., daughter of the King of Montenegro. Educated in Russia with her sister Stana, she married G. Duke Peter, second son of G. Duke Nicholas (brother of Alexander II). Her sister Stana married Peter's brother, G. Duke Nicholas, Commander in Chief of the Russian armies in World War I. The two sisters with their husbands were leaders of the "mystical set," blamed for bringing the last Empress under the influence of Rasputin.

Nicholas II, last Emperor of Russia, born 1868, son of Alexander III and MARIE FEDOROVNA. Succeeded to throne in 1894, and married Alix of Hesse-Darmstadt (Alexandra Fedorovna— "Alicky") the same year. Abdicated 1917 at outbreak of Russian Revolution. Murdered at Ekaterinburg with Empress Alexandra and their five children 1918.

Nicholas Alexandrovitch, G. Duke, eldest son of Alexander II, affianced to MARIE FEDOROVNA (Dagmar of Denmark) until his premature death in 1865. He persuaded his fiancée on his deathbed to marry his brother Alexander ("Sasha"), who later became Alexander III.

Nicholas Constantinovitch, G. Duke, son of G. Duke Constantine, brother of Alexander II.

Nicholas Michaelovitch, G. Duke, son of G. Duke Michael, the youngest brother of Alexander II. He was brother of G. Duke Alexander ("Sandro"), the son-in-law of MARIE FEDOROVNA.

Nicholas Nicholaevitch, G. Duke, brother of Alexander II, celebrated as a city fire fighter and for amorous adventures. He married Alix of Oldenburg and was father of Grand Duke Nicholas.

Nicholas Nicholaevitch, G. Duke, son of G. Duke Nicholas, the brother of Alexander II. He married Stana, daughter of the King of Montenegro. Nicholas became the Commander in Chief of the Russian armies in World War I. He has been blamed with his wife for bringing the last Empress under the influence of Rasputin.

Olga Alexandrovna, G. Duchess, daughter of Alexander III and MARIE FEDOROVNA. Born in 1882, she married first the Duke of Oldenburg, second Major Koulikovsky. She survived the Revolution.

Olga Constantinovna, G. Duchess and first Queen of Greece. She was the youngest daughter of G. Duke Constantine (brother of Alexander II) and married at the age of fifteen George I ("Willy") of Greece, the brother of MARIE FEDOROVNA and Queen Alexandra of Great Britain. Olga was grandmother of both the Duchess of Kent and the present Duke of Edinburgh.

Olga Nicholaevna, G. Duchess, eldest daughter of Nicholas II and Alexandra Fedorovna. Born in 1895, murdered at Ekaterinburg 1918.

Serge Alexandrovitch, G. Duke, son of Alexander II and brother of Alexander III. Born in 1856, he married Elizabeth of Hesse-Darmstadt ("Titinka"), the eldest sister of Marie Alexandrovna ("Alicky"), the last empress. G. Duke Serge was killed by a Nihilist bomb in 1905 in Moscow Square and Elizabeth shortly afterward took the veil, their only son Dmitri becoming the ward of the Emperor and later taking a leading part in the murder of Rasputin.

Serge Michaelovitch, G. Duke, youngest son of G. Duke Michael, who was the youngest brother of Alexander II. His brother Alexander ("Sandro") was son-in-law of MARIE FEDOROVNA.

Stana, Prs., daughter of the King of Montenegro. Educated in Russia with her sister Militza, she married G. Duke Nicholas, who became the Army's Commander in Chief during World War I. Her sister Militza married her husband's brother Peter, and the two sisters with their husbands were leaders of the "mystical set" blamed for bringing the last Empress under the influence of Rasputin.

Tatiana Nicholaevna, G. Duchess, second daughter of Nicholas II and Alexandra Fedorovna. Born in 1897, she was murdered at Ekaterinburg 1918.

Victoria Melita, Prs. of Great Britain and subsequently G. Duchess of Hesse-Darmstadt and then, after divorce, the G. Duchess Cyril of Russia. She was the daughter of Alfred Duke of Edinburgh and G. Duchess Marie of Russia (daughter of Alexander II and sister-in-law of MARIE FEDOROVNA). In 1894 she married G. Duke Ernst of Hesse-Darmstadt, who was brother of Elizabeth ("Titinka"), the G. Duchess Serge, and of Alexandra Fedorovna ("Alicky"), the last Empress. Thus, her divorce and marriage with G. Duke Cyril stirred up a bitter family quarrel among the Romanoffs and she with her husband was banished from Russia for several years. She escaped from the Bolsheviks.

Vladimir Alexandrovitch, G. Duke, son of Alexander II and most favored brother of Alexander III ("Sasha"). He married Marie of Mecklenburg-Schwerin. He and his wife had considerable behind-the-scenes influence. They made many enemies and were often seen in a sinister light. His wife overshadowed him, becoming the most notable figure of Imperial Russia after MARIE FEDOROVNA. He was great-grandfather of the Duchess of Kent by his daughter Helen, who married Pr. Nicholas of Greece.

Youssoupoff, Pr. Felix, married in 1914 Irina, only daughter of G. Duchess Zenia and G. Duke Alexander ("Sandro") and favorite granddaughter of MARIE FEDOROVNA, who sponsored the marriage against some opposition. Felix Youssoupoff was heir of the richest and most aristocratic family of Imperial Russia. In 1917 he murdered Rasputin, acting from patriotic motives, his companion being Dmitri, ward of Nicholas II and son of G. Duchess Elizabeth.

Zenia Alexandrovna, G. Duchess, eldest daughter of Alexander III and MARIE FEDOROVNA, born in 1875. In 1894 she married her cousin G. Duke Alexander ("Sandro"), who was a son of G. Duke Michael (a brother of Alexander II). Zenia had one daughter, Irina, and five sons, all of whom, with their parents, survived the Revolution.

Marie Fedorovna

EMPRESS OF RUSSIA

CHAPTER I

Two Sisters

IT WAS Dagmar's idea that the two of them should dress alike when the mood took them, or rather when the notion occurred to her. Dagmar always had the ideas, and since these were usually good ones, Alix, who was two years older, was inclined to adopt them in her usual impulsive way. The dressing-alike idea had first cropped up in the year of family excitement, 1862, after Alix had become engaged to Bertie, the Prince of Wales.

Lovely seventeen-year-old Alix had suddenly emerged blushing from the shades of Bernstoff to become the talk of Europe. Everybody was discovering that the eldest daughter of Christian, Crown Prince of Denmark, was the most enchanting young princess alive, and her delighted embarrassment and naïvely expressed bewilderment may have stirred a certain unconscious envy in the cleverer, more ambitious younger sister who had been her inseparable companion and confidante for at least the last three years. Hence, perhaps, Dagmar thought up her dressing-alike idea to make things more equal between them.

At fifteen Dagmar, with her limpid, dark violet eyes, soft yet piercing, and her ripening figure, gave nothing in stature, in womanly form or grace of movement to her older sister. But seen side by side, as the sisters so frequently were seen, in the streets of Copenhagen or in the rural privacy of Bernstoff, the two, so alike from the neck downward, differed in their features.

The classic, breath-taking perfection of Alexandra drew away the gaze of the beholder from the piquant, elfin, sparkling face of Dagmar. Yet, dress Alix and Dagmar alike, and there stood twin girls who offered a joint display of loveliness which deflected the vision and dulled the power of discrimination.

Their parents, Prince Christian of Schleswig-Holstein and Princess Louise of Hesse-Cassel, had always been poor; so poor in the days when the children were young and they had inhabited a little crumbling rent-free city palace as the guests and protégés of King Frederick's father, Christian VIII, that they had had to struggle desperately to keep up with the Guards set to which they belonged. It was not until 1852, when King Christian VIII was dead, that the Powers in conference, debating the troubled affairs of Denmark and the Schleswig-Holstein conundrum, agreed on the advice of childless King Frederick VII of Denmark to settle the problem of the Danish succession by making that easygoing, unambitious young guardsman Prince Christian the Crown Prince of Denmark.

From that time the Christians had been less poor. They had moved out of Copenhagen to the white mansion palace of Bernstoff, which stood in a modest park; but they were still poor for their high position.

In the year of the move to Bernstoff, Frederick, the eldest child, was nine, Alexandra was eight, William the future King of Greece was seven, and Dagmar was five. Thyra was born in the first year at Bernstoff, and Waldemar did not arrive until six years later.

To tall and dominating Louise, the mother of this family which from a prospectless future had suddenly acquired prospects more glittering than anyone then imagined, the change to the position of Crown Princess was delightful.

Crown Prince Christian, who liked to ride several different horses every day, was now affluent enough to buy some better mounts, and a smart phaeton with two splendid high-steppers. His endless cigars also gave off a more delicious aroma. Otherwise Christian was happy to let life flow on as usual. He still performed his rigorous daily bout of gymnastics and still threw aside his high-collared tunic before luncheon in preparation for putting his obedient family through the same exercises.

It might be thought that Crown Princess Louise, who gloried in the anticipation of future queenhood, would have wanted to train her children in a traditionally royal manner, but in actuality she was content to bring them up in a strictly bourgeois regime; for by nature Louise was rather bourgeoise herself.

Alix, as a result, was secretly bourgeoise all her life, in spite of her brilliant and apparently effortless success as Princess of Wales and later as Queen of England. Dagmar, on the other hand, did not spiritually conform to this family pattern. She wanted a stirring career for herself, and in that year of 1862 when Alix without making the slightest effort, indeed after being very silly and contrary, had engaged herself to the Prince of Wales, Dagmar was envious of those two extra years possessed by Alix, which had made it possible for her to obtain this glittering prize. Dagmar knew that those two extra years would have enabled Alix to secure an even more exciting prize—their cousin Nicholas, the Tsarevitch of Russia—if Bertie of Wales had not slipped in his claim first.

Empress Marie, the wife of Alexander II of Russia, was a Hesse-Darmstadt princess, belonging to the other ruling branch of the family from which came Louise, a Hesse-Cassel princess. The Empress of Russia was understood by the Christian family to be deeply upset that Queen Victoria had thwarted her own ambitions for the Tsarevitch. Empress Marie had coupled Alix with her eldest son for several years, and Emperor Alexander was supposed to approve of this matrimonial project. All Russians were indignant. Britain, having humiliated them in the Crimea, had now done it again by some typical underhand work.

Dagmar did not know if Nicholas himself was brokenhearted about Alix. He and Alix had always been such friends in Germany, or whenever he had come with his mother to visit them at Bernstoff. Nicholas had been wonderfully handsome for several years now, and of course, tremendously tall like all

Romanoffs. From that point of view Bertie of Wales was a pretty poor bargain. Dagmar believed the people who said that Nicholas would soon be the most accomplished Prince in Europe.

Nicholas had not been a friend of Dagmar. He was too old for that. But he had always been nice to her, and especially so during their last meeting, when she supposed she might have seemed rather more grown-up to him. She had known Nicholas for a long time, because he had often been at Schloss Heiligenberg, the Hesse-Darmstadt country seat of Empress Marie's brother Alexander, when the Christians had joined the Rumpenheim family parties, and Nicholas on his visits used to take more notice of the little ones than some of the others.

The Christians had traveled into Germany to Rumpenheim almost every second year of their lives. Their maternal great-grandfather, Landgrave Frederick of Hesse-Cassel, had willed Rumpenheim, the traditional family seat on the Oder, to his six children, desiring them to gather there for a family reunion every second year and live at the expense of a fund he had established. In this ancient white palace on the banks of the Oder near Frankfurt the far-flung Hesse-Cassels used to collect in summer, with children, grandchildren, suites and servants, each party opening up and cleaning out its own set of dusty apartments as they moved in.

For the adults Rumpenheim was a mart of international royal chatter and cheerful scandalmongering, as they sat over their embroidery or smoked their cigars on the terrace above the sleepy Oder. For the children it was a rambling, haunted paradise. Rumpenheim had provided almost the only holidays the Christians had known, because their stay cost almost nothing.

At the same time of year Empress Marie would often reach Germany from Russia—the fabulous land about which Dagmar used to hear so much—and would come over from her brother's seat, Heiligenberg, bringing her five eldest children, Tsarevitch Nicholas, Grand Duchess Marie, her only daughter, and the Grand Dukes Alexander, Vladimir and Alexis. Cousin Nicholas was the kind of boy who effortlessly wins the approval of the female sex, be they grown women or little girls. Alexander,

Vladimir and Alexis were barbarous bandits, scornful of petticoats, who headed a lusty gang as boorish as themselves.

*   *   *

The year 1862 passed into 1863, and as February drew icily to its
close the Christians, a rather awed, rather hysterical, rather sad
party, set out from Copenhagen for Windsor Castle, where the
royal wedding was to take place on March 10. Frederick, William, Dagmar and Thyra accompanied their parents and the
bride-to-be.

Dagmar had heard such conflicting reports of their future
hostess at Windsor, Queen Victoria, the royal ogress of Europe,
who some said was mad—Mama could not stand her, Papa shied
at her name—that she was in a mood of pulsing excitement and
awful curiosity. When the tired Danish party, several hours late
and escorted by the Prince of Wales, finally reached Windsor
Castle at 7 p.m. on March 7 in a sleetstorm, Dagmar's anticipa-
tions were surpassed by the experience which awaited her.

In the dimly lit entrance to the royal apartments at Windsor
Castle stood a small figure smothered in drooping veils, black
and ominous. The veils were lifted and the eyes of Queen Victoria regarded her guests with cold reproach. She had been waiting for hours. They had made her ill with worry. Suddenly the
Queen swept out her arms and enveloped Alix in a fervent, bat-
like embrace. Bertie was seized roughly from among them for
the next attention while they hovered uncertainly in the shadows.

The rudeness of Queen Victoria to Crown Princess Christian
had at a previous meeting "horrified" her uncle, King Leopold of
Belgium. Now this ruthless manifestation of a deep natural an-
tipathy startled and bewildered Louise's children. Dagmar saw
her father kiss the Queen's hand and stand back, unnoticed and
unaddressed. As for the three of them, Dagmar, Willy and Thyra,
it might be that the Queen, who had dropped her veils, failed
to perceive them through the meshes.

In clear, almost threatening tones the Queen proclaimed that
dinner would be served in half an hour in the oak dining room.
They had best go and rest for a few minutes. She herself was

"worn out," she told them, "worn out with this terrible ordeal of waiting." She could not face the sight of dinner. She would have to rest quietly, and she would look forward to seeing them "tomorrow."

The exit of the Queen was a relief to the party in the hall, yet they followed their conductors to their rooms in chilled and uneasy silence. Only Alix saw the Queen again that night; for after dinner and without invitation she went alone to the comfortable sanctity of the royal closet to call on her future mother-in-law.

Dagmar had never before seen a real queen. The Queen of Denmark—the former ballet dancer—was a mere country housewife, who preferred to be seen as little as possible. Empress Marie Alexandrovna of Russia never acted like an Empress in Germany or at Bernstoff. While Alix had greeted Queen Victoria with happy nonchalance, Dagmar had observed every motion of the Queen with inexpressible awe and admiration. She had watched the faintly shrinking, faintly flustered actions of the royal attendants, and indeed of the Queen's own sons and daughters. Queen Victoria had not yet reached her forty-fifth year, and traces of her youthful attraction still lingered in her face; but even then grief had bred an indescribable agelessness about that little figure, which terrified and yet drew people toward her at the same time. Here, Dagmar told herself, was a *real* Queen, a majestic presence beyond her dreams.

Further contemplation of Queen Victoria during the days which followed filled Dagmar with an ecstasy of wondering admiration, and it was on the wedding eve that she first disclosed her delight in the Queen to her amused elder sister. She had come to Alix's bedroom, and Alix, who seemed quite unperturbed by the thought of the morrow, was chattering gaily. Suddenly she began to imitate the Queen in a spirit of mischievous caricature, her imperious tone, her quick, decisive movements.

"No," cried Dagmar, "it's not like that . . ."

She then gave Alix a perfectly serious and much truer performance of the same speech and actions.

"Of course, you can laugh," she told her sister, "but I think the

Queen is magnificent, tremendous, terrible. No sovereign in Europe could stand up to her, I'm sure!"

"You might make quite a good queen yourself," laughed Alix.

"—Not as good as she is," rejoined Dagmar. "I should want to laugh a good deal if I were a queen—" and then she added hopefully "—or an empress."

No hint that she might attain such a high position had ever reached fifteen-year-old Dagmar. The field, however, was wider in those days. In Europe, apart from Britain and Denmark, there were three empresses—of Russia, of Austria, of France—and eleven queens, besides some very queenly consorts in the lesser German states.

Chances of unexpected kingship were going begging, too; for scarcely had Dagmar returned to Denmark with her parents after the royal wedding, when, without the slightest warning, her brother Willy was summoned from the naval cadet school and invited to become King of Greece.

When Dagmar thought back to her frugal childhood in the crumbling old Yellow Palace, it seemed fantastic the way things were happening in her family; but nothing happened to Dagmar, except that she attained her sixteenth year in good health.

Willy was to be crowned in Athens in lonely state that winter. Alix had protested wildly in her letters to Papa and Mama about letting Willy go to Greece. The Greeks were terrible people, brigands and assassins. Dagmar was secretly anxious about this, too, as she knew were Papa and Mama; but it was a wonderful opportunity for Willy, who like his father before him was cheerfully unambitious, and Dagmar wanted Willy to be King of Greece for the glory of it. If the Greeks had decided to have a queen—like Queen Victoria—and had invited Dagmar to rule them she would have been delighted to oblige them. In the meantime, she foresaw that life at Bernstoff was going to be even more boring and colorless with both Alix and Willy gone to their destinies.

When late that autumn Dagmar hurriedly returned home from her first stay with Alix and Bertie at Sandringham, it was to make her curtsy before an amiable but worried father, who by the sudden death of Frederick VII found himself King Christian IX of Denmark. The tall, bewhiskered Danish guardsman, who had risen so unexpectedly to the highest position in his country, had good cause for the anxiety which perpetually clouded his mild blue eyes. He fully believed that in a matter of weeks Prussia, with Austria and many of the German states, would invade his territory and seize Schleswig-Holstein. He would have to call upon his subjects to resist strenuously for the honor of Denmark; but he would send his troops into battle knowing that most of them were doomed men.

Bernstoff, except for future summer holidays, was a place of the nostalgic family past. Dagmar joined her family at the royal palace of Fredensborg, on the outskirts of Copenhagen. While King Christian worked late into the night at the hopeless task of organizing his neglected and feeble military resources, the Queen and Dagmar endeavored to revive, indeed to invent, the art of royal living in Denmark.

Now Dagmar, standing in her spacious bedroom before her ornate full-length mirror—she had had only a half-mirror at ill-furnished Bernstoff—told herself that she was observing the reflection of one of the most eligible and certainly one of the most attractive unmarried royal princesses in Europe. Her sister was the Princess of Wales. Her brother was King of Greece. And poor Papa, of course, was King of Denmark. Did not she belong to a "lucky" family?

But the delightful novelty of an income of her own and the fun of aiding Mama in creating items of royal procedure were spoiled by the sad smile of Papa, by that awful look of quiet despair with which he regarded them. They spent a miserable Christmas at Fredensborg.

On January 9 came startling news from England. Alix had given birth to a son at Frogmore during the previous night. The baby had not been expected for another two months! Everybody forgot the Prussian bogey in frantic anxiety for the mother, whom they believed to be in a dangerous condition.

Days of uncertainty followed. Then, scarcely had they received a truly reassuring letter from the adored patient herself before Dagmar was sitting at her desk at Fredensborg describing in her own weekly letter to Alix the first days of the dreaded invasion. "What is England going to do?" she asked hopefully.

Everybody in Denmark was beginning to ask that question. England was Denmark's only hope, and Denmark was full of rumors that the Royal Navy with its decks packed with redcoats was on the way. There were people who knew somebody who had already watched redcoats landing, but nobody had ever seen them themselves.

The truth of the matter was that the more Queen Victoria had assured the Danes that the match between their Princess Alix and her eldest son was a nonpolitical one, the more the Danes had winked at each other and been impudent and defiant to the glowering Bismarck, who, when any nervous Prussian tackled him upon this subject, declared confidently, "The English won't raise a hand to help them."

Alix, still weak and in bed, was ashamed to answer her sister's letter. She who had been all but torn to pieces by enthusiastic English admirers had believed Britons would race to the aid of her country. With dismay and personal humiliation she was now learning that the country which had thrown itself at her feet intended to do nothing to help Denmark in her distress.

In another fortnight all was over. Denmark was in mourning. Prussia and Austria held Schleswig and Holstein, and Dagmar's father had signed the capitulation.

Momentarily the flame of bitterness in Denmark burned so fiercely against England that it seemed as if Dagmar could not dare go visiting to her sister at Marlborough House for years; nor could the Princess of Wales venture to appear in the land of her birth. Danes in their first mad fury were calling the Princess Alix a traitor.

But a golden spring passed into a golden summer, the spirit revived in Denmark and feelings softened.

When it became known that in September the Princess of Wales with her baby son Albert Victor was coming to Copenhagen on a visit to her parents, the enthusiasm was tremendous. They talked of Albert Victor as if he were a Danish princeling.

They seemed to think that they all shared the responsibility for bringing him into the world. Danish faces grew glum, however, when it was realized that the Prince of Wales was coming too. Bertie, actually, had been one of the few Englishmen of high position frankly and loudly to sponsor the Danish cause during the fighting. His unrestrained abuse of the Prussians in the London clubs had infuriated and shamed his mother. But to the indignant Danes he remained the eldest son of Queen Victoria.

Dagmar, overcome with delight at the prospect of seeing her beloved sister again, scarcely took note of a letter received by her mother from Empress Marie Alexandrovna of Russia. In this the Empress announced her intention of joining the family party at Fredensborg and bringing with her her son Tsarevitch Nicholas.

But from the moment the carriages bearing the Empress of Russia and her glittering suite swung into the great courtyard of Fredensborg, accompanied by gigantic hairy, scarlet-coated Cossack orderlies, Dagmar began to discover another interest in life besides laughing and chatting and romping in Alix's boudoir. Dagmar had never had much liking for Empress Marie, who had always seemed to take a dismal, disapproving view of the doings of young princesses. In the past when Empress Marie had addressed her she grew awkward and scared, imagining that she disliked her. Now she was bewildered to find that Empress Marie liked her very well, singled her out, in fact, for tender and rather embarrassing little chats. It was almost as if Empress Marie had come all the way from Russia to see her.

The handsome and exclusive Nicholas also surprised Dagmar. It was true that she was the First Princess of Denmark; but even so, it was flattering at seventeen to see the most accomplished prince in Europe frequently and elegantly disengage himself from other company to approach her with a charming smile.

Some of the better features of Fredensborg Castle, with its rambling spaces and lofty halls, were the alcoves and cozy corners shut off by tall potted palms and screens, where people might retire from the company to converse on settees in restful seclusion. Dagmar was guided by the Tsarevitch to these refuges with increasing frequency. He listened with amusement to her lively flow of ideas. He told her many fascinating things about Russia and the imperial court. He explained the problems of Russia. He confided to her the troubles of those who had to rule Russia. He praised her intelligence and understanding.

It was on the night of October 5—Alix and Bertie had returned earlier that day from their unofficial visit to Sweden—that Nicholas sat with Dagmar after dinner gazing out upon the groups of guests from the haven of some potted palms. It was surprising, but for the first time in Dagmar's experience Europe's most accomplished prince seemed unable to furnish a subject for conversation.

At last Dagmar named a matter which never failed to absorb him—Russia. Nicholas gave a start, glared at the youthful princess beside him, and then seemed to be fighting for words as if her suggestion had terrified him.

Suddenly he spoke in French so breathlessly rapid that momentarily she missed the significance of his utterance.

"—Would you like to be a future Empress of Russia?"

If Dagmar had begun to expect some kind of declaration, the manner of its delivery was a shock. Having fully understood the nature of the question, she was cooler than she might have been in the face of more romantic advances.

"Do you want me to be a future Empress of Russia?"

"Yes—"

"Then I would like to be a future Empress of Russia."

But if seventeen-year-old Dagmar had been self-possessed and graciously obliging to the Tsarevitch of All the Russias—as became the dignity of a future empress—she was in floods of tears, a typical young maiden of her generation, when later that night she sought out Alix alone in her boudoir to make her the first recipient of the wonderful news. It was a foregone conclusion that Alix, too, should break into frantic weeping over her sister's joy; for nothing delighted these two better than mutual bouts of emotional sentiment.

Thus occupied, the two devoted sisters were found by the Prince of Wales, whose startled curiosity was quickly satisfied.

The second recipient of Dagmar's secret appeared genuinely delighted. Both sisters were somewhat surprised at this, for, aware of the British attitude toward Russia, they had been doubtful of Bertie's reception of the idea of a Russian Imperial sister-in-law.

"The wedding will, of course, be in St. Petersburg," announced Bertie, "and I shall certainly come to it."

This remark was not simply the enthusiastic outburst of a fond brother-in-law. It was a royal proclamation of tremendous political significance. No member of the British royal family had ever visited Russia. The Russians hated Queen Victoria, all her children, all her subjects and all her works.

When the Tsarevitch returned to Russia the words of the Prince of Wales would soon become known. The youthful, amiable and so garrulous Bertie, not satisfied with being the Haroun-al-Rashid of London night life, was showing the first signs of his brilliant flair for international diplomacy.

By this union between his wife's adored sister and the Tsarevitch of Russia he envisaged a change in the balance of European power. He knew that the Germans would be infuriated and insulted, because Russia, departing from her custom, had omitted to seek out a German princess for the future Empress. He saw the breakup of the endless flirtation between Russia and the Germans and the decline of German petticoat rule within the Russian state.

When the Prince of Wales reached London a few days later his glowing views upon the coming Anglo-Russian *entente* were widely spread in the London clubs. Few men of mark took him seriously. The Russian Bear was a crafty, treacherous and savage beast, immune to the blandishments of civilized man.

Nevertheless, the Prince of Wales intended to be in St. Petersburg in the near future. Nor was his political flair at fault concerning the possibilities inherent in Dagmar's marriage into the Russian Imperial family, although decades of time must pass before his own perseverance and that of his wife and his sister-in-law bore fruit in an Anglo-Russian alliance against the power of Germany.

CHAPTER II

Dreadful Betrothal

PRINCESS DAGMAR, fiancée of the Tsarevitch, bound on her first visit to St. Petersburg, traveled majestically in an imperial train from the Russian border on January 5, 1865. Nicholas had been awaiting her with his private train at the frontier station, and the Danish visitor, stepping nervously from the humble dinginess of an ordinary passenger carriage, had little inkling of the splendors ahead.

The magnificence of the imperial train was accentuated by the flat bleak land stretching in white loneliness to the leaden skies of the horizon, and Dagmar as she alighted knew that she had entered another world. Like so many newcomers to Imperial Russia, she was suddenly frightened and troubled. Some mysterious, intangible force seemed to grip her spirit in cruel, icy fingers.

The frontier platform was crowded, yet everything seemed dead in the cold stillness. For the first time that choking Russian smell of rancid leather grease, majorka tobacco and filthy garments assailed her throat and nostrils. She gazed at the splendid furs of Nicholas and his suite and at the bared and bowing heads of the wild-bearded moujik porters with their unwashed faces and their huge padded greatcoats, spreading from belted waists

31

like befouled old tents. She saw behind them the shivering clusters of women and children in their muffled squalor, who dropped their eyes servilely when she gazed at them. She observed a policeman kicking and beating a too-curious peasant youth.

At St. Petersburg the imperial Romanoffs stood on the platform in terrifying array: Emperor Alexander II, Empress Marie, the grand dukes and the grand duchesses. She was placed beside the Emperor in the first carriage, and presently amid a cloud of Guard Cossacks with fluttering lance pennants, she was traveling swiftly through the immensely broad and swept streets of the world's strangest capital toward the doors of the mammoth Winter Palace. Dagmar as a child had met her future father-in-law, Alexander II, the Emancipator of the Serfs; yet he had scarcely ever spoken to her. A tall man with grizzled side-whiskers and a pale attractive face full of dignity and kindliness, he at once inspired her with confidence to face the experiences ahead.

At Fredensborg that winter life had been cold and drafty, and so it had always been at Bernstoff. The white-piled enormity of the Winter Palace scarcely suggested warmth to the stranger; but when the Danish guest stepped into the great entrance hall she reeled and gasped for breath as the hot perfumed air of the palace enveloped her. Entering suddenly from the intense cold of the street she slipped into a dazed and dreamy condition, out of which she had scarcely roused herself when, several hours later, she sat beside the Emperor at the imperial banquet given in her honor.

In a pale-blue and silver hall, tall as a cathedral, which seemed to stretch like a road into the distant shadows, an army of candle flames danced down an incredible table, flanked by men and women in fancy dress who rose suddenly in glittering ranks to toast her with shrill clamor. She looked down at the table, and the flash of gold and silver plate blinded her; she looked up and the flaming jewels in hundreds of kakosnik headdresses made her lower her eyes. Behind her a melee of gorgeous servants stumbled, pushed and shouted at one another. Gigantic Abyssinian Guards in scarlet coats, bearded Cossacks, a handsome young page in a black-crested helmet, who gracefully handed her gold cups of wine, weird music which throbbed and surged somewhere out of sight—this was the Arabian Nights, or Dagmar was lost in some barbaric fairyland.

Next morning the fiancée of the Tsarevitch awoke from the sleep of exhaustion with a clearer mind. She left her bed cheerfully. She was once again the same young princess who had left so recently the somber halls of Fredensborg. Could the memories of the previous night be part of her dreams? But presently Dagmar was adrift in fantasy once again.

The day was January 6, Epiphany, and that morning the Emperor in a traditional ceremony was to bless the waters of the River Neva, which flowed beside the Winter Palace—a ceremony so ancient that neither the Emperor nor the Metropolitan knew the reason for it.

Dagmar, awaiting a summons to she knew not what, gazed down from her windows upon the Neva. The sun shone and the wind shrieked savagely down the broad snow-white belt of river dividing the Winter Palace from the grim Fortress of Peter and Paul on the farther bank, where all the dead autocrats of Russia lay in their tombs. Below, upon the Neva, stood a pavilion draped with crimson velvet beside a huge circular gap in the ice, and around the hole men in round ostrich-feathered hats stirred the dark water with long poles to keep it from freezing.

All the imperial family had their part in the Blessing of the Waters, and a high court dignitary presently arrived to conduct the fiancée of the Tsarevitch to join spectators at the lower windows of the palace. Her escort brought her through an endless succession of huge mirrored halls, blazing with Byzantine decoration on walls and ceilings and stagnant like tropical hothouses. From hall to hall they passed between towering avenues of Guard Cossacks in red, white, black, blue and brown, between Guard Lancers, Red Guard Hussars, and white Gardes aux Chevaux in black breastplates and brazen eagle-crested helms.

Twice on their way they were halted by pages of the Imperial Cadet Corps while processions moved out from side halls. First, with a jingle of spurs, came the Emperor's procession on its way

out to the Neva. Behind Alexander II followed the grand dukes,
the great officials, the generals, the admirals and Church dignitaries in brilliant vestments.

The second procession, filing out from the chapel between the
marble pillars of St. George's Hall, caused an absolute stillness to
fall among the crowd. Even Russians, seasoned to the imperial
court, held their breath at the sight year after year of this slowly
advancing spectacle.

With whispering skirts the procession of the Empress and the
grand duchesses passed on its way to the imperial balcony. No
color of the rainbow was missing in that glorious array of old
Russian costumes. The transparent white head veils floated from
the tall kakosniks, on which the encrusted gems burned and scin-
tillated. Empress Marie in white velvet with a long ermine train
walked before the grand duchesses, and behind, two by two,
came the ladies of the grand-ducal courts. The fiancée of Tsarevitch Nicholas could not but reflect that one day she in place of
Empress Marie would marshal this enchanting procession.

At last Dagmar was brought to a tall window overlooking the
Neva, evidently reserved for her by an Imperial Cadet; for at the
windows on each side officers, ladies, court dignitaries and
gilded diplomats jostled without restraint for a view of the river.

Already the Emperor's procession was on the ice, bending to
the wind with banners and standards flapping like gunshots.
Several generals were clutching at their toupees, and one indignant gray-beard chased his wig across the snow. The shaven
heads of the Cossacks of the Imperial Escort jerked agonizedly
from side to side in the cutting gale.

Clouds of incense floated up. The chant of the bearded priests
blew away on the wind. The Metropolitan in his gorgeous robe
with the tall Emperor beside him stepped forward to the hole in
the ice and, dipping a great silver crucifix three times in the
water, raised his arm in the blessing. On the farther bank spurts
of orange flame vanished in gray smoke as the guns thundered
from the Fortress of Peter and Paul. The clashing of bells came
from the dazzling golden domes and cupolas of the cathedral
across the river.

It was over, and the medieval pageant on the Neva turned and almost ran into the Winter Palace like children released from school. Those scenes during Dagmar's first day in St. Petersburg stuck vividly in her memory all through her life.

Dagmar had arrived in Russia in the height of the Petersburg season, and the second court ball was to take place two days later. The official court balls always began with the Imperial Polonaise, in which the Emperor and Empress, hand in hand, followed by the Tsarevitch with a suitable partner, the grand dukes and duchesses and the lesser princely relatives of the imperial family, marched to stately music through the principal halls of the Winter Palace. The guests, numbering several thousands, were marshaled by chamberlains so as to form a broad and magnificent avenue for the imperial progress.

Dagmar heard with trepidation that in the Imperial Polonaise her lot was to proceed with Nicholas behind the Emperor and Empress. The fiancée of the popular Tsarevitch would be the target of every eye in all those halls. She had wanted to go to Worth's of Paris for her best evening gown; but Mama would not hear of the extravagance. It was bad enough that every lady in the Polonaise would have the advantage of her by wearing court costume. Worse—she told herself—that every lady among the spectators would wear a Parisian gown, and worse still that every one of them would instantly note that her gown was out of date. The thought of the terrible Polonaise filled her with dread. On the eve of the court ball she passed a restless night.

Next morning Nicholas did not make his appearance. He was in bed with a feverish chill contracted at the Blessing of the Waters. Having satisfied herself that Nicholas was not seriously ill, she could scarcely hide her delight at the verdict of the doctors that he must keep to his room for several days.

But the fiancée of the Tsarevitch was not destined to escape so easily from the Imperial Polonaise. What actually happened to Dagmar on the occasion of the second court ball has a strange interest in view of after events in her life.

Vladimir, the third son of the Emperor, a gay nineteen-year-old ensign in the Preobajansky Guards, arrived in her sitting-room with a verbal message from Nicholas.

"Nicky says that Sasha [Alexander] is to partner you in the Polonaise tonight and to look after you at the ball, as he is the next oldest of us. You have to take part because it is promised and the guests can't be robbed of the object of universal curiosity!"

Vladimir had a tremendous, startling bass voice, and his words usually seemed to hold a mocking ring. At that moment they sounded like a death knell to Dagmar. She could have murdered this big, smiling Guards officer, who actually had been charming to her ever since her arrival, and whom she secretly suspected of understanding her better than anybody else in the imperial family.

"Sasha is very lucky," announced Vladimir. "It is an honor for him. I wish I thought he had the sense to appreciate it," and he winked at her.

Alexander, known to the family as Sasha, was the tallest of the Emperor's tall sons. His tight red hussar jacket emphasized his sacklike waist and he shambled awkwardly about in a peculiar crabwise manner. Sasha had not spoken a word to her since greeting her gruffly at the station. He was not bad-looking, but he was frightening—like the giant ogre in the fairy tale—and she had several times seen his sharp, rather bulging blue eyes peering at her with apparent dislike. Now, not only the Polonaise, but the entire evening, was going to be one horrible embarrassment. She had a feeling that he might omit to speak to her at all.

Vladimir had settled himself comfortably.

"My brother Sasha is simple—a blockhead," he announced condescendingly. "Do not be surprised at him whatever he does. He is not talkative by nature. He may be rude. Father nicknamed Sasha the 'Bullock,' because he is always pushing his head forward and hunching his shoulders. His soldiers call him the 'Bull,' because his temper is worse than a mad bull; but they like him all the same."

Vladimir informed her that he had just left Sasha, who since hearing about his assignment for the evening had become unapproachable. It was simply that he was terrified of "grandes dames" like herself, he assured Dagmar.

"—Sasha is a ladies' man with a vengeance among the gypsies and the dancing girls down at the Novaia Deresvnia quarter; but don't be dismayed. Sasha and I are very fond of one another. Treat him gently and he may like you too."

The day fled away miserably for Dagmar, and with each hour her dread increased. She dressed herself for the ball. She joined the imperial family assembling for the Polonaise. Her hulking partner, like some fantastic red hussar of nightmare, took his place beside her in grim silence. They were lined up and ready. With a fluttering heart Dagmar watched the scarlet footmen swing open the double doors of the anteroom. A roar of voices and women's laughter floated in to them. She shrank with nervous terror. She felt supremely ridiculous beside this man. All those people would laugh, and Russians apparently did not trouble to hide their laughter. The military band struck up, drowning those wild-beast voices. She saw the Emperor and Empress brace themselves and glide forward with the easy grace of long experience. They might have been moving in their sleep. She forgot the "Bullock" beside her, and tried to force her body to imitate the gait of Aunt Marie as they emerged into the first hall.

Perhaps Dagmar profited that night by a Beauty and the Beast contrast set up by the actions and uncouth bearing of her elephantine partner. This was her first appearance before the general society of Petersburg and the great landowning families from the provinces; but far from displaying herself at a disadvantage, the fiancée of Tsarevitch Nicholas—the future Empress of Russia—aroused universal admiration and satisfaction, which the Russian crowd, as ready to exhibit unrestrained delight as openly to manifest blighting disapproval, made plain as she passed through their midst by clapping, hurrahing and pointing with audible compliments.

To her the measure of the change from a dreadful, uneasy progress to triumph was apparent not only by the sight of the buzzing crowds flanking the imperial parade like some vast and sumptuous opera chorus, but by the tightening grip of Sasha's bearlike hand. The sweat shone on his brow and instead of talking to his partner as was customary during the Polonaise, he glared ahead in ferocious embarrassment, crushing her fingers till, but for her joy, she could have fainted.

The imperial family took their seats on the dais, and the dancing began. It was not the custom for the Emperor and the Empress to take part in the waltzes and mazurkas which followed the Polonaise; but the grand dukes and duchesses were expected to do so. The Grand Duke Sasha sat morosely beside Dagmar gazing disgustedly at the dancing throng. He had placed a chair for her with an awkward bow, but still he had not addressed a word to her.

At midnight, the dancers, including the imperial party, proceeded to the magnificent supper hall, where Imperial Cadets collected tickets from the guests and led them in parties of ten to circular tables, out of the hollow centers of which sprouted full-sized palm trees rising from a bed of hothouse flowers. The high ceiling was painted dark blue like the night sky and powdered with golden stars. The palm trees rose like a forest and thousands of colored paper lanterns that hung between the stems lit the scene.

For Dagmar the ball took a more lively turn; for seated in a circle she benefited from the company of others, who amply made up for the taciturnity of her own partner. Sasha's brothers, Vladimir and Alexis, with two young Guards officers and their four partners, made up the table. While they refreshed themselves with strange delicacies, Sasha added nothing to the gaiety of the party. He swallowed champagne with startling rapidity. He smiled at his partner and attended to her needs, but never spoke. Later on he addressed a few remarks to his brothers.

Supper was almost ended when Dagmar with amazement and indignation felt Sasha brusquely nudging her bare arm. Her scared glance met his, and he gave her a sheepish grin. He picked up a heavy chased silver plate, brushed the little iced cakes off it among the flowers, held up the glittering plate in both hands, bent it between his thick fingers till the outer edges touched, and sharply smacking the ruined plate between his enormous palms, reduced it almost to a perfect half-moon of sheet metal. Then, starting with herself, he bestowed a broad wink upon the party round the table.

Sasha snatched up a big silver fork and in a flash he had turned it into a silver corkscrew. Behind him stood his personal servant, a trooper in the Red Hussars. Sasha glowered round at him.

"Cards!" he grunted.

The soldier without apparent surprise pulled a yellowed pack of cards from his pocket. Sasha snatched the pack from his hand. With one ferocious jerk he ripped the pack in half and hurled the pieces like a snowstorm into the air. The Emperor, who in accordance with custom on such occasions was walking from table to table chatting with his seated guests, stood watching the antics of his second son without enthusiasm.

But Sasha's performance was not yet at an end. He rose abruptly, smiled at his astonished partner, but offered no apology as he walked from the table toward the brightly lit platform of the military band. Presently he was pushing his way among the musicians. The tune was in full swing and the players ignored him. The bandmaster wielded his baton, unperturbed by the huge figure jostling among his players.

Sasha took an instrument from a bandsman. The man abandoned his chair to the Grand Duke, who sat down and began to play. It was plain that Sasha was playing his instrument with gusto; yet no discordancy came in the music. He rose, handed back the instrument and grasped another. Without surprise the second bandsman vacated his seat. Again Sasha took up the tune. Soon, tired of the instrument, he was on his feet once more. Then he was playing a third instrument, seated in a third chair. Sasha was making a round of the band. Not once did he give the bandmaster cause for complaint.

It was in this wise that Dagmar of Denmark had her first experience of the ways of Alexander Alexandrovitch, the second son of the Emperor, who was to play such an important part in her destiny.

Early in March Dagmar returned to Denmark. Nicholas and

his mother had accompanied her to the frontier, and there, while she changed to a passenger train, returning homeward in the same humble manner in which she had set out, the imperial train was diverted to the German railways, as mother and son were bound for the imperial villa at Cannes.

The wedding was to be at St. Petersburg in June, and April and May were going to be busy months of preparation for Dagmar. Mama had at last agreed that she must visit Paris for Worth to fit her with some of his famous creations. In a few days, also, a dignitary of the Russian Orthodox Church was to arrive at Fredensborg to prepare her for entrance into the Byzantine faith.

Yet, despite the activity and excitement at Fredensborg, Dagmar felt flat and depressed, as some person might who had just returned out of Fairyland into a drab world. But there was something deeper than mere youthful discontent in her restlessness and her low spirits. As the days went by, Dagmar afterward confessed to a friend, she began to experience a sense of foreboding and even a kind of constant dull fear of something unknown, which puzzled her.

The first week of April had passed when, one morning, Queen Louise entered Dagmar's room. She held a telegram in her hand, and her face was pale and drawn.

"This is from Empress Marie at Cannes," she said. "She asks me to break bad news to you. Nicholas is very ill. He has had an accident. He is asking for you. We shall leave for Cannes today."

Three days before, the horse of Grand Duke Nicholas had bolted and thrown him heavily against a tree trunk. He was carried unconscious to the imperial villa. Nicholas had recovered consciousness within a few hours, but he was almost unable to move. The doctors declared that he was suffering from shock and a bruised spine.

Yet two days later they had sought the Empress with dismay on their faces. No doubt remained that the Tsarevitch had developed cerebrospinal meningitis. His condition had suddenly become so serious that they believed he could live only a few days and they advised that he should be warned of his approaching end.

It had, indeed, been suspected that Nicholas had harbored this disease in his system for several years, for maladies of this kind were inherent in the Romanoffs, and the severe blow seemed to have brought it out.

Dagmar traveled to the Riviera with her mother and her eldest brother, Crown Prince Frederick, a close friend of Nicholas. At Cannes the Empress met the Danish party at the station. They read the truth in Empress Marie's stricken face before she spoke.

They reached the imperial villa. In the hall a lady in waiting hurried to the Empress, who turned to Dagmar.

"Nicky has asked to see you as soon as you arrive. You are to go to him alone. I will take you to his room."

Dagmar had been only a few minutes at the bedside of Nicholas, and he had spoken little, only held her hand and smiled, when a heavy knock sounded on the door. The door opened hesitantly and the great figure of Sasha filled the aperture. He wore civilian clothes, which hung clumsily from his immense shoulders, and his eyes were red-rimmed with weeping.

"You sent for me, Nicky?" he asked.

"Yes, Sasha. Please come to the bed," said his elder brother.

When Sasha stood beside Dagmar, Nicholas began to speak in firmer tones. His eyes turned to his fiancée.

"I want you to take Sasha's hand," he declared, and she wonderingly obeyed. "I have known you long enough to feel sure that you are a person well fitted to be the future Empress of Russia," he continued. "It is God's will that I shall soon cease to be the Tsarevitch. You are holding the hand of the Tsarevitch who will take my place—and it is my dying wish that you two should marry. You may entrust yourself to Sasha without fear, my dear. He is a better man than I. He will make a greater Emperor of Russia than I would have done."

Nicholas asked them to kneel. Then he feebly placed a hand over theirs.

"Do you agree to marry her, Sasha?"

There was a pause.

"I do . . ."

Dagmar heard the same question addressed to herself.

No wonder Dagmar, too, hesitated at that solemn and awful moment of decision with the hand of her dying fiancé touching hers. She could not ask for time to think. She must there and then bind herself to this strange man kneeling beside her—or, she must unclasp her hand, rise from her knees and tell Nicholas, who would presently be in his grave, that she would not do it.

"—I promise to marry Sasha," she replied.

"May God bless you both."

They rose and left the room, still hand in hand, but unaware of this till they stood in the corridor. Several persons were waiting there. Nobody spoke a word. Perhaps those in the corridor did not observe that the fingers of the Grand Duke Alexander and the Princess Dagmar were intertwined. Their hands fell apart and for a second their eyes met. At that moment neither of them had anything to say to the other. Dagmar asked a servant to take her to her room, and Sasha, ambling like a drunken man, sought his own quarters.

Two hours later the Tsarevitch Nicholas died in the presence of them all, and it was almost with his last breath that he revealed painfully and very briefly to those around his bed that Dagmar and Sasha had promised to marry one another.

Even in the hour when the Tsarevitch was breathing his last at Cannes, and several hours before the telegram announcing his death reached the Russian capital, a sensational rumor was growing like a rolling snowball in Petersburg and Moscow. This rumor declared that if Tsarevitch Nicholas died the Emperor intended to vest the succession to the throne in his third son Vladimir, of whom he thought very highly, and that he considered the Grand Duke Alexander incapable of ruling Russia. Nor was such an action without precedent in Russian history. Within living memory Nicholas I had superseded his crazy elder brother Constantine.

At Cannes the same rumor was the subject of general gossip and speculation among the Russian suite and the household staff throughout that day, and the story had reached Queen Louise by her lady in waiting within an hour of her arrival. Dagmar, upon leaving the sickroom, had said nothing to her mother, for she considered that her lips must be sealed until Sasha informed his father and received the imperial assent to the marriage.

Thus, to Queen Louise the news that her nephew Alexander might be superseded in the Russian succession was only an item of secondary interest. She thought little of him, had heard he was a libertine who had been involved in many low scandals, and was not surprised.

Later, Louise stood by the deathbed and listened with dismay and incredulity to the announcement of the dying Nicholas. Such was the shock that she appeared on the point of fainting, which was attributed to her emotion at the tragic scene.

But the Queen of Denmark was envisaging her daughter married to an uncouth madman with a vicious reputation, who might be repudiated by the Emperor and forced to live a life of disgrace or even exile.

Louise was appalled. The transaction seemed sinister, even macabre, to her. As she blundered from the death chamber she determined that it was her duty to warn her daughter of the information concerning Sasha which had reached her ears.

Back in their own apartments Dagmar heard her mother out in silence.

"I have given my word," she said when her mother had finished. "I shall marry Sasha if the Emperor allows it."

If tall Louise was a woman of resolution, so was her small daughter. There for the moment the matter rested, with the imperial villa in a state of grief and bustle as the elaborate preparations began for the ceremonial removal of the corpse of the Tsarevitch to the Russian capital.

The rumor about the supersedure of Grand Duke Alexander and the naming of Vladimir as Tsarevitch had gained tremendous strength in Russia when the imperial funeral train with the Emperor and Empress, the grand dukes and duchesses, and the Danish party arrived in Petersburg. Up to that time the Emperor, who had been in deep distress since the death of Nicholas, had kept his silence.

But deputations from all parts of the Empire, come to express their condolences at the death of the Tsarevitch, awaited him in the capital. When the Emperor received the Poles he called Sasha to stand beside him. The Poles were the most troublesome subjects in his vast domains, and even on this occasion of sorrow he could not resist speaking to them like a disapproving headmaster, who hoped for better things in future. But the final words of his brusque speech killed a rumor.

"—Here beside me stands my son, my *heir*," he exclaimed. "He bears the name of the emperor who formerly established the kingdom of Poland. I hope he will know how to govern his inheritance worthily, and that he will not endure that which I myself have not tolerated."

Whether Alexander II had really contemplated the possibility of depriving Sasha of his rights in case of the death of Nicholas, and if so whether he changed his mind after hearing the deathbed disclosure of his eldest son, is not known. It may be so; for he had been heard to express a flattering opinion of the character of his Danish niece, and he may have arrived at the conclusion that the unsatisfactory personality of his second son might greatly adjust itself under Dagmar's guidance.

CHAPTER III

Bride cAmong the Grand Dukes

Princess Dagmar of Denmark was married to Tsarevitch Alexander on November 9, 1866, in the chapel of the Winter Palace at St. Petersburg. She was nineteen, within a few days of her twentieth birthday. Sasha was twenty-one.

The incredible sumptuousness and extent of their wedding presents and of her own trousseau, which when displayed filled a huge hall of the Winter Palace, were such as to render speechless any bride who had not been born a Russian grand duchess. Dagmar stood before the dazzling mass of gems which loaded the jewelry tables, and made the Russians laugh by her naïve declaration that she would be dead before she had time to wear half the pieces presented to her. Her amazing trousseau owed its magnificence in a generous degree to gifts from the Emperor, as was customary when foreign brides came into the imperial family. Superb furs, coats, mantles, jackets and caps were piled high on tables in one corner of the hall, and silk stockings, gloves for every occasion, articles of fine lingerie, dressing-gowns, fur boots, shawls and scarfs were repeated by the score. Even bundles of lace handkerchiefs had not been omitted from the imperial munificence.

The wedding day of a Russian grand-ducal bride was a harsh

ordeal, especially if she was a stranger. Entangled in a web of incomprehensible Romanoff ritual and tradition, she was the harassed slave of a relentless master of ancestral ceremonies. Dagmar, like many an imperial bride before and after her, scarcely emerged to full consciousness on that day, until she found herself buried in furs in a covered sleigh, with Sasha looming silently beside her, and the icy winter darkness surrounding them, as they swiftly sped through the countryside to Ropsha, the little country palace where Romanoffs spent their honeymoons.

That morning she had stood for a terrible three hours in the Malachite Drawing Room of the Winter Palace for the ceremonial bride-robing, while dressers borrowed from all the grand-ducal ladies jostled and argued angrily around her.

Every Romanoff bride must be dressed before the celebrated golden mirror of Empress Anna Joanovna, and she had gazed in patient wonder at herself as her glory grew painfully upon her: her hair rolled into the long traditional side-curls, resting on the shoulder after the mode of Catherine the Great, her body imprisoned in the stiff, immensely heavy antique gown of genuine silver tissue, her shoulders torn by the sweltering ermine train, dropping in endless folds behind her, tugging her backward and setting the perspiration oozing from her back in the merciless palace heat. Clusters of ancient jewels were snatched from red velvet cushions and violently affixed to her person, to be as roughly torn away and replaced by others, till their mocking light filled her with nausea. Empress Marie and her mother had sat nearby in chairs, offering contradictory suggestions which increased the ill-natured confusion.

She had been exhausted before she reached the dazzling splendor of the altar, she had reeled, sick and choking, amid the thick clouds of incense. At the never-ending imperial reception, where she had to drag her ermine train without trainbearers, she had heaved herself from place to place in a nightmare of physical misery.

But even in the midnight peace of Ropsha Dagmar discovered that she had not yet left Romanoff ritual behind her. The old palace was silent and she was alone in the bridal chamber. Certainly the bridal chamber in the dim lamplight had an ancestral and ghostly air, with the shadow of the towering and forbidding baroque four-poster blackening the colors of the painted ceiling; but at least she was alone, her few remaining attendants having retired with knowing looks. Doubtless they were not far away, peering excitedly from dark crannies in the corridor; for the hour had struck when the imperial bridegroom, garbed in the "wedding-night uniform" of the Romanoff grand dukes—but alone, thank heavens!—must issue from his dressing-room and traverse the corridor to enter the nuptial chamber.

Sasha had not warned her to expect a shock. He had been so silent. She heard the creaking of an opening door, and heavy dragging footsteps slowly grew louder in the corridor. The door swung open dramatically, as if some very angry person had pushed it. The monstrous vision which met her startled gaze was too much for her strained emotions. She collapsed in peals of hysterical laughter.

Sasha, with his head thrust forward to clear the lintel and enveloped in a kind of high silver turban, crowned in its turn by the fat nude flesh-tinted cupids sprawled over the doorway, glared at her with bulging eyes and an expression of shamefaced indignation. From his tremendous shoulders to his ankles, like a canopy, hung a gleaming silver gown, which seemed to have the solidity of armor, while from under it his huge feet stuck out, encased in silver slippers with long curling metallic points. He was like some theatrical Bluebeard whose beard had dropped off, or a gigantic operatic Caliph of Baghdad.

❈   ❈   ❈

One aspect of this marriage between the sister-in-law of the Prince of Wales and the Tsarevitch was the strong political significance it was deemed to have at the time for Great Britain. The Prince of Wales, in accordance with his promise made two years before at Fredensborg, made his appearance in the Russian capital for the occasion. He had not achieved his ambition without difficulty.

Alix, to her bitter disappointment, had been unable to accompany him. She lay in bed at Marlborough House in the first stages of recovery from a nearly fatal attack of rheumatic fever. Alix had been desperately anxious for Bertie to attend the wedding; but her personal feelings on this subject did not in the least move Queen Victoria, who thought "a visit to St. Petersburg by one of the Prince of Wales's gentlemen would be quite sufficient."

In the end, the Prime Minister had prevailed with the Queen where Bertie had failed, and Emperor Alexander in his reply to the notification from Windsor that the Prince of Wales was coming had, in fact, seemed to be extremely flattered.

Three days before the wedding Bertie had been greeted at Petersburg by the Emperor and the grand dukes. There could be not the smallest doubt that his visit was a good idea. Language presented no difficulties, for strangely enough they all talked English, as well as French, despite the twelve years of bitterness which had existed between Britain and Russia.

Bertie's boyish exuberance had delighted the young grand dukes, amused the older ones and charmed the grand duchesses. Carefully instructed to avoid the pitfalls of politics, his social success was sensational.

He had cheerfully made the round of Petersburg's low night haunts with Sasha, Vladimir and Alexis. The underworld of Petersburg was, indeed, the proudest exhibit of Russian grand dukes to all princely visitors, for they boasted—rightly—that their capital was the most depraved in Europe, and regarded it almost as their personal property. Nothing, therefore, could have pleased them better than the assurance given by the royal connoisseur of London night life that his own capital could not compare with it.

It was, perhaps, in this tawdry and erotic environment that the Prince of Wales caught the imagination of Sasha; for only in these crude haunts did his Russian brother-in-law feel really at home. One of the most surprising features of the English royal visit to the imperial court was the nonchalant ease with which the Prince of Wales penetrated the façade of taciturnity which the stolid Tsarevitch presented to everybody else, except perhaps to his brothers Vladimir and Alexis.

Whatever Bertie did in Russia was generously applauded, and he finally surmounted all previous successes at the British Ambassador's ball in honor of the wedding by taking the floor first in full Highland costume with Dagmar as his partner.

Before Bertie left for home, having established a lifelong friendship with the future Emperor and Empress of Russia, he was able to report to his mother that "every moujik in the streets seems anxious to show me some signs of good will."

In Alix's bedroom at Marlborough House, Bertie upon his return painted a colorful picture of the fairy-tale life her sister was going to live as the Tsarevna of Russia. He said nothing about the black side of things, concerning which the Tsarevna would soon enough be sadly cognizant, for he then knew nothing of this himself. His optimism about the political good he had done would presently prove to be pathetically overrated. Nevertheless, it was his enthusiasm on that day of return from the wedding which fired Alix with the desire to form a real Anglo-Russian *entente,* to be established by the efforts of herself at Marlborough House and of her sister in St. Petersburg. During the years ahead the weekly letters of the sisters would constantly harp on this theme.

          ○   ○   ○

In Petersburg, Tsarevitch Alexander and Tsarevna Marie Fedorovna, for such was the Russian name given to Dagmar, took up residence in the large Anitchkoff Palace on the Nevski Prospect.

But that the interior walls and the ceilings of the principal apartments in the Anitchkoff were covered by a tracery of the fantastic and beautiful paintwork of Russian eighteenth-century artistry, their Petersburg home would have repeated the bleak and dingy spaciousness of Fredensborg.

An army of servants awaited them, proudly bowing them into a scene of dirt and disorder. Dirt and disorder, Dagmar was to discover, were the most difficult enemies to combat in Russian imperial homes; for the servants, who looked so impressive in their costly liveries, seemed to think this a perfectly natural state. The principal members of the household awaiting the Tsarevitch and the Tsarevna at the Anitchkoff consisted of two young married couples, the Count and Countess Obolensky and the Count and Countess Vorontsow-Daskov, and the association of this quartet with Dagmar and Sasha was destined to be a long and intimate one.

The two men were officers with whom Sasha had served in the Guard, and both were well acquainted with his peculiarities. Their wives, as ladies in waiting, had each of them something to teach the unsophisticated Tsarevna. Tania Obolensky soon established herself as the favorite. Tania bubbled perpetually with fun and mischief, and she speedily set to work to demonstrate to Dagmar the joys to be found in wanton extravagance in dress and the delightful excitement which could be experienced in the pursuit of high-life intrigues and scandals.

Tania's levity was offset by the stately Tatiana Daskov, who came from the haughtiest of "old Russian" families. Tatiana Daskov offered a pattern for grace and majestic bearing to the Tsarevna, which she closely observed, and to Tatiana has been ascribed that air of splendid and effortless regality which one day would make Dagmar famous throughout Europe.

It was not long before a whisper passed in Petersburg society that the enchanting and gay young Tsarevna had a *bad* husband and that she was to be pitied. While Dagmar sat at home of an evening with her ladies the Tsarevitch was wallowing in the wildest orgies with his brothers Vladimir and Alexis at Novaia Deresvnia, the notorious "Islands" quarter in the Neva. Such was the vile nature of these orgies, and such was the quantity of champagne alleged to be consumed by the young grand dukes, that it was said the Tsarevitch would soon ruin his health, if he did not kill himself.

Perhaps the bride of Tsarevitch Alexander was less perturbed by these things, which she had good reason to believe were really taking place, than those who sympathized so dismally with her pitiable lot. For Dagmar was aware that her huge, awkward and silent Sasha was a tender husband, and that possibly the dead

Nicholas had not been wrong when he spoke so well of his brother on his deathbed. Dagmar had married a wall of obstinacy. She had also married a savage bull. Whether or not she had married as big a blockhead as was generally supposed, she was about to set out to discover for herself. This crude giant was the man at whose side she would one day have to appear as the Empress of Russia, and it seems that in those early days of their marriage Dagmar had more confidence in the future of Sasha than anybody else.

The education of the Tsarevitch began, and it was the Tsarevna who undertook the task. An emperor autocrat requires some knowledge of the history of the people he has to rule, some knowledge of world history, some knowledge of political and economic science. But Sasha was as ignorant as a peasant. Each of his four living brothers, even ten-year-old Serge and eight-year-old Paul, appeared to be more fitted by their scholastic accomplishments for an imperial throne than did he.

If Sasha chose to drive away into the Petersburg night to his horrible orgies with that dogged, defiant air, which secretly amused his wife, she had no pity on the sagging ruin who sprawled in an exhausted mound under the bedclothes next morning. She told him shortly to get dressed, and went to set out the books which they were to read together for that day. At first Sasha had obeyed her command in shocked astonishment, and the educational process had been cold and painful. But not many days had elapsed before Sasha so far forgot himself that he entered into discussion with his wife on items which cropped up in their reading. That was the signal for Dagmar to hand him several exercise books and tell him to make notes. There were witnesses at the Anitchkoff who presently declared that Tsarevitch Alexander actually emerged from his study periods with a smile on his face.

There was one person who observed this development in the life of the Tsarevitch with deep interest and amazement. He was a lean, tall, hungry-looking, middle-aged man, with a pale, sharp nose and gimlet eyes which gleamed blackly through gold-rimmed spectacles. His name was Pobedonsteff, and somebody had once said of him that he always walked about as if he were leading a never-ending religious procession. He had, indeed, started life as a divinity student; but he had abandoned religion for the law, and finally he had been chosen as head tutor for the Grand Dukes Nicholas, Alexander, Vladimir and Alexis by the Emperor.

Pobedonsteff had utterly neglected Sasha. He was hopeless. When some elder member of the imperial family or some favorite minister of State visited the schoolroom in the Winter Palace, as happened from time to time, Pobedonsteff would draw them aside if he saw that they had inspected Grand Duke Alexander's exercise books.

"Our darling dove," he would whisper in his coldly supercilious voice, and with a glance toward the oafish Sasha, "has been sent into the world with the shabbiest of intellectual outfits."

But from the day on which Sasha had been proclaimed Tsarevitch, Pobedonsteff had made a new approach to his old backward pupil, and after his marriage the tutor became a frequent guest at the Anitchkoff. Dagmar was impressed by Pobedonsteff —not that he was a ladies' man, but because of his intellectual power. Everything he said came out with a kind of cold, fanatical earnestness which defied contradiction.

One day at the Anitchkoff Pobedonsteff declared, "Outside the imperial palaces, Russia is an icy desert, the abode of the Bad Man!" and Dagmar had heard this brutal observation with a shudder. Yet she was deeply interested in this glaring unlikable man; nor could she believe that he would ever utter words in which he did not passionately believe. She perceived that Pobedonsteff watched her husband with mingled scorn and curiosity, but that he was, nevertheless, intensely anxious to ally himself with him in his function as Tsarevitch. She knew that Sasha feared and held in respect above all men the tutor who had mockingly neglected his youth. She was aware, also, that in one respect Pobedonsteff had strongly influenced the boyhood of Sasha: he had succeeded in instilling in his mind a kind of blind, primitive passion for the Orthodox faith.

Dagmar began to encourage Pobedonsteff in his approaches to Sasha. He was in her opinion a man fitted to groom an autocrat; or at least he might with her connubial aid imprint upon her husband's limited mind many valuable maxims for the future. If Sasha could be made to acquire a truly keen comprehension of his own shortcomings, to know at what point he became inadequate and must turn to another for advice, that of itself would be of great use to him. She believed that the born stupidity and obstinacy of Sasha would always make it painful for him to accept advice from other men. But what if the adviser—the imperial mentor—was Pobedonsteff, the old tutor whom Sasha so revered?

Thus there appeared in the circle forming around the clever and fascinating young Tsarevna a forbidding figure, who puzzled and frightened many of her friends by his cool assumption of authority. This was the heartless cynic whom liberal exiles would label the Evil Genius of Russia.

But one of the first new tendencies to become apparent in the Tsarevitch had nothing to do with Pobedonsteff. This was his growing, and soon startlingly outspoken, anti-Germanism. It was entirely due to his wife. Dagmar, like her sister Alix, bitterly hated Germans from the day they robbed her father of Schleswig-Holstein.

Germanophobia appeared as an odd characteristic to most Russians in the late 'sixties; for Emperor Alexander II loved Germans, the Empress was a German, the grand duchesses were Germans and many of the best administrators in the Empire were the Russians of pure German descent from the Baltic states. German names were, in fact, very common in Russian high life; for it was the ancestors of these people who had helped Peter the Great to civilize Russia.

As might have been expected with Sasha, the tempo of his Germanophobia soon moved to ridiculous lengths. Dagmar had set off a steam roller and she could not stop it.

If, when Sasha was at court, he perceived that some eminent visiting German was being led up to him to be introduced, he deliberately turned his back on him and ambled away. If he was taken unawares by the stranger's approach the Tsarevitch stood glaring morosely at the floor without offering a word of conversation, till the victim shriveled and shrank away in humiliation. Brother officers with Sasha in the Guards, who bore German names, and who formerly had spent many a mad night with him in the Petersburg underworld, asked their friends in bewilderment what they had done to offend the Tsarevitch.

Sasha, soon after his marriage, was appointed by his father to be Colonel of the Probajansky Regiment, the oldest corps of Guard Infantry, and as a result a story came out of the Anitchkoff which subsequent happenings proved to be true.

The Tsarevitch asked for a list of the names of the officers of the Probajansky, so that the Tsarevna could personally send out invitations to a party to mark his appointment. This list was handed to him one evening as the household was waiting to proceed to dinner, and he immediately passed it to his wife. She perused the list, and then without a word handed it back in a rather deliberate way to her husband, lifting her eyebrows quite perceptibly as she did so. He looked surprised. His eyes ran down the list. The expression on his face grew longer and longer, and then positively black. Every officer on the list bore a German name, except the last one—Ensign Woronzoff, the junior officer.

Suddenly the Tsarevitch startled the assembly by shouting out, "Thank God for Woronzoff!"

"Yes," murmured the Tsarevna with a mischievous smile, "Woronzoff should have a bright future in the Probajansky."

"He will soon be the officer with the longest service in the Probajansky," grunted the Tsarevitch, "because I shall get rid of the others as quickly as possible."

He kept his word. Within a few weeks the Commandant of the Guard Corps was astonished to receive applications for a transfer of regiment from every officer in the Probajansky from the Lieutenant Colonel downwards, except one—Ensign Woronzoff. From that time on the Probajansky was referred to jokingly in Guard messes as the "All Russian."

These antics of Sasha greatly offended and irritated his father, and were the cause of the first coldness between them after he became Tsarevitch. The climax of the Germanophobia at the Anitchkoff was reached when the Crown Prince of Prussia was expected on a visit to the Emperor. Sasha was in the Emperor's study with several of the elder grand dukes, his uncles, and various distinguished officers when Alexander II, while discussing the arrangements for the visit, chose to give deference to his eldest son by asking his opinion on some item.

"It is of no consequence to me," said the Tsarevitch. "I don't intend to meet him during his visit."

There was a horrified silence. The Emperor, pale with rage, ordered him to retire to the Anitchkoff and remain under close arrest until further orders. Upon Crown Prince Frederick William's arrival it was explained to him that the Tsarevitch was unfortunately ill and confined to his room.

The state of arrest at the Anitchkoff was short-lived, for Dagmar exercised the same charm over her father-in-law as did Alix with Queen Victoria. Strangely enough, Alexander did not seem to connect his daughter-in-law with his son's Germanophobia.

Dagmar saw her father-in-law the Emperor only infrequently. The private life of Alexander II had already become involved in a scandal, which would one day rock the whole of Europe. He was on bad terms with the Empress, and he seldom ascended to her apartments in the Winter Palace except to fetch her to dinner, which was a meal of ceremony. The Empress, perhaps to solace herself, was becoming deeply concerned with mysticism, and taking less and less interest in people and happenings around her. Dagmar soon discovered that in Petersburg a moment of strained silence occurred if mention was made of the Empress.

Alexander II lived in his large study below the apartments of the Empress. Here he slept on a camp bed, when he slept at all; for he suffered severely from asthma and often preferred to work at his desk through several nights at a stretch rather than risk lying down. Some said that he drank heavily. Nearly everybody liked Alexander II, and even those who were genuinely shocked concerning the unpleasant nature of his feminine entanglements were inclined to regard him with pity rather than bitterness.

Marie, his little daughter, then on the threshold of her teens—
she was destined to become Duchess of Edinburgh—was his
closest friend in the family; and in both winter and summer
Alexander II, dressed in a general's undress uniform and accompanied by Marie and two large dogs, might be met almost
every day walking on the Quai de la Cour, the fashionable
promenade which ran alongside the Winter Palace by the Neva.
In the later 'sixties clusters of vigilant police appeared on the
promenade before the Emperor strolled from the Palace. Not
long before Dagmar's marriage Alexander II, while walking
totally unguarded on the Quai, had been shot at by a young
Nihilist at point-blank range. The bullets had missed. The Emperor disarmed the youth and held him till somebody fetched
a policeman.

A sad expression usually played over the pale, handsome features of the tall Emperor, who was said on state occasions to be
the most dignified sovereign in Europe. In spite of all Alexander
II had done for the people of Russia the sinister underground of
Nihilism, controlled by mysterious individuals at Geneva, was
coiling itself into secret cell upon cell throughout the vast Empire. Preaching the atheism which was necessary to its macabre
purpose, it impressed upon its gullible disciples the need of
bringing humanity to the foul equality of worms in the dunghill,
so that out of the horrible midden a grand new world could
arise, free of all the faults and injustices of the old world.

Relations acquired by marriage must always be of some concern to a young bride. Dagmar found herself with three uncles-
in-law, three aunts-in-law and twelve first cousins, the grown-up
or growing children of these three couples.

The uncles, brothers of the Emperor, were the Grand Dukes
Constantine, Nicholas and Michael, and it was with the family
of the senior uncle, Constantine, that Dagmar at first became
most friendly. This was chiefly because in the year after her own
marriage her brother Willy, the King of Greece, married fifteen-
year-old Olga, the youngest of the four Constantine children.

The young Greek King had been invited to Russia by the

Emperor to find a bride, and after a nine-months' sojourn, during which he was much in the company of his sister the Tsarevna, he astounded everyone by picking as his wife a schoolgirl, who happened to peep at him over some banisters at the Marble Palace.

Uncle Constantine himself, a sharp, sinister, unpredictable man, was as frightening to his Danish niece as to most other people. A gaunt, hawklike giant with sly, hooded eyes under pale eyebrows, it was whispered of him, even in the family, that he was constantly under supervision of the Secret Police. He was supposed to have been discovered contributing to Nihilist funds, with the object of achieving the murder of his brother the Emperor so that he himself might somehow usurp the throne.

Uncle Nicholas, a more amiable and picturesque eccentric, pursued the strange hobby of attending every fire in Petersburg, night or day, and was a popular figure among the mob in the city. The colorful love affairs of Uncle Nicholas also aroused perpetual gossip, and though people praised the dignified forbearance of his wife, Alix of Oldenburg, they hinted that the beautiful and good-natured Grand Duchess knew how to solace herself for her husband's unfaithfulness. But Grand Duchess Alix was not too absorbed in her own disturbed domestic affairs to be a kind and helpful adviser to her niece, the young Tsarevna, in the bewilderments of Russian imperial life.

Dagmar had met her youngest uncle, Michael, and his wife, Olga of Baden, only at her wedding, for Michael was Governor of the Caucasus; but it was this couple and their children who were destined to come closest to her among the Romanoffs.

Imagination must supply the regiment of imperial cousins in their various states of removal from the Romanoff fountainhead, the lesser princes and princesses of the blood, who made up the fantastic kaleidoscope which was the wealthiest, the most bejeweled, the most ceremonious, and the most scandalous court in Europe. Few of these people knew the meaning of money, or if married into the family from abroad they, like Dagmar, soon forgot it. It was inevitable that most of them should indulge their every whim. Who can wonder that these highborn Russians were human beings apart, at whom the rest of the world wondered? They were unique, and the most incredible stories told of them were often the truth.

The cosmopolitan sophistication of this self-indulgent court was contradicted by the actions of many of its most notable inmates, who developed a greedy appetite for crude medieval mysticism and magic. The mirrored halls of the palaces reflected holy miracle-workers in greasy moujik gowns passing among the elegant groups, and horribly deformed cripples and epileptics, dumb and gaggling, screeching and thrashing their twisted limbs, were exhibited by the grimy ecclesiastical charlatans like organ-grinders' monkeys. The sickening performances of these pitiful horrors were reverently listened to as the oracles of God, and people who in appearance were cultured Europeans avidly begged the holy men to translate the noises they emitted.

In this charged atmosphere of sacred conjuring, of pantomime gallantry and beautiful intriguing women, of stately processions and pageantry and imperial clowns and madmen, walled off from the "icy desert of the Bad Man" by an army of secret police, the second daughter of the bourgeois King of Denmark carved herself a place with charming equanimity. Her wit, her loveliness, her mischievous gaiety, her quiet dignity and sympathetic manner, brought her many devoted friends and admirers.

Dagmar was very young, and it is difficult to believe that at her age she was wholly unmoved by the prevailing temperature of imperial Petersburg; yet the impression remains that then, as afterward, she stayed remarkably cool, when other young foreign wives abandoned themselves with mind and body to the languorous vapors of the hothouse.

During those last years of the 'sixties and the opening years of the 'seventies life for her was comparatively uneventful, except for those supremely important personal items in the career of a young wife—the birth of her children.

In August 1867 her firstborn came into the world, a son, who was christened Alexander. He was a magnificent baby, large and healthy, and everybody agreed that Alexander looked just the right kind for a future Emperor.

Nicholas was born in May of the following year. Members of the family looked at Nicholas, and then regarding his mother almost reproachfully announced, "He is going to be small!" In the Romanoff family it was a crime to be puny. It gave ground for deep foreboding. The small princes of the Romanoffs had a bad record.

It was in the Summer of 1869, in a hot August, when the doctors told the Tsarevna that her eldest son, who had developed a bad cold and cough, was suffering from pneumonia. Two days later Alexander was dead.

Thus it came about that puny little Nicholas, destined to be the last of the Romanoffs, became the heir after his father to the Throne of All the Russias.

One of the court priests, who was ministering to the grief-stricken mother as she knelt beside the dead child, assured her that since Holy John of Tobolsk, the guardian Saint of the Romanoffs, had allowed the Grand Duke Alexander to die, then clearly it was because the Saint had singled out the Grand Duke Nicholas for the highest honors. This solemn declaration by the holy man was heard by the attendants in the room and soon the words were widely broadcast through Russia. But although this prophecy offered just that brand of mystical claptrap which awed Russians, many of those who had actually seen the weakling Nicholas still persisted in regarding him with dismay.

Two years later, in the dawn of a May morning, George was born, a handsome and winning child, who presently showed all the promise and the determined character of his dead brother Alexander.

One notable item concerning the coming of a family to Dagmar and Sasha must not go unrecorded. Sasha was already qualifying as one of the better husbands of the imperial court, even if he underwent occasional relapses. Now, with the mantle of paternity upon him, he was beginning to display another characteristic, which many had not expected of one so taciturn. He began to take a great delight not only in his own children, but in all children of all ages. "Uncle Sasha" was launched on his Pied Piper career as the inspired buffoon and beloved friend of an army of small nephews, nieces and cousins of the future. Perhaps the truth was that Sasha had never ceased to be a child himself.

CHAPTER IV

The Tsarevna

In 1872 a new and colorful personality entered Dagmar's life, a woman who was to be her friend and ally, and also at times her rival, during the half-century ahead.

On an April afternoon of this year Grand Duke Vladimir, the usually gay brother-in-law of the Tsarevna, called upon her. Dejection and dismay showed in his face. Vladimir had been called to his father the Emperor that morning. Emperor Alexander had told Vladimir that he had found a wife for him.

It appeared that Vladimir's future bride had seen him when he was in Germany in the previous autumn and had decided that he was her destiny. After reflection she had informed her doting parents of her resolve to marry him, and they had written to the Emperor.

This determined German princess was Marie of Mecklenburg-Schwerin, who would one day be a grandmother of the present Duchess of Kent.

Marie of Mecklenburg was tall, beautiful and commanding. She was a close friend of Bismarck, who was said to have praised her force of character, her energy and her intellect in the highest terms. That Vladimir, unwilling to sacrifice his carefree life to any woman, was perturbed at the prospect of this formidable partner was sympathetically appreciated by his sister-in-law, but she could offer him no comfort. The word of the Emperor was law.

The wedding of Marie and Vladimir took place in the autumn of 1872, and afterward it was natural that the newly married couple should be frequently at the Anitchkoff. Firstly, this was because Sasha always sought the company of his more gifted younger brother and always liked to listen to Vladimir's opinion with the closest attention, and secondly, because Grand Duchess Marie, finding herself the third lady in the land, wished to ally herself with the Tsarevna in the leadership of the fashionable world.

Up to this time the acknowledged leader of society had been the Tsarevna. The Empress was an ailing and embittered woman and was rarely seen. Now, and for the next nine years, the elegant Grand Duchess Marie was in a better position to shine than the Tsarevna; for Marie had equipped herself with a husband who was able to give her brilliant support in salons and ballrooms, whereas Sasha was no ornament to Dagmar and was frequently notable by his absence.

Sasha did not like his brother's bride. Whether or not he became aware of the whisper soon current in Petersburg that Grand Duchess Marie was an agent of Bismarck, his sister-in-law certainly sinned in his eyes by being a friend of the Prussian statesman. Marie's constant flow of clever repartee, her sparkling displays of intellectuality, left Sasha groping and indignant. But chiefly his German sister-in-law offended him because in defiance of Romanoff tradition she had done a thing which no imperial bride had done for 150 years: she had refused to abandon her own faith, the Lutheran, for the Greek Orthodox Church. Sasha, with the narrow faith instilled into him by Pobedonsteff, was shocked and outraged by a matter which his father, the Emperor, had accepted with placidity.

The dislike of Sasha for Grand Duchess Marie was not hard to perceive. Marie saw it, but she was unmoved, for she secretly despised the stolid Tsarevitch. She observed how her husband dominated his elder brother. She could picture herself and Vladimir in the role of Tsarevna and Tsarevitch, parts they could have played with such accomplishment, and she believed it was her duty as the wife of Vladimir to conduct herself toward Sasha with the same condescending amiability as did he. Eyewitnesses told of the giant Tsarevitch grinding his teeth behind his sister-in-law's back.

The summer of 1873 was a memorable one for Dagmar. It was the occasion of the celebrated visit to London of the Tsarevitch and the Tsarevna as guests of the Prince and Princess of Wales at Marlborough House.

In the years since Dagmar's marriage she and Alix had met every year in Denmark at the family gatherings at Fredensborg, either at Christmas or in the summer; and the sisters had met once or twice at Schloss Heiligenberg, the hilltop Hesse-Darmstadt country palace above Jugenheim. The London visit had been Alix's idea. It was to be semiofficial, a gesture by the British royal family to the Romanoffs. Moreover, an event had happened in 1871 which gave the sisters high hopes that Anglo-Russian relations might take on a new color. In that summer Bertie and Alix, with his next eldest brother, Alfred Duke of Edinburgh, were guests at Schloss Heiligenberg. Emperor Alexander II with Empress Marie and their only daughter Grand Duchess Marie were also of the house party. They had all got along so well together that both parties confessed afterward that the same thought had occurred to them: a close friendship between the British and Russian families might truly bring the two countries to a better understanding of one another. Something else had also happened at Schloss Heiligenberg. Alfred of Edinburgh had been enchanted by sixteen-year-old Grand Duchess Marie.

The parties had met again at the Schloss in the following summer. There, Alfred of Edinburgh had asked Alexander II for the hand of Grand Duchess Marie.

The Emperor had at once given the pair his blessing. This was accepted by all as a solemn token of his good will to Britain, and more especially as his intense dislike and mistrust of Queen Victoria was well understood.

For the moment the engagement, which would certainly stir a sensation throughout Europe, remained unofficial, and therefore private. It was agreed that in Britain the official announcement should be made by Mr. Gladstone, the Prime Minister, to Parliament in April 1873. Mr. Gladstone was to assure the House that the match was a love match: a family union without political significance. But the Waleses did not doubt—as proved to be the case—that the announcement would be received with amazement and uneasiness. Was this the prelude to some kind of jiggery-pokery bargaining with Russia about spheres of influence in the Middle East?

The visit of the Tsarevitch and the Tsarevna was, therefore, Alix's contribution toward stressing the family angle, the coming friendship which was to exist between the British and Russian royal families. The visit was to be the event of the London season and society lent itself enthusiastically to the project.

One original feature of the coming visit, which today would probably be hailed as crude publicity, was that Alix and Dagmar agreed to dress alike, day and night, throughout the entire visit, which was to last a month. In pursuit of this end the letters of the sisters, crossing one another in a most aggravating fashion between London and St. Petersburg, grew very fat; for these were stuffed with sketches and patterns of gowns, with designs for hats and with endless arguments about bustles, buttons, braids, ribbons and jewelry.

Then in the midst of these exciting preparations a bombshell struck Marlborough House, and rebounded upon Whitehall and Windsor. Shah Nasr-el-din of Persia announced his intention of touring the great capitals of Europe in May and June. First the Shah would go to St. Petersburg and nobody could doubt the glory of the reception this greedy Anglo-Russian shuttlecock would receive in that quarter. After that he was visiting Berlin and thence he was coming on to London.

One thing was certain: the reception given to Nasr-el-din in London must equal, if not surpass, that of St. Petersburg. In fact, the coming of the Shah would have to be treated as a full-dress state visit, with the added disadvantage that the Shah, having invited himself, would almost certainly stay longer than the customary three days allotted to such occasions.

Shah Nasr-el-din was going to arrive in London in the middle of the semiofficial visit of the Tsarevitch and the Tsarevna, which was to have been the great event of the season. Now, Sasha and Minnie—Dagmar was known as Minnie to her intimates—would have to play second fiddle and appear on all occasions in the wake of this oriental potentate. Society, of course, would tumble over itself to entertain the fabulous Shah, and the Russian imperial guests would be eclipsed by his magnificence. In Russia everybody would be indignant at the apparent slight to the Tsarevitch and the Tsarevna. The Russians would also be extremely jealous and suspicious of anything the British did for the Shah.

At Marlborough House Alix wept: all the good which had been done was going to be undone, and Britain and Russia would be at loggerheads again. Even Minnie and Sasha might themselves be upset at having to trail about after the Shah, and who could blame them! The wonderful London season they had planned so carefully was spoiled. Bertie ranged about his study in high wrath; for he knew that his mother would do practically nothing about the Shah, except to send him contradictory instructions concerning the things which he and Alix were to do for the Shah. In fact, between them they would have to do nearly everything and entertain Minnie and Sasha at the same time.

A bright June morning arrived when the Russian imperial yacht drew into Woolwich, while the Prince and Princess of Wales waited on the quayside with most of the inhabitants of the town. The gangway went down and the Prince and Princess of Wales went aboard.

Presently they reappeared with their guests and came down to the quay. Suddenly it dawned upon the crowd that the white dress and the little straw bonnet with cherries of the Princess of Wales exactly corresponded to the ensemble of her imperial sister. People gasped at this ravishing picture, as the sisters stood side by side on the quay. Nothing like it had ever before been seen on royal occasions. The crowd roared with delight. They were thrilled by the spectacle of the tremendous Tsarevitch, towering grimly above the rest of the royal party and looking in his embarrassment so exactly like a huge Russian bear. Behind the Tsarevna stood her two small boys, Nicholas and George: a sight that especially pleased the ladies among the spectators.

The carriage procession set out for London with an escort of the Third Dragoon Guards. The Queen had vetoed Bertie's request for Household Cavalry. It was true that the Shah would have to have the household troops, but the Russian visit was only semiofficial! Throughout the long drive to Marlborough House the vision of the twinlike sisters, sitting side by side in the open carriage, stirred the crowds to frenzy and many people to tears.

Some glorious days lay ahead before the arrival of Shah Nasr-el-din, and the sisters determined to make the most of these. Every morning crowds gathered at the railings in Hyde Park to see the Princess of Wales and the Tsarevna, dressed entirely alike, drive by in a victoria drawn by two gray ponies. At the great ball at Lansdowne House a royal quadrille was the feature of the evening. In this the Tsarevna was partnered by the Duke of Teck, the father of the future Queen Mary; and such was the eagerness of the massed guests to watch all the royalties dancing together and the celebrated sisters in their matching evening gowns, that footmen had to go round the ballroom pulling down hysterical ladies from chairs, tables, sofas and even from pillars and potted palms. Bridgewater House, Dorchester House, Apsley House, Grosvenor House, all the great houses gave elaborate balls, which were perhaps more enjoyed by the royal sisters than by most of the guests; for at moments the ballrooms were almost battlefields from which magnificent gowns emerged comically bedraggled.

The Princess and the Tsarevna, still dressed alike but in a much more subdued pattern, arrived in the East End of London, then a place of indescribable squalor and smells, where they alighted at various houses of refuge in which Alix was interested. Such localities the Tsarevna could not conceivably have dared to visit in Russia; but there can be no doubt that as a result of what Alix showed her in London she was stimulated to exercise a strong behind-the-scenes influence in the development of such charitable institutions in Petersburg, where in the murderous winters the poor underwent terrible sufferings.

For Sasha the visit had its trying moments, for he hated balls and receptions, and he was shortly, with the arrival of the Shah, going to become somewhat taciturn and out of temper, as had been anticipated by his brother-in-law. In the meanwhile, the Tsarevitch enjoyed himself in the nursery at Marlborough House, where his own two small boys lived with the Wales children, Eddy, George, Louise, Victoria and Maud, aged from 9 to 4. He found satisfaction in exhibiting his astonishing feats of strength to parties of Bertie's male friends. At a debate in the House of Commons the Tsarevitch was observed to listen with the closest attention, and was said to have declared that he was impressed with the parliamentary system: an interesting fact, if true, when the actual circumstances of his autocratic reign come to be considered. With the Prince of Wales he visited Woolwich Arsenal, Aldershot and many national institutions, and sometimes remarked with apparent annoyance that Russia had nothing as good.

Imperial Russian grand dukes were inclined to be subjects of scorn and suspicion to Englishmen of that day and liable to be the targets of criticism; but the huge and awkward Tsarevitch seems to have given an impression of dignity and restrained affability, which he probably would not have achieved before his marriage.

On June 18 the Shah arrived in London. Rumor had flown ahead of him concerning the three Georgian female slaves who were to join him at Buckingham Palace, which had been placed at his disposal by the Queen. Nasr-el-din seemed to have peculiarities which had much disturbed the Court of Berlin.

Nasr-el-din surpassed all expectations. What were a Tsarevitch and Tsarevna of Holy Russia compared with this! Ropes of blazing gems adorned the chest of his black frock coat like a breastplate, his epaulets were of emeralds and diamonds, a high aigrette of diamonds sprouted from the front of his tall astrakhan cap, his coat buttons were huge rubies, his belt and sword were encrusted with colored jewels. He was tall, with piercing black eyes and handsome mustachios. Society was mesmerized, and so were the people in the streets. The imperial Russians had become back numbers.

The first great event in honor of the Shah was the banquet at Marlborough House on the evening after his arrival. It had already been learned from Berlin that Nasr-el-din had disgusting table manners, that his freedom with ladies was quite shocking, that he had insulted the elderly German Empress and that his bland arrogance was insufferable. The party at Marlborough House and the guests bidden to the banquet were all agog.

The Shah did not disappoint them that night. He arrived an hour late. At the table he sat down while the guests stood awaiting the Prelate's Grace. Gripping the elbows of the Princess of Wales and the Tsarevna, he jerked them down at each side of him. He thought their matching gowns a joke especially for his benefit.

Nasr-el-din pulled food out of his mouth, held up the morsel muttering "Good!" and replaced it. Other rejected bits he tossed under the table with a grimace. He shouted at footmen, which frightened elderly dowagers, and he thrust his bejeweled fingers into the dishes. His knife and fork were soon abandoned and he nonchalantly wiped his greasy hands on the tablecloth. Occasionally the Shah was seen to have risen to his feet: a position from which he could better examine some beautiful woman at the far end of the table. He lolled back and belched with his arms embracing the chair backs of the Princess of Wales and her sister. The favorite drink of Nasr-el-din was strong spirits and he did not spare himself. Wine the Shah waved aside with an indignant protest. People began to watch for the moment when His Highness fell under the table, but his vigor was unimpaired.

Somehow the Shah would have to be persuaded to behave himself at the Queen's luncheon at Windsor on the next day. An important member of his suite, when diplomatically warned of the rigid table etiquette expected at Windsor, was petrified with terror at the prospect of having to approach His Highness. No help could be looked for there. Even in Buckingham Palace the Shah would not have hesitated to strike off the head of an offending subject. Nasr-el-din had even advised the Prince of Wales that when he became King he ought to behead the Duke of Sutherland. *"Trop riche—n'est pas?—dangereux!"* Many conjectured that it was the gruff Tsarevitch who bluntly explained to the Shah in language he could understand that he must restrain himself at Windsor. However that may be, Nasr-el-din did not displease the Queen at Windsor, and the royal luncheon was frigidly correct.

For the general public the most memorable occasion of the dual Russian and Persian visits was the famous gala concert given in honor of both parties at the Albert Hall. There, many thousands had the pleasure of observing the Shah, sparkling all over with gems, sitting in the royal box between the Princess of Wales and the Tsarevna, who in their identical white gowns and matching tiaras framed him like a picture. But that was not all: Nasr-el-din was in gallant mood, and doubtless he would have been unmoved even had he been aware of the grim immensity of the Russian Tsarevitch, which from time to time reared dramatically over him from the gloomy depths of the box. The Shah was seen to pass his arm first round the chair of one royal sister. Then he abandoned her and put his arm round the chair of the other. Later he sat complacently embracing both chairs at the same time. Nasr-el-din appeared at one time to be enfolding not the chair backs, but the bare shoulders of his partners. Some said that he fed the Princess of Wales and the Tsarevna with sweets. He certainly nudged and ogled them from time to time. He may, as others declared, have fondled them. The royal sisters were clearly rocked with hysterical laughter. Their behavior was not quite decorous, and was remarked upon with surprise.

In one respect the imperial Russian guests did rise superior to the Shah of Persia. They spent three days as the guests of Queen Victoria at Windsor. But at the Crystal Palace, to which all distinguished visitors were taken in those days, the great set piece of the fireworks displayed the Shah amid Persian emblems. At

Guildhall it was the Shah who dominated the occasion. At the opera it was the Shah who jostled to the front of the royal box, dazzling all eyes at Covent Garden, and drawing more applause than the prima donnas.

But the first public occasion upon which the Tsarevitch and the Tsarevna noticeably and humiliatingly had to give way to Nasr-el-din was at the great Windsor Review.

Sasha may well have been in ill-humor at that splendid spectacle, for apart from the mortifications of the day, *The Times* had that morning at last exploded at the fierce abuse which the Russian newspapers, all of them passed by the Imperial Censor, were aiming day after day at Britain.

The St. Petersburg *Mir* had finally caused the eruption of *The Times.*

—Proud Albion is doing all she can by the pomp of her receptions to astonish the Shah [proclaimed *Mir*], and to what end, only to outdo Russia and to efface the pleasing memory the Shah took with him from St. Petersburg. In all the British festivities England is showing her spite against Russia rather than her friendship for Persia.

The Times, after mocking at the childish "rant" of *Mir,* had got into its stride:

—There is a portion of the public in St. Petersburg who likes to hear England spoken of as "Bloody Albion," which enjoys such delicate figures of speech as "the hidden growl of the perfidious and cruel tiger," and is able to tolerate as true the description of the Sepoy Mutiny as sustained by English gold to supply an opportunity for the plunder of the Indian Princes. Our Russian friends must not suppose we are always thinking about them. Our Queen, her Ministers, the Lord Mayor, the Lessees of the Opera, the directors of the Albert Hall and the Crystal Palace, have not the slightest desire to make a demonstration against the Russian Government. In fact the Tsarevitch and the Tsarevna have borne a chief part in all these ceremonials. Is it to be supposed that they, too, have been aiding the moral conquest of the British tiger?

Thus the visit which had opened so brilliantly for the Russian imperial guests petered out in anticlimax. Dagmar, perhaps, did not much care. She had thoroughly enjoyed herself with Alix. But Sasha, bearing the honor of Russia on his shoulders and tormented by that terrifying flame of envy inherent in the Russian temperament, had been growing impatient. While Nasr-el-din was bringing bare-knuckle prize fighters into Buckingham Palace gardens and loose women into the building, while he was soiling the palace carpets by eating on the floor, ordering goods from shops for which he never paid and declaring cheerfully that he intended to prolong his stay, the Tsarevitch and the Tsarevna departed quietly to Russia.

At Petersburg Dagmar found that Grand Duchess Marie was already busy with the preparations for her wedding, which was to be in the Russian capital in January; and her "niece," for Marie called her "Aunt Minnie," was eager to consult her about Queen Victoria and royal life in England.

Nobody seemed to be happy about the marriage, except Marie, with her youthful self-confidence. The Emperor and the Empress scarcely mentioned it. Queen Victoria was uneasy and secretly prejudiced against her future daughter-in-law, and her own daughters were always inclined to follow the same line of thought as herself. After the bad feeling stirred up by the Russian newspaper campaign Bertie, dismally convinced that a great gap still yawned between Britons and Russians, had expressed himself on the Russian marriage. He had said that he "hoped for the best," and Dagmar had heard of this from her sister. Back at the Anitchkoff, Sasha and Dagmar, recalling their recent memories of the Windsor atmosphere, began to question whether spoiled Marie would ever find her place in that quarter.

It was on January 18, 1874, that Bertie and Alix arrived in Petersburg for the wedding. They were to stay at the Anitchkoff as the guests of Sasha and Dagmar. Prince Alfred, who had reached Russia a few days before them, was lodged at the Winter Palace. To Bertie it seemed at first that the imperial atmosphere was somewhat cool, but this was perhaps because he himself was uneasy. He had been forced by his mother to refuse the colonelcy of a Russian regiment offered him by the Emperor: such a custom, she said, was "un-British," and as a result Bertie feared he had caused much offense. Nevertheless, the feel of Petersburg outside the walls of the Winter Palace filled the Prince of Wales with excitement. He meant to enjoy himself, and there were ample opportunities for so doing.

The wedding took place in the Winter Palace, with all the ritual magnificence attending the nuptials of a grand duchess. Shortly afterward the Grand Duchess with her British husband left St. Petersburg for her new home; nor was it long before the imperial family were discussing with indignation and dismay the information contained in Marie's first letters from England. Marie wrote that her mother-in-law was "a silly obstinate old fool." Her father had warned her about Queen Victoria, and now she agreed with him. The Queen, wrote Marie, was obviously jealous of the tiara she had worn in London. It was, in fact, a magnificent one, given as a parting present by her father. At a Drawing Room the Queen had glared at Marie's tiara, ruffled her shoulders like an angry parrot, and scowled meaningly at the less distinguished ornaments adorning the brows of her own daughters. The Queen had even thought fit to hint that she thought Marie's tiara "too good" for a young princess. At Balmoral Marie had ordered a fire to be lit in her icy bedroom. When she was out the Queen had entered the room and had ordered a maid to put out the fire and open the windows. Marie declared one might as well live in an iceberg as in an English home in winter. There was no court life in England. The cooking in the royal homes was terrible. The only person who was *very* nice was the Princess of Wales.

To Dagmar, with her keen anxiety to bring together the Romanoffs and the British royal family, the bitter complaints of Marie were disheartening, and impelled by the fascination which Queen Victoria exercised upon herself, she endeavored to make the somber glory of the Windsor ménage comprehensible to the incredulous Russians.

It was in April 1875 that the Russian newspapers reported a

happy event at the Anitchkoff Palace. The Tsarevna had given birth to her first daughter.

The baby was chistened Zenia. She was a dark-eyed child with the elfin beauty of her mother, and soon gave promise of developing her lively intelligence. Everybody about the imperial palaces knew that the clumsy and elephantine Tsarevitch was delighted by the sex of his fourth child, for his customary brusqueness was conquered by his enthusiasm concerning Zenia. There had been a gap of three years since the birth of George, and it was known that the young parents were beginning to wonder if they would have any more children. There would be another gap of more than three years before the family was complete with the birth of Michael in December 1878.

With the middle years of the 'seventies Dagmar had almost lived through a decade in Holy Russia; yet she was only beginning to see that vast strange empire and its people in some perspective. "Russia," Pobedonsteff, the former imperial tutor, had told her, "is outside the Imperial palaces an icy desert, the abode of the Bad Man!" and now she could in part discern the significance of those grim words. During her first years in Russia she had remained under the spell of the weird and colorful life of the Imperial Court of St. Petersburg.

But with the 'seventies certain pressures had come to bear upon the Tsarevitch, as a result of which Sasha began to move more in the outer world of Russia. He was neither impressionable nor receptive, but he learned many things. He came into the company of people whom the narrow court circle would have considered peculiar, if not dangerous. Gradually he unburdened himself about many disturbing items to his wife.

Russia was alive with revolutionary forces. The mysterious Nihilists were organized into self-contained cells of five persons, each cell a secret known only to the sinister agents of the Internationale. The members of these cells were expected to fulfil any order which might fall to their lot.

Many of these sworn Nihilists were but vaguely aware of what they might be called upon to do. Most of them were young, and many of them were women. In their secret conclaves the members of the cells prattled endlessly of "the Day." They lived in a feverish, enthralling little nightmare world of their own, suspecting their neighbors of being in the Secret Police, or associates of another cell set to spy on them. They feared the emissaries from Geneva, who from time to time appeared in their town to "inspect" them; for as a result of the visit four members of a cell might be ordered to destroy a fifth.

Secret printing presses worked in the attics of every town, and the members of the cells, be they army lieutenants, girl students, civil servants, artisans, midwives, or society women, set out obediently to distribute the inflammatory leaflets placed in their hands.

The Tsarevna herself had read a revolutionary leaflet, blood-curdling but comically crude, which had been picked up in the Anitchkoff kitchens. Citizens of the most impeccable respectability were caught slinking about with parcels of savage and ungrammatical exhortations to revolt; but the police could seldom beat or torture the culprits into disclosing the whereabouts of the hidden printing presses.

Leaflets bearing the same slogan mysteriously circulated in several different provinces simultaneously, proving the existence of a directing brain. One day the peasants were the target of the Nihilist manifestos:

Poor Peasants—victims of the Landlord Oppressors—go out in the morning with your pitchforks: return at night lit by the flames of the great houses with the money which is your due in your pockets!

Another day the revolutionary message was addressed to the whole of Russia:

> Close Your Churches.
> Drive Out the Priests.
> Break Your Marriage Vows.
> Abolish the Rights of Inheritance.
> You are the Equal of the Emperor.
> Arm Yourselves with Knives and Pistols,
> for the Day of Your Deliverance Approaches!

In a sense Alexander II himself sympathized with the aims of the Nihilist moderates, in that he, having already released the serfs, was secretly ambitious to end autocracy in Russia. Nevertheless, he was disgusted when he learned that the Tsarevitch, whom he knew to be simple and gullible, had been observed in the company of "higher liberals." Dostoyevsky, writing at the time, has called "higher liberals" clever talkative persons "without any aim whatever." But "higher liberals" when associating with liberals of less immaculate views were sometimes swept into the whirlpool of Nihilism.

The Anitchkoff was opening its doors to liberals, and it must be assumed that Dagmar at this period of her life was inclined to liberalism in Russia; for her country of birth was outstandingly liberal. Pobedonsteff, the retired tutor, sardonically squinting through his gold-rimmed spectacles at the liberals gathering in the halls of the Anitchkoff, was himself no Liberal. But doubtless in his calculating wisdom he foresaw that the grim march of events would in due time force his protégés to take refuge in his own political beliefs.

The Tsarevna, in the meanwhile, found herself presiding at the Anitchkoff as the leading liberal hostess in Petersburg. She did not rule over a brilliant salon of loquacious intellectuals, as certain great ladies of Russia had done in the past. Such smooth and pompous occasions were not in keeping with the times. The atmosphere in the Anitchkoff soon became electric, conspiratorial. The voices were raised, the faces flushed. It was all typically "new Russian," with the arguments waltzing, pirouetting, twisting back on themselves and toppling into absurdity. Dangerous things were uttered and repeated and denied. Furtive glances flickered to and fro. Doubtless there were evenings at the Anitchkoff when some distinguished Nihilist and a secret-police agent shared the same settee. Dagmar confided to a friend that she entertained this odd company because Sasha wanted it, and that even if some of her guests admitted to strange ideas, she tried to please them, because she believed that anybody who could broaden Sasha's mind and make him speak out was doing a service to the future ruler of Russia.

Many Russians believed that if the Russo-Turkish War had not broken out in 1877, whereby the whole life of Russia was disrupted, an open clash would have occurred between the Emperor and his eldest son, which might have resulted in Sasha being cast from the succession. They suggested, in fact, that the Emperor had held his hand so long only because he feared that if he challenged his eldest son about his liberal activities the Tsarevitch in his turn would openly attack his father for the scandalous circumstances of his life, which everybody agreed was one of the chief causes of the Tsarevitch reforming his own way of living.

Sasha was appointed to command the Army of the Lom. It was, perhaps, a prudent appointment, for the line of the river was unlikely to be strenuously assaulted by the Turks, and the Tsarevitch would have little chance to blunder.

Dagmar was called upon to deputize for the ailing Empress as head of the Russian Red Cross. She insisted upon training as a nurse in a leading Petersburg hospital. Many ladies in high positions went to train as nurses at this time in the hospitals, and the presence of the Tsarevna was unknown among the staff. As always with her, she became universally popular, and everybody treated her with familiarity. Russian military hospitals of the 'seventies were scarcely more inviting than those which Florence Nightingale had set out years before to reform in Britain. The Russian peasant soldiers were incorrigibly filthy, and traditionally had little respect for any but their own officers. Life was hard in the wards for a woman of refinement; but Dagmar proved herself willing to do everything and was considered capable.

Her identity was discovered when the ward sister under whom she worked reported her absence one morning to the matron.

"Don't worry," said the matron. "She is in the building. She will be here in a few minutes."

Presently the door of the ward opened, and in came a solemn procession of inspection, headed by the Tsarevna as head of the Russian Red Cross.

For a time the Tsarevna continued unperturbed at her work

in the wards; but it soon became evident that if, as head of the Russian Red Cross, she was to tackle the chaos which always reigned in Russian organizations and which people seemed to regard as inevitable, she must give her entire attention to the task.

She was thirty in the year the Russo-Turkish War broke out, and in Petersburg it was the general opinion that, fascinating as the Tsarevna had always been, she now possessed an altogether richer quality of enchantment than when she had come as a bride. Ten years of the Petersburg court and in Petersburg society had left her with poise, which was said to be matchless in a woman of her age. Yet her stateliness was of a singular kind, for it allowed her to be perfectly easy and lighthearted with everybody without losing its effect. She had great self-confidence, and spoke her mind in a firm, even voice. Nor, for good measure, did she lack those whimsical characteristics of her sister Alix which so amused the British: unpredictability and cheerful obstinacy. Her services as an administrator in the Russian Red Cross were tremendous in the latter part of the war when the casualties were very heavy.

The war ended with the Russians at the gates of Constantinople. Sasha returned from the Lom. It would soon appear that, if his record was not distinguished, he was nevertheless the only Russian commander to emerge with a clean record from the war. Upon his arrival in Petersburg the Emperor summoned the Tsarevitch to the Winter Palace. When Sasha left the palace he had been made president of the commission set up by his father to examine into the almost incredible accusations of corruption and peculation being made against every commander in the field, *except the Commander of the Lom.* Army boots made of paper, bread stuffed with plaster of Paris, putrid meat, parcels of dirty rags labeled "Bandages," bayonets which twisted like corkscrews, trainloads of greatcoats which never reached the front, swindling contractors alleged to be in league with the Grand Dukes Nicholas and Michael, the senior commanders—these were the items for investigation placed before the Tsarevitch's commission.

Sasha grimly exposed his uncles Nicholas and Michael and, to a lesser degree, Vladimir, the brother whom he idolized. The elder grand dukes were placed under arrest, and the resounding scandal rocked Russia. But in the Russian system little could be done against imperial offenders, except to impose severe mortification upon them. Indeed, the incomes of members of the imperial family were so fantastic that the only real crime of the Emperor's brothers was probably neglect, whereby dishonest subordinates had been able to plunder in their name.

Russians were beginning to look askance at the imperial family. Two of the brothers of the Emperor were under arrest for criminal war records, which had caused the deaths of thousands of soldiers during the Caucasian winter. The Grand Duke Constantine, who commanded the Fleet, was alleged to be constantly shadowed by the Secret Police, because he was a Nihilist. The Emperor himself, who was sacred, was living an openly immoral life, and was said callously to inflict cruelty and humiliation upon the Empress, who was dying of cancer. His sons, the Grand Dukes Vladimir and Alexis, had proved themselves to be abandoned rakes, notorious not only in Petersburg but in the Continental resorts; and the Grand Duchess Vladimir, who scorned the ancient faith of Russia, was reputed to be a spy of Bismarck. Some said that the Tsarevitch was mad; others that he was merely a hopeless simpleton. Certainly he and the Tsarevna had been hand in glove with some very queer liberals before the War. Nevertheless, the Tsarevitch and the Tsarevna emerged much the most satisfactorily from the storm of criticism which even rigid conservatives leveled at the Romanoffs, and they found themselves the only popular members of the imperial family.

The Romanoffs, estranged and bitter among themselves, were united in only one thing: whether brothers or sisters-in-law of the Emperor, or sons or daughters-in-law, they were disgusted by the frantic and pitiful infatuation of Alexander II for a woman young enough to be his daughter, and horrified at his treatment of Empress Marie.

To Sasha and Dagmar, however, Emperor Alexander was now plainly making overtures. He began to come to luncheon every Sunday at the Anitchkoff after attending the usual inspection of regiments of the Guard Corps in the Michael Riding School. He seemed eager to forget for an hour the unhappy atmosphere of the Winter Palace, and to share in the happiness of a gay and untroubled family. To the children of the Anitchkoff the shadow looming over Alexander II meant nothing. Nicholas, George and three-year-old Zenia thought Grandpapa Emperor, with his glittering dark green uniform, his glossy side whiskers and his handsome, kindly face, an exciting and entertaining addition to Sunday luncheon with Papa and Mama.

An inevitable result of these scandals and accusations was that the slumbering fires of Nihilism leapt into a hotter flame than before the War. The presence of unknown Nihilists was suspected in the staff of the Winter Palace. It was widely put about that, no matter what precautions were taken, the Nihilists would murder the Emperor in the end. Noblemen and women of fashion were arrested as Nihilists, and even the Secret Police were believed to contain Nihilist cells.

Earlier in the decade Dostoyevsky, the novelist, had made one of his characters in *The Devils*—Verkovinsky, the Nihilist—shout out: "There's going to be such a to-do as the world had never seen. Russia will become shrouded in a fog, the Earth will weep for its old gods!" Many thinking Russians feared that this frenzied prophecy, one day to be so horribly fulfilled, was coming to pass in the late 'seventies.

The feeling of amiability between the Emperor and his eldest son was not to last long. The liberals returned to the old center of attraction, and the Autocrat of All the Russias, who had been taking his heir more into his confidence, decided that his son was taking advantage of him, and was seized with jealousy and resentment. He continued to attend the Sunday luncheons at the Anitchkoff; but his good nature was forced and his smiles were frigid.

One result of all these things was that at the turn of the decade, when many Russians felt in their bones that somehow a change was coming, the Tsarevitch and the Tsarevna were spoken of highly even in Nihilist circles. It was declared that they could be the salvation of Russia.

CHAPTER V

Terror in February— Scandal in December

IT was on the evening of February 17, 1880, that Dagmar had her first blood-freezing encounter with Pobedonsteff's Bad Man of the icy Russian desert. The experience left her with one of those nightmare memories which came to haunt her dreams all through her life.

❀   ❀   ❀

Shortly after half-past six that evening a young carpenter ascended from the basement of the Winter Palace and stood shivering in the wind while a policeman examined his pass under the gas lantern. His teeth were chattering and his feet shifted restlessly, which the police officer attributed to the cold. The workman had come up at least a quarter of an hour later than his mates, and the officer had not at first realized that he was one of the gang which had been at work in the basement for the last three months. The pass was in order.

The carpenter received it back with a curt nod and muttering, "I'm late for an appointment with a lady friend—must hurry!" he winked at the officer and started at a trot across the broad square toward the Nevski Prospect Archway. The trot had turned to a brisk run before he vanished through the archway, but the policeman was not interested.

In the basement of the Winter Palace a slow fuse was burning its way toward a fulminate-of-mercury detonator resting amid one hundred pounds of dynamite packed in an old wooden case. The carpenter—a Nihilist university student—had brought in the sticks of dynamite in his tool bag day by day.

The box of explosive lay in a room next door to the guard-room, which was occupied that night by the Finnish guard. Immediately above the dynamite, on the ground floor, was the small imperial dining room, and beside this was the Great Hall, from which the grand staircase ran up to the imperial apartments on the first floor.

Emperor Alexander was accustomed to dine at 6:30 p.m., and the time was nearing the quarter to seven. But the dining room was empty except for a few servants, who were putting final touches to the table. Dinner had been postponed till 7 p.m. that evening because the Emperor was giving a family party to welcome his young protégé Prince Alexander of Bulgaria. Alexander of Bulgaria himself would have reached Petersburg in time for the normal imperial dining hour, but his father, Alexander of Hesse, who had been invited to Russia to join him, arrived by a later train.

At a quarter to seven Alexander of Bulgaria and his father crossed the hall and were about to mount the grand staircase. Above, Alexander II with the Tsarevitch, the Tsarevna and the grand dukes and duchesses came out from the Lesser Field Marshals' Saloon and stood at the top of the staircase in readiness to welcome the guests.

For a moment the two parties seemed to pause like tableaux of arrested action, the one gazing down the stairs, the other upward. Then the building shuddered. The huge chandelier over the staircase well rushed past the imperial party and struck the stairs. Plaster poured down on their heads. Below, the wall of the dining room split asunder and a fiery flash filled the hall.

There was a roar like thunder, and smoke belched up the stairs. The gaslights flickered and went out.

In total darkness the imperial family sprawled on their backs, choking in the acrid fumes and groping and clutching at one another in efforts to regain their feet. The terrifying noise of crackling wood, tumbling stonework and splintering glass seemed to continue for several minutes. For a split second absolute silence followed, and then up from the black depths rose bloodcurdling screams and agonized cries, ringing and echoing again and again round the vault of the stairwell. In the wreck of the basement forty officers and men of the Finnish Guard lay dead and fifty-eight seriously injured, while the smoldering woodwork which trapped them threatened to burst into flames and roast them if help did not come quickly. At the foot of the staircase Alexander of Bulgaria and his father lay uninjured.

Wild confusion reigned on the first floor, caused by servants rushing to and fro in the darkness, and several with shouts of terror tumbled headlong down the stairs. Candles and lanterns were kept in the lower rooms of the palace. Ten minutes had passed before lights were brought to the head of the staircase. The stairs were seen to be undamaged. Emperor Alexander hurriedly descended, followed by his sons and brothers. The dazed German guests were helped up the stairs by footmen and the Emperor and grand dukes rushed out into the freezing night to aid in the work of rescue.

Since the Empress was not present it fell upon the Tsarevna to decide what the grand duchess should do. The urgent necessity was a temporary hospital to which the injured could be carried as quickly as possible out of a temperature many degrees below freezing-point. Dagmar led her party down to one of the lower halls, ordering the footmen to bring lights, sheets and all kinds of linen, mattresses and buckets of hot water.

It must have been a macabre scene in that dimly lit hall, where the fetid air was alive with moans of pain; such a scene as Florence Nightingale and her nurses had often known at Scutari —but the women who knelt by the wounded soldiers here glittered with gems, and dark stains smeared their magnificent evening gowns.

This year of 1880 had started grimly for the members of the imperial family, and many of them admitted later that after the disaster of February 17 they were gripped by an uneasy dread that this night of horror was the prologue to evil things. Nor did their secret convictions of coming calamities play them false.

From the beginning of the year it was plain to all of them that short of a miracle Empress Marie would be dead of the cancerous growth which had long troubled her, before another New Year came in. Little could be done for her physical sufferings, but one human being could have eased her mind. This was the Emperor, and he was horribly indifferent. None of them believed for an instant that Emperor Alexander would undergo a change of heart. He was without pity, incapable of any soft feelings for the tortured Empress, engulfed as he was in his insane old man's passion for the Princess Dolgorousky.

This was the quarter from which the next calamity was to come, and the cause of it was the conjunction of two factors: the death of Empress Marie and her husband's overwhelming love for the Dolgorousky.

The Dolgorousky scandal, which had long cast its shadow over the Romanoff family, had its origins in an event of the early 'fifties, when Prince Michael Dolgorousky, a favorite boyhood friend of Alexander II, had died. Michael Dolgorousky was a widower, and on his deathbed he had asked Emperor Alexander to become the guardian of his two small daughters, Mary and Catherine. This Alexander II had willingly agreed to do. He placed the two little girls at the Institute of St. Catherine for daughters of the nobility in Petersburg.

In 1868, Catherine Dolgorousky, the younger sister, reached her eighteenth birthday. She came to live in the Winter Palace as a maid of honor. Catherine had grown up the lovelier of the two Dolgorouskys. She was tall, slender and graceful, with a mass of golden hair.

Presently a story began to spread in Petersburg which created a wave of disgust and incredulity. The fair-haired Catherine

Dolgorousky had left the Winter Palace and the service of the Empress on the plea that she was going to set up house with a female relation in the city. She had moved to a luxurious house on the English Quay, which the Emperor had given earlier to her sister Mary as a wedding present. Almost every afternoon Catherine Dolgorousky was visited by the Emperor, who stayed many hours at the house. Alexander II had fallen madly in love with the younger Dolgorousky. At the house on the English Quay the presiding genius, the custodian, the impresario who displayed Catherine Dolgorousky in the manner of greatest allurement, was thirty-year-old Mademoiselle Schebeko, a distant cousin. She was a clever and ambitious woman, interested in the liberal side of politics, a fact which was to affect future events.

The appearance of infants in the house on the Quay soon became known, and the public scandal grew the greater. It has been said that out of all the imperial family it was Dagmar who found the conduct of the Emperor most painful. She was bitterly ashamed and humiliated because she belonged to a family which Queen Victoria called disreputable and libertine, and was troubled by a sense of almost personal guilt. By the marriage of Alexander's daughter Marie with Alfred of Edinburgh the golden-haired Dolgorousky had turned into a skeleton in her own family cupboard.

In 1875 the Nihilist menace had grown so dangerous that the Emperor decided to bring Catherine Dolgorousky with her family to the Winter Palace.

In all that great space of apartments, many of which had stayed empty for a century, it was strange that Emperor Alexander should have chosen the rooms immediately above the suite of the Empress as lodgings for his mistress and her family. For him it would be convenient, after he had arranged to drive a secret staircase up through the thickness of the outer palace wall from the imperial study to Dolgorousky's rooms, which would enable him to bypass his wife's apartments in between.

The first inkling of unusual things was given to Empress Marie by strange hammerings and clatterings inside her walls. She was left to guess the explanation, which was not perhaps difficult when she heard the noise of children overhead. It was not long before one night she had to listen to the disturbing sound of a confinement over her head; for Catherine Dolgorousky's third child, a girl, was born in the Winter Palace.

Empress Marie was beyond doubt dying of cancer at the beginning of June 1880, and the Duchess of Edinburgh was summoned from England. When she arrived she found that her father was paying no attention to her mother, who was lying in agony. Marie of Edinburgh, although aware of the liaison with Catherine Dolgorousky, did not know that she was lodged on the floor above her dying mother. When she complained of the din above the sickroom the truth was revealed to her. She was inexpressibly shocked. Furious with indignation, she rushed to her father. Almost for the first time in their lives father and daughter faced one another in anger. Their voices grew loud. The door was not shut and the servants heard what was taking place. It became the talk of the palace.

An hour later the Cossacks of the Imperial Escort were warned of an immediate journey to Pavlovsk. Few people knew that the Emperor was leaving the Winter Palace until he climbed into his carriage. He had not visited the Empress. Princess Dolgorousky had preceded him to Pavlovsk with the three children.

Alexander II never saw Empress Marie alive again, and she died on June 16 in the arms of the Duchess of Edinburgh.

Forty days later, on July 26, while the imperial family and, indeed, all the royal families of Europe, observed court mourning, after the strict custom of those days, Emperor Alexander married Catherine Dolgorousky at a private ceremony in his study. Apart from the agitated court priest who conducted it in accordance with the imperial order, the only witnesses were two generals who had long been the Emperor's friends. Alexander gave Catherine and their children the family name of Yourievsky, and declared that henceforth she should be addressed as the Princess Yourievsky. No official announcement was to be made for the present, and the Emperor's secret seems to have been surprisingly well kept. For instance, Victoria, the Crown Princess of Germany, the brilliant eldest daughter of Queen Victoria, who generally knew everything, did not hear of the Russian imperial marriage until November. Victoria was unsure if her mother had heard anything when she reported the marriage to Windsor on November 12, and one passage in her letter especially is interesting in that it relates a detail concerning Dagmar and Sasha to be found nowhere else.

After writing of the secret wedding ceremony, the Crown Princess states that she knows from another source that *"after the ceremony the Emperor sent for Minny* [Dagmar] *and the Tsarevitch and presented his wife to them and asked them to be kind to her."*

Crown Princess Victoria, also, tells her mother that the Russian marriage is not to be made known officially until December 3, and so it was to be. The imperial family, who already knew unofficially, and who expected to be the first recipients of the official news on December 3, were conjecturing fiercely, and with some confidence, what they were likely to learn on that date. They believed that the Emperor, moved by certain secret pressures, such as that of Mademoiselle Schebeko and some interested liberals who were her friends, intended to make Catherine—"the Yourievsky," as she was now referred to in hissing tones—*the new Empress of Russia.*

The private interview between Alexander II and his eldest son and daughter-in-law, which the Emperor must have opened hopefully, can only at best have been a cold, painful and noncommittal one, if Count Vassili is to be relied upon for his account of the course of conduct pursued by Sasha and Dagmar in the days that followed the marriage.

"The heir to the Throne and his wife," declares Vassili, "openly put themselves at the head of the party of those who repudiated every possibility of a *further* triumph for Catherine Yourievsky. They had to see Catherine every Sunday at Mass, where she appeared and stood near the Emperor, in the chapel of the Winter Palace, but beyond that official meeting they paid no attention to her."

It was during the last unhappy months of 1880 that Alexander II at last determined to risk the hazards of granting Holy Russia a limited constitution, as a first step toward the abolition of autocracy, and Vassili declared that it was Catherine Yourievsky who moved the Emperor "to enter upon the road to the most important of all his reforms." The somewhat extraordinary and dramatic denouement of this transaction, in which the Tsarevitch was so closely involved, was vitally to affect the careers of Sasha and Dagmar till the end of their lives.

On the evening of Sunday, December 3, the entire imperial family gathered at the Winter Palace in the Saloon of the Lesser Field Marshals, as was customary when they were to dine with the Emperor.

As Victoria of Germany had forecast, this was the day when Princess Yourievsky was to be acknowledged by the Emperor as his wife, and more than that, when the Tsarevna and the grand duchess were to be told that Catherine Yourievsky was the leading lady of the imperial family—and worse things, perhaps, than even this had to be learned, if the settled opinion of some of the grand dukes proved to be right.

The events of that dramatic dinner party have been recorded by one who was then a fourteen-year-old boy, for all but the youngest members of the imperial family were required to be present. He was Grand Duke Alexander (Sandro), who afterward became a son-in-law of Dagmar. Alexander was the fourth son of Grand Duke Michael, the Emperor's youngest brother, who with his family had just returned from the governorship of the Caucasus.

The boy Alexander, like other young Romanoffs, attended the imperial dinner in some bewilderment, but *he* already had some inkling of what might take place. As the train bearing his family party from the Caucasus neared Petersburg his father had summoned his sons abruptly and declared in gruff tones: "I have something to tell you—be prepared to meet the new Empress of Russia at your first dinner party at the palace!" Their mother, very agitated, had protested angrily at their father's words.

It was a grim and silent party, with only a few whispers passing among them, which awaited the Emperor on that Sunday evening. The battery of glowering male and female eyes which was ready to blast Yourievsky upon her first appearance and, indeed, to shoot her through and through until her final exit, was likely to be so merciless in its execution that, even if the victim was no more than the brassy adventuress she was thought to be, she was likely to remember that terrible dinner party to her dying day.

The Tsarevitch and the Tsarevna stood apart with their two eldest sons, Nicholas, aged twelve, and George, aged nine. As the outcome of that evening their portion of humiliation was likely to be greater than any of the others. The brothers of the Emperor clustered together: the Grand Duke Constantine like a ruffled bird of prey, the Grand Duke Nicholas, gross and surly, and only the soldierly Michael with a look of stern and tranquil resignation. The sons of the Emperor, Vladimir, Alexis and young Serge and Paul, formed another group, and the others of the younger generation yet another: Constantine and Dmitri, the sons of the Grand Duke Constantine, and Nicholas and Peter, the sons of the Grand Duke Nicholas, four haughty young Guards officers; the four eldest sons of the Grand Duke Michael, Nicholas, Michael, George and Alexander, the little-known cousins from the Caucasus, who were all in their teens and who were examining the disgruntled assembly with grave curiosity.

Young Grand Duke Alexander, who in his time had to listen to so many Grand Masters of the Imperial Courts intoning their cool and measured pronouncements, realized long afterward when he came to recollect the tense events of that Sunday evening that on this occasion, when the veteran Grand Master of the Emperor's Court entered the Lesser Field Marshals' Saloon, even he, a monument of human impassivity, rapped his ivory staff on the floor with nervous indecisiveness and cried out with a voice almost on a hysterical note:

"His Majesty the Emperor and Princess Yourievskaya!"

Alexander had seen little of his uncle the Emperor, who entered "with a strikingly attractive woman on his arm." To the youngster his imperial uncle appeared to be an old man, and he watched with shocked surprise when Alexander II swaggered in jauntily, "like a boy of eighteen," and winked at Grand Duke

Michael in passing. But the Emperor had no friendly look for the huge Tsarevitch. Momentarily the Emperor stared coldly at his eldest son.

The grand duchesses bowed icily, and young Alexander thought that Princess Yourievsky, whose "nervousness was obvious," acknowledged them with graceful elegance. "My mother," says Alexander, "turned her head away in plain disgust. My future mother-in-law, then wife of the Heir Apparent, lowered her eyes. She would not have minded it so much for herself, but she was thinking of her sister Alexandra married to the Prince of Wales." Alexander had doubtless heard his mother-in-law, with whom he was very intimate, enlarge on her awe of Queen Victoria.

In speechless procession the family trailed in the footsteps of the Emperor and Yourievsky to the dining room. There every eye bored into Catherine Yourievsky as she sat herself beside the Emperor at the head of the table in the chair of the dead Empress Marie Alexandrovna.

In the dining room the stillness of the tomb prevailed. What they had just seen was unforgivable. Yet not one in the room could have suggested where else Catherine could have sat under the circumstances.

At the foot of the table, side by side, sat the Tsarevitch and the Tsarevna. It was as if the pairs facing each other from the ends of the table were opposing pieces on a chessboard; and chiefly it was the demeanor of Sasha which gave the impression of alert hostility. His massive body was frozen, with the thick head thrust forward from the square, epauleted shoulders and the eyes fixed and bulging like some evil dead fish.

Catherine Yourievsky addressed her neighbors with a smile. They answered abruptly in low monosyllables and tried to shift their gaze in the other direction. With nobody speaking the elaborately served meal was more like a religious ceremony than a family dinner party; except that the scarlet footmen performed their duties with a kind of brisk and knowing insolence.

Young Alexander confesses that he could not look away from the beautiful Yourievsky, for whom he personally felt sorry. She was facing her ordeal with courage. "Frequently she turned to the Emperor, and he patted her hand gently." Nerved, perhaps, by this kindly notice from her husband, the Princess in the later part of the dinner, when some desultory general conversation did begin to pass, several times attempted to join in. The conversation instantly died away, the participants averting their eyes and examining their plates. Young Alexander formed the opinion that in the end the Princess could "have succeeded in conquering the men, had not they been watched by the women."

As it was, a state of practically open family rebellion reigned at the table. Alexander II could not have remained unaware of this; but he appeared to be so. His face was cheerful, and every time he looked at Catherine Yourievsky his tired eyes visibly glowed. With the dessert the Emperor was chattering away like a high-spirited ensign, turning to his guests on right and left, but except when he was conversing with his wife he was largely delivering an unflagging monologue.

Dinner had ended when a door behind the Emperor opened and in came an English governess with a small boy and two lovely little girls. They were the children of Emperor Alexander and Catherine Yourievsky. Unlike their mother, often seen beside their father in recent months, the children were unknown to most of those present.

The boy, about seven years old, was dressed as a sailor. He looked lively and attractive, with fair hair like his mother's. The sight of the bejeweled and uniformed company did not abash him in the least, although in his almost secret existence he could never have seen such a sight before. He especially of the trio at once became the target for many penetrating glances. This boy, if his mother was proclaimed Empress, would move into the line of imperial succession after the sons of the Emperor's first marriage; or worse, if he grew up ambitious and unscrupulous he might one day set himself up in rivalry to his half-brothers and put himself in the hands of revolutionary elements.

When the Emperor looked round and saw this boy his eyes filled with delight. Not one of his sons at the table could remember ever having seen such a light shine in his face for them.

"A—h, there is my Gogo!" exclaimed Alexander II. He beckoned to the boy, who ran to him. In another moment Gogo had been lifted up by his father and set on his shoulder. The Emperor turned to his horrified relatives, who regarded Gogo as nothing but a bastard, and confronted them with the triumphant smile of an acrobat who had just put his partner through some spectacular feat.

Then Emperor Alexander uttered words which made them all sit up in their places. It must have been almost possible to hear the intake of breath round the table. This was what they had been waiting to hear; although they had not expected it would come to them like this. When he had finished a pin could have been heard striking the floor.

"Tell us, Gogo," asked the Emperor loudly, "what is your full name?"

"I am George Alexandrovitch Yourievsky," declared Gogo with animation, and he began to smooth the Emperor's side whiskers with his hands.

"Well, we are all very glad to make your acquaintance, Prince Yourievsky," exclaimed his father. The Emperor paused for a moment. "By the way, Prince," he went on, *how would you like to be a grand duke?*"

There could be only one meaning in that: Gogo's mother would presently be the Empress of Russia.

No sooner had the Emperor spoken than young Alexander saw Catherine Yourievsky blush.

"Please, Sasha, don't!" she pleaded in an urgent tone.

Her hand went out to the Emperor in agitation.

"For the first time during the evening," observes Alexander, "she [Catherine] forgot all about etiquette and addressed her husband by his little name."

Perhaps Alexander II had expected Gogo to render a decisive affirmative to his question in front of the family, which would give him an opening to make clear his own intentions. But Gogo answered nothing, and continued to stroke his father's whiskers. Nor did his father press him for an answer, but pushed back his chair and, with Gogo still balanced on his shoulder, his wife on

his other arm and his little daughters behind him, led the outraged and horrified imperial family into another room, where
chairs had been set for a performance.

It would not have been possible in all probability to choose a
kind of family entertainment which would have aroused enthusiasm on the troubled evening of December 3; and a smiling and
voluble Italian conjurer, who pranced about the room with a
zeal for comic effects, was doomed to failure, except among the
youngest members of the party.

Looking back on that Christmas season and the New Year of
1881 in the light of the appalling horror which so soon changed
everything, there seemed to be a tragic and pitiful irony in the
fact that Alexander II used that time in giving an unprecedented
series of splendid court festivities for Catherine Yourievsky.

The Petersburg season of 1880-81, although ornamented with
so much imperial magnificence, was not gay. It was unhealthy:
haunted by sharp peering eyes and alive with cruel and heartless
whisperings. People who went through that season, till its abrupt
and terrible ending, thought of it in after days as downright
macabre.

At the great January court ball, the most elaborate and sumptuous of all the festivities, Emperor Alexander with Princess
Yourievsky led the Imperial Polonaise through the echoing halls
of the Winter Palace before a huge assembly of curious Russians
—and few doubted that the Emperor's morganatic wife would be
the Empress of Holy Russia before the year was out.

CHAPTER VI

The Day of the Murder

DAWN WAS only a dim light over the eastern rooftops of St.
Petersburg on Sunday, March 13, 1881, when police, acting
on information received, broke into a newly established cheese
shop in the Sadovaya, the main shopping street. They expected
to discover that the proprietor was Jelaboff, a notorious Nihilist,
who had too widely boasted of his intention to kill the Emperor
that day as he returned along the Sadovaya to the Winter Palace
after reviewing the Guard Marine Regiment in the Michael
School.

Jelaboff was caught. They grappled with him in his nightshirt
at the top of the stairs, where he stood brandishing a revolver.
But an open skylight in the roof and various male and female
garments strewn about left them in no doubt that others had
escaped from the house.

Perhaps the police, having captured their quarry—a notable
achievement—persuaded themselves that they could relax for the
remainder of that Sunday. The Emperor would be safe for the
day. They searched the premises from roof to basement. Behind
some packing cases in the basement a gallery had been dug
under the roadway, but the policemen were in too much of a
hurry to remove the boxes; nor did they trouble to set a guard
on the shop when they left it.

Sophia Peroskaya, the highborn mistress of Jelaboff, was a woman of resolution. She insisted that the four young men who had escaped with her over the roofs should follow her back to the cheese shop when the police walked out of it. Under her instructions they laid a mine in the gallery below the Sadovaya.

But the womanly intuition of Sophia suggested to her that the Emperor, contrary to his custom, might choose to return to the Winter Palace by the other route, which ran alongside the Catherine Canal. She gave to each of the young men a nitroglycerine hand bomb.

"Post yourselves at intervals along the Catherine Canal opposite the Summer Garden," she said. "He might come that way. One of you will succeed if he does. Draw lots for the order in which you stand."

With a hard glitter in their eyes they walked into the street, leaving Sophia in the cheese shop. The snowbound city shone in the sunlight, and soon afterward the clocks struck ten. From that hour Emperor Alexander was a doomed man.

✱   ✱   ✱

At nine o'clock that morning Alexander II attended Mass in the Winter Palace Chapel with the Princess Yourievskaya, their children and all the members of the imperial family. Vassili relates that when the Tsarevna came up to take her leave of her father-in-law after Mass, she ignored Princess Yourievskaya, who stood beside him.

The Emperor caught at his daughter-in-law and pushed her toward the Princess.

"*Dites donc adieu à la Princesse!*" he cried out.

Everyone was startled. The Tsarevna, who had almost turned her back, appeared unmoved. She gave a second "profound curtsy" to the Emperor, then hastily, with her face expressionless, she bowed her neck to the Princess and glided from the chapel, followed by the Tsarevitch. For a moment it looked as if the Emperor would pursue her. His mouth twitched. But he turned to the waiting members of the imperial family.

As soon as the Emperor reached his study he sat down at his

desk and wrote a note to say that he would not be lunching at
the Anitchkoff after the parade. It was half-past ten, and as he
sealed his note Count Melikoff, the Prime Minister, entered with
some documents. These were drafts of a manifesto in which the
Emperor granted to Russia a Consultative Assembly. At last
Alexander II was doing what he had long planned to do: he was
giving Holy Russia a national constitution and launching her
upon the first step toward representative government. It was not
much; but Emperor Alexander, like Pobedonsteff, was too well
aware of the presence of "the Bad Man of the icy desert" to venture further for the present. He signed the manifesto, and told
Melikoff to send a copy to the head of the Government Printing
Press to appear in the *Official Messenger* (Court Circular) on
Monday morning. The nature of this manifesto was known at
that time to the grand dukes, who had not seen it and who were
divided in their opinions as to its wisdom, and to a few statesmen, but otherwise its existence was a secret.

At the door of the study Melikoff passed Princess Yourievsky.
Vassili says that as she approached the desk the Emperor was in
the act of locking the signed copy of the manifesto in a drawer,
and knowing she would be pleased he smiled and said: "I have
just signed a paper which I hope will give a good impression in
Russia, and show I am willing to give her all that it is possible
to give. Tomorrow it will be published. I have given the order."

He went down with her to tea and the children joined them.
Presently he was driving away in a small closed carriage to the
Riding School. He had told his coachman that he wished to go
and return that day by the Catherine Canal.

Meanwhile, at the Anitchkoff, Sasha had just driven away to
join the Emperor at the parade, and Dagmar, finding that her
father-in-law was not coming to luncheon, had ordered an early
lunch and was going skating. The sky was blue and cloudless,
and the afternoon promised to be magnificent. She had bought a
new pair of special skates the day before and she was looking
forward to trying these out. She was proud of her skating. Nicky
was coming with her, and her five tall and handsome Michaelovitch nephews were going to join them. They were to meet at

the Winter Palace. For the morning scene in the chapel she was neither disturbed nor repentant. In her feelings for her father-in-law deep pity mingled with exasperation. He was demented by a siren. To behave as he had done to her aunt, Empress Marie, was beyond the bounds of human normality. In common with all the Romanoff ladies she was honestly convinced after the happenings of the last six months that Yourievsky was nothing but an intensely cunning adventuress.

After the Marine Regiment had been dismissed from the Michael School Emperor Alexander dropped in at the Mikhailoffski Palace to lunch with a favorite cousin, the Grand Duchess Catherine. He did not stay long, and at 2:15 p.m. the imperial carriage passed out of the gates of the Mikhailoffski. Cossacks of the Escort rode with the carriage, and behind came a line of sleighs. In the first traveled the Chief of Police, in the second another high police official, in the third the Grand Duke Michael and behind came the general officers of the Petersburg garrison.

News had reached Sophia Perovskaya at the cheese shop that the Emperor was lunching at the Mikhailoffski, and she judged he must be returning by way of the canal. Leaving the shop, she visited the young men at their posts. Perhaps if this cold-blooded woman had not arrived to steel them to their duty they would not have dared to act. She told them that she would stand at a place on the Summer Garden side, where she could see both the gates of the Mikhailoffski and along the Catherine Canal. When she waved her handkerchief they would know that the carriage had left the gates.

The procession was moving at speed when the first bomb hit the road behind the imperial carriage. The air flamed, a deafening crash followed and the road vanished in smoke. The smoke blew off in the wind, displaying the imperial carriage at a standstill, but unscratched. People were running up from the sleighs behind. One Cossack and his horse twitched on the ground in a red smear of snow. A butcher's boy lay on his face with his basket split beside him. Two Cossacks tumbled slowly from the saddle. Several among the crowd wiped bloody faces and a young woman collapsed in a faint.

The Emperor jumped from the carriage and looked about him. At that the gray-bearded coachman started to shout roughly at him.

". . . Get in, Sire! Get in! Drive on to the Winter Palace, in the Name of God!"

The Police Chief pulled himself from under his overturned sleigh and staggered toward the Emperor, crying, "Are you unhurt, Sire?"

"Yes, by Heaven's mercy," came the answer.

A voice behind the Emperor growled, "It is too early to thank Heaven for her mercy!"

There stood Russiakoff, the bomb-thrower, who had been dragged forward by a soldier and a policeman. The Emperor confronted him, demanding his name. The haggard young man glared at him silently with blazing eyes, and the Emperor shrugged and told them to take him away.

"We must look to these wounded," declared the Emperor.

"Drive on, Sire!— Drive on, Sire!" exhorted the old coachman in a voice of desperation, as the Emperor bent over a Cossack.

Nobody had noticed an ugly, thickset student, who had been clinging agitatedly to the Canal railings. As the Emperor spoke to the Cossack the student hurled the second bomb.

Everything vanished in the smoke of a thunderous explosion. It was altogether greater than the first. Glass could be heard tinkling down from distant windows and repeated screams of agony broke out in all directions. Momentarily no gust of wind came, and the smoke-cloud hung. Then it drifted off slowly as if a curtain had risen.

Emperor Alexander, a terrifying red torso, hatless, coatless, legless, seemingly faceless, stained the white pavement as he rolled across it. His brother Michael rushed up to him.

"For God's sake get me to the palace to die," croaked a strange distant voice.

They lifted the Emperor upon a sleigh, and with blood pouring over the snow it raced toward the nearby Winter Palace, with the other sleighs plowing wildly after it over the stained track.

At the Anitchkoff, Sasha, who had taken a cold leave of his father at the Michael School, was still lunching upstairs. Dagmar and her eldest son had finished lunch. She and Nicky, skates in their hands, stood waiting in the entrance hall for a sleigh to take them to meet the Michaelovitches at the Winter Palace.

The Tsarevna, in her small white ermine jacket and tilted ermine cap, her short, full, ermine-bordered skirt of deep blue velvet and her high ermine-topped red leather boots, carried with her an exquisite jauntiness at horrible variance with the scene of blood-freezing terror, tragedy and frantic emotion into which she was about to enter.

At the roar of the first explosion Sasha came hurrying down the staircase. His face was pale, and husband and wife stared at each other with frightened eyes. The second explosion shook the Anitchkoff. In that instant they both knew instinctively that this had done its work. They remained horror-stricken and speechless, while glass tumbled down from the windows. Footmen and maids ran into the hall, saw the Tsarevitch and Tsarevna, and stopped dead, watching them with anxious, questioning looks. Some started to pray and cross themselves.

A rapid thudding of horses' hoofs stopped outside, and an officer plunged blindly in through the entrance. He was wild-eyed and gasping.

"They have killed the Emperor!" he screamed. "They have taken him to the Winter Palace. God have mercy on Him—I never saw such a sight in the Turkish War," and he tumbled sobbing against a pillar.

The sleigh was at the steps and they tremblingly scrambled into it. Swiftly it swept them along the canal road. They passed a swaying cluster of people and heard their cries. Men, women and children, weeping and praying, were fighting to dip handkerchiefs in the blood of the Emperor. The shrinking gaze of Dagmar and Sasha followed the stained trail which ran from the crowd to the Winter Palace. The Preobajansky Regiment debouched at the double with fixed bayonets from a side street and blocked their progress. The faces of the tall guardsmen, usually so wooden, twitched with savage bewilderment and they glared menacingly at the civilians running toward the Winter Palace.

The Tsarevitch's sleigh stopped at a doorway at the back of the palace. The Emperor had been brought in that way. The sight was sickening. Sasha supported his wife up the stairway, pulling her aside from the blackening clots of blood. Her skates were still clutched in her hand, and Nicky, pale with terror, fiercely grasped at her ermine jacket.

Behind them, stumbling and whispering, the five Michaelovitch brothers half-pushed, half-dragged their moaning mother up the stairs. They had been leaving for the skating party when an excited messenger had informed them that their father Michael had been carried dying into the Winter Palace with the Emperor.

It was fourteen-year-old Alexander Michaelovitch who recorded his boyish impressions of that nightmare Sunday afternoon. Trembling and frightened as he never had been before, Alexander felt afterward as if every face, every action in the imperial study had been indelibly printed on his mind. It was like watching some appalling macabre scene in a theater.

The door of the study was open. Already the large room was full of people, members of the imperial family, ladies and gentlemen of the household, court dignitaries, ministers, generals. At the door the air choked them with its stench of fresh blood and chemicals, mingled with Parisian perfumes.

At their entrance Grand Duke Michael met them, and at the sight of him Grand Duchess Olga broke from her sons and fell fainting into his arms. People turned at the disturbance in the doorway and seeing the Tsarevitch and the Tsarevna they stepped aside, forming a respectful corridor; for none of those who had been gazing with stupefaction at the spectacle upon the couch beside the imperial desk could doubt that in a few minutes these two would be the Emperor and Empress.

The white room with its gilded plasterwork, its rich Empire furnishings, its bibelots cluttered with small valuables, personal souvenirs and family photographs, presented a setting of shocking unreality for the tattered imperial remnant exposed nakedly to the terrified eyes of his family and subjects.

Blood oozed, no longer capable of flowing from a mass of open wounds. One eye, wide open, moved to and fro lazily in the red mask and the black gap of the mouth twitched hideously. Dr. Markus and Dr. Botkin, with their instruments, bottles and lint, bent helplessly over a wounded man beyond their aid. At the head of the Emperor the Metropolitan knelt and prayed, his long beard, his clasped hands, his cassock smeared in blood, for he had tried to administer the Last Sacrament.

The boy Alexander, clutching in his terror the hand of his friend Nicky, who in his turn clung to his mother, wrenched his gaze away from the couch, and looked toward his Aunt Minnie, who he knew must soon be Empress. To Alexander she appeared "stunned," as she stood perfectly still in front of the crowd, a few feet from the Emperor whom but a few hours before she had defied and humiliated. Alexander heard the jangling of steel, and glancing down saw the new skates, which flashed and trembled in her fingers.

The Tsarevitch stood rigidly, awkwardly, peering from his great height at the torn trunk of his father. His big face was impassive, expressionless. Soon he would know what it felt like to be Emperor of All the Russias, the most powerful autocrat in the world, the only living sovereign whose life no insurance company would dare to cover, however high the premium.

"How long has my father got to live?" he asked the doctors.

"From ten to fifteen minutes," answered Botkin, offering the Tsarevitch no title.

The Tsarevitch grunted, and with bald head hunched forward in that bull-like movement which had once amused his father, he shambled through the weeping women and praying men to the window, where he stood watching the wailing crowds flowing in through the Nevski Prospect Archway.

One figure flitted restlessly through the throng in the death chamber, out into the corridor and back to examine with a pale, shrinking countenance the dying Emperor. It was his brother Constantine, concerning whom Petersburg rumor would soon be whispering that it was he who had paid the Nihilists to do this deed.

Nobody in that room full of emotion and horror had noticed the strange absence of Princess Yourievsky. Had she been in a deep sleep when the explosions occurred? Had none troubled to tell her? Had none dared tell her?

Suddenly, as if a scythe had swept a passage from the door to the couch, Princess Yourievsky, in white and half-dressed, flashed through the crowd and threw herself flat upon the body of the Emperor. "Sasha, Sasha!" she screamed, till everyone's blood froze, and she passionately started to cover with kisses the terrible hands.

To young Alexander the moment was "unbearable," as the pale, grief-stricken form writhed in her husband's gore. Women who had silently wept in pity and nervous revulsion—the grand duchesses who had hated the Princess—broke into loud sobs and men covered their faces. The Tsarevitch at the window—who had examined the scene of bloody mutilation with the impassivity of a commander on a battlefield—was emitting loud throaty sobs and shuddering from head to foot. A tall, cool, bewhiskered, youngish officer, wearing the epaulets of a general, stood at the Tsarevitch's elbow with his demeanor of dignity and authority apparently quite unruffled. This was the Grand Duke Vladimir, and he presently removed his arm gently from around his elder brother's shoulder, and slipped away to resume the orders and instructions which he knew the occasion required. Indeed, here was the man whom a stranger might have mistaken for the expectant Emperor. Evidently he had understood instantly all that ought to be done in such an unprecedented imperial crisis, and he was seeing that these things were done. The tones in which Grand Duke Vladimir could be heard speaking were peremptory—perhaps too loud in this place of approaching death, for he had a great voice.

If there was one woman among those in the imperial study who matched in equanimity the Grand Duke Vladimir and who observed all that went forward with a controlled and sensible mien, it was his wife Marie Pavlovna, the girl of whom Bismarck had thought so highly. If a stranger in that overwrought assembly could have mistaken Vladimir for the new Emperor, he might equally well have selected Marie Pavlovna as the waiting Empress.

That Sunday afternoon when, perhaps, the Empire was about to topple, the Vladimirs instinctively started to play those parts in which they saw themselves in the days ahead—the uncrowned Emperor and Empress of Russia, the power behind a feeble throne. Poor sluggish Sasha was dumb and hopeless; and as for Minnie, would she want more than to be universally adored, the Fairy Queen of ballrooms, the blazing star of Court processions, the Empress of the dress salons?

Count Vassili, with strange facts to reveal about the later happenings of that day, is emphatic upon the attitude of keen expectation at once manifested by the Vladimirs, and is struck by the quickness with which Sasha understood what was taking place. Yet it would be unjust to discern the shade of the Macbeths in the Vladimirs. Rather, these two, with ready self-confidence and without one word passing between them, saw themselves at that hour as fated to fulfil high duties for the salvation of weaker vessels, and accepted almost exultantly the prospect before them.

"Silence, please," a loud voice proclaimed, "the end is near!"

People averted their eyes, drawing nearer to the dying Emperor, as if in a spontaneous last act of homage. The imperial study was perfectly silent; but outside in the square, where a triple line of bayonets now glimmered along the whole face of the Winter Palace, the wails and moans of the crowd had changed into cheers and shouts for "Our Little White Father, Alexander III." For several minutes the word had been passing among them that Alexander II was already dead.

Dr. Botkin gently pulled the red hand of the Emperor from under the Princess Yourievsky and felt the pulse. He rose, releasing the stiff and lifeless hand.

"The Emperor is dead," he declared in ringing tones.

Princess Yourievsky rose up from the body, and a shuddering gasp greeted the frightful sight she presented to the room. One frenzied, ear-splitting shriek burst from her and she tumbled rigid as a pillar beside the couch. Her friend, Mademoiselle Schebeko, who had seen her protégée Catherine Dolgorousky rise so nearly to the throne, knelt bleakly beside the unconscious widow.

All fell upon their knees, crossing themselves, and the room was filled with the sound of murmured prayer.

The skates of Empress Marie Fedorovna tinkled as she rose and holding the hand of Tsarevitch Nicholas crossed to the window to join her husband, the Emperor. Sasha got ponderously to his feet. He would have taken the hand of his wife, but seeing that between the skates and Nicholas both hands were occupied a flicker of a smile passed over his face, and he bowed to her affectionately. His glance passed to the kneeling assembly in the study and then turned to his excited subjects below the window. The Grand Duke Vladimir had also risen and he had brought to his feet the Chief of Police, to whom he appeared to be giving some earnest instructions in an undertone. The official appeared to be attending to him with impatience, and at the first opportunity turned to the Emperor.

"Has your Majesty any orders to give?" asked the Police Chief.

Grand Duke Vladimir began to speak again. The Emperor interrupted him.

"Yes, I have," he exclaimed bluntly. "The police have lost control. The Army will take over for the present. Where is the Prime Minister? I want to see all my ministers at once at the Anitchkoff Palace."

Young Grand Duke Alexander observed his Uncle Sasha with astonishment. "In less than five minutes he had acquired a new personality. Something much bigger than a mere realization of the imperial responsibilities had transformed his massive frame."

Alexander III beckoned to Marie Fedorovna. She dropped the hand of Nicky and took his. He began to walk toward the doorway, erect and with—for him—a surprisingly measured stride, and the new Empress, tiny beside him, incongruous with her tilted cap and swinging skates, too sick from her horrific experience to notice the bowing and curtsying, and the avenue of livid faces which endeavored to give her looks of homage, was dragged across the corridor into another room. Involuntarily falling in behind them, came the grand dukes, the brothers, the uncles, the cousins; and the grand duchesses, finding themselves deserted, threw fearful glances at the couch and scurried after them.

The French valet of the dead Emperor, who had stood silently tearing handfuls of hair out of his own head in the agony of his grief, now came forward with a sheet and covered the remains of his master. With breathless speed the imperial study emptied, and when the flight was over only the faithful valet remained, with Schebeko on the floor by the blood-stained couch using a bottle of smelling salts to revive Princess Yourievsky.

Meanwhile, the Emperor and Empress were descending without ceremony to the main hall of the Winter Palace, where all in the building had been hastily marshaled to swear the Oath of Allegiance to Alexander III before the Metropolitan. Outside priests passed down the long ranks of troops, raising their arms with crucifixes and ordering them to bare their heads and declare the Oath to the new Emperor.

A red sunset lit the golden domes of St. Petersburg in a rosy light by the time this was done, and Emperor Alexander III and Empress Marie Fedorovna were ready to depart to the Anitchkoff Palace.

First, out upon the main steps came the Grand Duke Vladimir, walking backwards nimbly with bared head and gripping his sword, then swinging round and staring defiantly at the mob as if to challenge bomb or bullet meant for the Emperor—not that this was likely on the marble steps with so many bayonets massed below, but the gesture was heroically, officiously symbolic. The vast striding bulk of Alexander III, with the Empress almost running, lurched out after his brother so suddenly that Vladimir was all but tumbled over the steps among the military topboots below. The Emperor charged purposefully downward, dragging Marie Fedorovna, and the flashing skates were plainly visible, as the roar of greeting from the crowd rent the air. They plunged through a gap in the troops and into a closed carriage, which was hedged about by a sea of lances. As the horses of the Escort backed into their places the closed window of the carriage was seen to be slammed down and the bald head of the Emperor was thrust out toward the people. He nodded stiffly, appeared to be scowling and waved his fur cap abruptly. He vanished and pulled the white-faced Empress into the window aperture. She tried to smile and seemed on the point of collapse. The window was jerked up and with a sharp whip-cracking the imperial carriage began to roll forward at gathering speed through the Petersburgers.

They swept through the Nevski Prospect Archway at a gallop with the air shuddering at the clamor of human voices, with the nearby church bells chiming and the distant ones tolling, while a whole regiment of scarlet Don Cossacks thundered around them with lances lowered for the attack.

Thus dramatically the new Emperor and Empress arrived with a clatter before the wide-open portals of their old home. The household of the Anitchkoff, down to the youngest scullery boy, all with glistening eyes, awaited them in the hall.

Sasha the Bull and Dagmar the adored scrambled over the familiar threshold as clumsily as they had left the Winter Palace. The household fell on their knees with tears pouring over their cheeks. It was the lot of old Ivan, the valet who had tended Sasha from his ponderous babyhood, to limp forward offering the traditional bread and salt on a golden tray, begging the Emperor in halting words to be "Little Father to our People."

There had been, and there would be, many occasions when ceremonies and civilities would fire those fishlike blue eyes of Alexander III with a light of scornful impatience. But at that moment all who looked up at the Emperor grew startled at the extraordinary sight of their beaming benevolence.

Closely clutching the arm of the little Empress, Emperor Alexander III growled in a loud voice, "Yes, Ivan, I will try to be a Father to my People."

The dull cold look reappeared in his eyes. The passage through the throng was wide, but he seemed to push his way through it with lowered head, while Marie Fedorovna as she was whisked along enveloped them all in a wan but enchanting smile. Behind them came Nicky, with his eyes still horror-stricken, oblivious of the nods and smiles which everybody tried to accord him in his new dignity. At the top of the stairs Sasha left his wife and son and went to his study, where the ministers already awaited him.

But before Sasha addressed them he asked them to be patient for a moment, and sitting down at his desk he wrote a short and abrupt letter to his stepmother the widowed Princess Yourievsky. After expressing his sympathy for her, which he said he had been unable to do in the study, he told her that he believed that his father had made no proper financial arrangement for her and the children in case of his death. He assured her that she need not worry. He knew what his father would have wished and he would see to the matter himself.

*   *   *

We must return to the imperial study in the Winter Palace, where the dead Emperor lay upon the couch under a stained sheet, and where only two people remained: the Princess Yourievsky, now restored to calmness, and Mademoiselle Schebeko. A weird stillness reigned in the corridors outside. It was as if the entire palace had been emptied of inhabitants.

It is not known how much was revealed to Marie Fedorovna of the strange and dramatic events which took place in the imperial study in the later hours of that day. It was the habit during the years immediately after the accession of the new sovereigns to say that the Empress was a "nonpolitical woman," who heard and sought to discover nothing in affairs of state; but knowledgeable opinions formed later incline strongly to the contrary view. Probably as much became known to her the next morning as had come within the experience of Sasha himself. The events, in any case, are an essential part of her story, for these vitally affected not only her own future, but the future of her children and everything around her. Indeed, as a direct result of the transactions of that night, life for her had always a sinister and nightmarish background and her husband was dogged by them until the hour of his collapse into a premature grave.

Only Count Vassili seems to know the details of those odd scenes in the death chamber at Winter Palace, or only he dared to reveal them, in the days when Russia was still ruled by the Romanoffs.

Vassili recounts that as soon as Princess Yourievsky appeared sufficiently recovered Mademoiselle Schebeko ceased her attempts to comfort her. She turned to the widow and addressed her in earnest tones.

"Where is the Manifesto? You told me it was signed. You must take it. It may be of tremendous use, if it does not fall into *certain* hands for the present!"

The sharp words electrified Yourievsky into life. We must suppose that these two ardently liberal women both had the same suspicion: that the new Emperor, generally supposed to be a Liberal, but known for his unpredictable ways, might, after the cruel murder of his father, be no longer inclined to Liberalism. If this was the treatment Russians gave to the man who had liberated the serfs, he might well begin to see Liberals with eyes of disgusted disillusion. But, while the signed Manifesto of the dead Emperor remained in safe hands, and the words of the Manifesto were actually passing out of the government presses, Russia was yet on the threshold of a new era.

Princess Yourievsky had seen her husband place the Manifesto in a drawer of the desk. She knew where he had hidden the key. She quickly found it, and with a hand shaking violently she inserted the key in the lock of the drawer.

The corridor outside was lighted by gas, but in the imperial study only one small lamp burned on the desk. At the moment when the Princess put the key in the lock a shadow from the open doorway fell across the floor. A very tall figure stood watching them in the aperture. In the dim light of the study his features were indistinguishable to the two women, but they saw the glitter of epaulets as an officer silently approached them. When he stood before the desk they recognized the Grand Duke Vladimir.

The key was in the lock, but the Princess had not turned it. Without a word the Grand Duke gently brushed aside her hand from the key. He pulled out the key and slipped it into his pocket.

"I will attend to everything, Mother," he said quietly. "I have come to see to some last duties for the body of the Emperor." There was a pause while he and the Princess eyed one another. "I think it best that I shall do this so that you shall not be needlessly distressed," he went on, and his tone grew in firmness. "I suggest that you now go to your room and rest."

Princess Yourievsky and Mademoiselle left the room without speaking. Grand Duke Vladimir did not attend to any last duties to his father's corpse when the study was empty other than to light two candles and set them on a small table at the head of the couch, and to place another table at the foot of the couch upon which he set two more lighted candles. For a minute he stood thoughtfully regarding the drawer from which he had taken the key. Then he extinguished the lamp on the desk and walked out into the silent corridor. He went to the head of the stairs where there was a speaking-tube beside the chair usually occupied by the duty footman of the corridor. He ordered the officer of the Guard to come up to him, and while waiting returned to the door of the imperial study. When the officer arrived he told him to place a sentry outside the study till further notice. As soon as Vladimir had seen the sentry in position he descended and drove hurriedly to the Anitchkoff.

At midnight the stiffening corpse of the Emperor still lay under the stained sheet in the dim study, lit only by the light of four fresh candles. Not a sound could be heard in the Winter Palace. The sentry had just been dismissed. Four people stood by the desk: Emperor Alexander III, his brothers Vladimir and Alexis and *one other*, whom Vassili describes as a "trusted adviser in whom the Emperor had the utmost confidence." They had met a few minutes before, and they were talking urgently in whispers, but otherwise they were apparently indifferent to the presence of the corpse.

Alexander III held the key of the drawer, which Vladimir had taken from Princess Yourievsky. He inserted the key, opened the drawer and pulled out the first paper. This was the Manifesto.

Somebody relit the lamp and the Emperor held the paper to the light and began to read it slowly, the others peering from behind him. Nobody will ever know what ideas were passing through his mind as he held the signed Manifesto of his father, the substance of which was already passing through the presses, and which he was expected to honor. A hand appeared in the ring of light round the lamp. It snatched the Manifesto out of the hand of the Emperor, ripped it in several pieces and quickly thrust the pieces in the flame of the nearest candle. Soon the Manifesto was nothing but a few smoldering fragments on the carpet.

"Now, your Majesty," said the "trusted adviser," who had done the deed, "you can punish me, but at least it cannot be said that you stepped upon the throne of Russia with tied hands!"

Count Vassili, whose name is undoubtedly a pseudonym, always published his revelations outside Russia in the French language. Usually he does not shrink from mentioning his characters by their true names; yet he never disclosed the identity of "the trusted adviser in whom the Emperor had the utmost confidence." But one name in this connection does immediately spring to mind: *Pobedonsteff.* The action is in character. Moreover, this was the man whom Alexander III was about to raise to a high office, and who during the coming reign was always said to be the only man to whom the impatient and obstinate Emperor would invariably listen with deference.

It was not long after midnight when the head of the Imperial Printing Press was awakened by an officer bearing an order signed by Alexander III. He was instructed immediately to stop the printing of the Manifesto of the late Emperor. All copies of the *Official Messenger* carrying the Manifesto which had already passed out of the presses were to be counted and counter-checked and then destroyed in his sight. When this was accomplished he was personally to report to the Emperor. If we have to rely upon Vassili for the midnight scene in the death chamber, this is not the case in regard to the order received in the early hours of Monday morning by the Imperial Printing Press. The latter is vouched for by every chronicler of the reign of Alexander III.

The hands of the Nihilists were everywhere. When the copies

of the *Official Messenger* already printed were checked a number of these had vanished; and even while destruction was under way the missing copies were being read aloud to hastily summoned congregations of Nihilists in carefully guarded cellars and attics throughout the capital.

This now worthless Manifesto of the Emperor they had murdered too soon did not offer them much; nevertheless, it had been unmistakably a step in the right direction. They did not doubt that whatever the new Emperor might deign to offer them —if indeed he did not make the Russian yoke heavier—would be something less generous than the thing he had destroyed.

For a few days they agreed to leave the Emperor in peace to contemplate the obligations of his high office. After that, if no good came out of this imperial holiday, the new persecution should begin. And a fresh line of attack was settled upon, which might have its effect upon the Emperor: let the persecution creep into his domestic life, let that light-hearted enchantress, Empress Marie Fedorovna, have her spirits crushed and her blood curdled by the next terror campaign.

That Monday morning before dawn the imperial Romanoffs were not irretrievably condemned to extinction. But from that day onward there was no hope for the dynasty unless they changed their ways and freed Russia from the shackles of Sacred Autocracy. By discovery of the existence of the abortive Manifesto of Alexander II the Nihilists had tasted blood. They wanted a whole carcass and nothing would stop them from getting it. Delay would only stir in them ferocious exasperation, and pave the way for the terrible and insane extremists who reveled in the thought of the great Destruction and the "equality of worms in the dunghill."

CHAPTER VII

The Days of the "Holy Band"

IT HAD BEEN customary for the Emperors to inhabit the Winter Palace, and the question of the move from the Anitchkoff arose after breakfast on Monday morning. One thing was certain: the Emperor and Empress would have to go into residence at the Winter Palace during the Lying-in-State and the long and elaborate funeral obsequies. But after that?

Sasha was of the opinion that they would have to live at the Winter Palace, and the more experienced members of their household agreed with him. Marie Fedorovna did not hide her distress and agitation. In the feverish stress of that terrible Sunday afternoon and the night of disturbance which had followed it, the thought of having to leave the Anitchkoff had not occurred to her. She had never been known to speak in very glowing terms of her home, which beside the Winter Palace was meager and almost shabby—quite unworthy to house the Sacred Autocrat; but now she was gripped by a passion of womanly sentiment for the Anitchkoff. For fifteen years the Anitchkoff had been their home. All their family roots were there. She was sure the children would not want to go.

"—All the same, we shall have to go," said Sasha. "The people will expect it of us."

"Are you or are you not the Autocrat of All the Russias?" demanded Marie Fedorovna with a boldness which but for her overwrought state she might not have dared to offer; for she knew that openly to goad him could produce an appalling outburst of rage.

"Yes, I am—" growled Sasha.

"—Very well then—the Autocrat does as he wishes! What do you want to do? Of course, we should have to give important entertainments at the Winter Palace—but if you insist on living there they will expect you to put up with all the fuss and nonsense, which is the regular thing in that place. How you will hate that!"

The Autocrat grunted. The mere thought of the ceremonial stranglehold of the Winter Palace filled him with loathing and disgust.

"We will live here," he declared, "and the people will have to put up with it."

St. Petersburg was a city of fear. An Englishman on business in the Russian capital at that time wrote home describing it as "reeking of dynamite—a nest of invisible assassins."

Lord Dufferin, the British Ambassador, who had shaken hands with Alexander II at the Sunday parade an hour before his assassination, wrote to Lady Dorothy Neville in words which aptly depict the Petersburg scene as the imperial obsequies began, and the mood of hysteria which gave vent to strange outbursts.

—I attended the transportation of the body from the chamber where it had been laid out and embalmed to the [Winter Palace] chapel. It was a most melancholy scene. The whole palace was lit up as if for a gala festival, and the people present formed themselves into two rows, between which at a given signal the procession moved. The crowd was so enormous that I had great difficulty in making my way to the chapel, and I was almost crushed to death. In the midst of it I found myself wedged up against a young, rather pretty, and very plump lady with her back towards me. She was pressed against me, and I was pressed against her, for we were both equally powerless. Suddenly she was seized with a fit of nervous impatience, to which she gave vent by using her behind as a battering-ram, with which she made the most desperate plunges. If she had not been rather soft I should have been brayed as in a mortar. . . . The ceremony of the removal of the body from the palace to the cathedral in the fortress took place on Saturday week. As the procession had to make a long round of about four miles, I was able both to see it and attend the service in the church. Though there was a high wind the sun was shining, and the sight would have been striking if only the individuals and groups, of which the procession was composed, had struggled less and comported themselves with a little more attention to effect. But octogenarian generals carrying crowns on cushions, and decrepit old priests over ninety, can hardly be expected to walk four miles through streets deep in slush without falling into disarray.

Lord Dufferin was among those who advised that the Prince of Wales ought to attend the funeral of Alexander II. At Marlborough House Alix had already declared that she had to be with poor Minnie at such an awful time, and that whatever Bertie did she was going to St. Petersburg with Charlotte Knollys, her lady in waiting. Bertie wanted to go, and having consulted various people in London was confirmed in his opinion that he should do so. A confidential telegram from Petersburg had also reached him from his brother Alfred of Edinburgh, urging him to come because he and Alix were expected. Alfred and Marie of Edinburgh had set out from London as soon as the news of the assassination had reached Britain.

"Every one I have spoken to expects that I am going," wrote the Prince of Wales querulously to the Prime Minister. One of the persons he had not spoken to was his mother. He knew what she would say— "Too dangerous, far too dangerous. Somebody suitable can represent you." But Lord Granville, the Foreign Minister, who agreed with the Prince, had a way with the Queen, which her eldest son lacked. Always prepared to do her duty, the Queen gave her assent with a sigh of unwillingness. According to Sir Alfred Lyall she telegraphed to Lord Dufferin that if the

Prince was blown up, or if any mishap occurred during the funeral, she would hold him entirely to blame.

Bertie and Alix reached St. Petersburg on March 25 and were met by Sasha and Minnie, who took them at speed, and enveloped amid an enormous escort, to the Anitchkoff. When Alix expressed disappointment at not being with her sister in the Winter Palace, they answered that they had thought it "too risky," but promised to join them at the Anitchkoff as soon as the funeral was over.

Shortly afterward, Alix in a conversation with Count Loris Melikoff, the Minister of the Interior, inquired anxiously if her sister was in great danger. He shrugged his shoulders and with the inconsequential fatalism of the Russian declared that as he unfortunately had evidence that the Secret Police were "honeycombed with conspirators" he would not care to commit himself. But they themselves, he informed them cheerfully, should be perfectly safe as long as they avoided the proximity of the Emperor and Empress in public.

The long-drawn-out and tedious imperial funeral was over by the end of March, and the Emperor and Empress left the Winter Palace and returned to the Anitchkoff. Alix and Bertie, who met them in the hall, could all but hear their sighs of relief as they crossed the familiar threshold. Alix saw with dismay the tense and feverish light in her sister's beautiful eyes. The new Empress had, indeed, some grounds for being disturbed at that moment. Alix was not informed at the time. The thing was too terrifying to be mentioned even between the two sisters.

The Nihilists had struck for the first time during the new reign. Two days before Marie Fedorovna had entered her sitting room in the Winter Palace. Lying on the table was a fat letter addressed to "His Majesty the Emperor."

When Sasha came in she had handed him the letter without a thought. He remarked that he did not know the handwriting, tore it open and began to read. Suddenly his face suffused with scarlet, his eyes glared and she watched the sheets of paper tremble in his fingers. Sasha glanced at her and started hastily to fold the letter.

She caught at his wrist before he pushed it into his pocket, demanding to see it.

"It's nothing to do with you!" he shouted roughly.

When she pulled at the letter it slipped from his hand. She stood there defiantly waiting for a huge fist to strike her. But the look she saw dawning on Sasha's contorted face was probably relief that someone would share the secret.

The letter was from the "Central Executive Committee of Nihilists."

Marie Fedorovna read to the end with rising terror and hopelessness.

No ferocious threat met her eyes. The letter was a table of political demands which the Nihilists made to the new Emperor. The words which frightened her constituted the "Address" of the Committee to the Emperor. In those sentences the pattern of the future was plainly declared, *if the demands were ignored.*

. . . Yes, your Majesty, do not be deceived by the words of flatterers and parasites. In your position there are only two outlets—either the inevitable revolution, which cannot be obviated by capital punishments; or voluntary compliance with the Will of the People on your part. . . . Be sure, Sire, that as soon as the supreme power ceases to act arbitrarily, and only thinks of recognizing the rights of the people, you can safely dismiss your spies, who only do your Government harm, disband your personal escort, and burn your scaffolds.

We solemnly declare, in the face of the Fatherland and the whole world, that we shall never be guilty of any act of violence against the measures of a Government created by a popular Parliament. Your Majesty has to decide. You have two ways before you; it is for you to choose which you will take!

There was the pattern. Surrender while there was yet time, or defy the storm. Neither of them, reading those words, could fail to recall the sickening sight of that bloody and tattered torso lying on the couch in the imperial study. Such was the fate of one condemned by the Nihilists.

In the mind of Marie Fedorovna there was little doubt as to

what her husband, for his part, intended that the shape of the future should be. While his murdered father still lay unburied he had shown his hand. Already Sasha had dismissed *five* of the liberal ministers of Emperor Alexander II in one day. He had replaced them by "old Russians" suggested by Pobedonsteff. For Sasha the tragic Sunday afternoon was the end of liberalism. The Bad Man of the icy desert had proved by his brutal deed that he was a Beast. Only the whip of a Master could keep him docile.

The wife of Sasha knew that he was terrified as he read the letter, *because he did not mean to give those people what they demanded.* She realized the grim significance of the letter being placed upon her table—that *she* was to be identified with the Emperor by the Nihilists, that they must have an accomplice in the Winter Palace, and that this person, man or woman, might be one of those who would accompany them back to the Anitchkoff.

It was plain that Sasha also wore a tired and drawn expression when he reached the Anitchkoff. His brother and sister-in-law thought that even his huge bulk seemed to have shrunk, whereby his great height gained an added impressiveness. While Alix submerged her sister in light-hearted chatter and brought the light back into her eyes, Bertie, adopting a rather more serious line of conversation with his solemn brother-in-law, met with equal success. Bertie, the born diplomat, sensed exactly what was wanted. Sasha was so grateful for his company that he went to his desk and wrote a letter to Queen Victoria, thanking her for allowing the Waleses to come and assuring her that their "presence has been a great consolation for me and the Empress."

Bertie had brought with him the Order of the Garter to bestow upon Sasha. The ceremony took place in the study before the Empress and the assembled household. The Garter was the most coveted of all honors among the sovereigns of Europe, and Sasha, standing before the little assembly with the ribbon almost stretched to bursting-point across him, presented a picture of smiling and childish pride, very different from the aspect of the gloomy giant who had plodded into the Anitchkoff a few days before.

While Alix and Bertie had been on their own at the Anitchkoff the guards had been comparatively light; but now they watched with amazement and misgiving as the palace became the center of an armed camp. Even so, poor Sasha and Minnie were not allowed in the garden. Bertie informed his mother with dismay that the only place in which it was considered safe for them to take open-air exercise was a back yard which was "unworthy of a London slum." The Autocrat of All the Russias and his Empress were close prisoners in their own capital; and still many Russians believed them in grave danger. Whenever Sasha accompanied his wife to Denmark from that time onward he would always talk of himself with jocund grimness as having "come out of prison," and people who did not know the circumstances thought his words in rather bad taste. Even state visits abroad, which Sasha detested, would have one compensation: they were "escapes from prison." A return to Russia would always be drearily hailed by the Russian autocrat as "going back to prison," which the uninitiated considered an unprincely remark in even worse taste.

Alix stayed on for a week with her sister after Bertie and the Duke of Edinburgh had left for London. Of the imperial couple, Minnie, with her highly strung and imaginative temperament, was most in need of comfort, and Alix, who in these respects was so like her, was well fitted to bring her back to normality.

It was only a month or so after the departure of the Princess of Wales that Marie Fedorovna, who had astonished her intimate circle by the quick revival of her spirits, suffered a setback, which resulted from a gruesome and horrible shock. The time of the happening was in the late afternoon, and as before her sitting-room, on this occasion at the Anitchkoff, was the scene of the incident.

In her room she always kept a large album of family photographs, starting with the day when she and Sasha had been married and continuing with the children as they made their appearance and developed year by year. On the afternoon in question she noticed upon entering the room that the family album, which normally rested upon a small side table, lay upon the large central table. She attributed this to the carelessness of a housemaid, a phenomenon of which she had bitter experience in Russia. It in no way surprised her. But the album being where it was, and she herself being for the moment unoccupied, she walked toward it and idly opened it at the first page.

The picture that should have met her eyes was one of herself and Sasha taken at the Winter Palace after the wedding. But the face and bare chest of a corpse confronted her. The picture showed it lying in a lidless boxlike coffin. The head of a flabby-cheeked young man with thick lips and nostrils and shaggy hair rested on a rough pillow. The eyes were closed, which would have given the dead man a kind of tranquility, but that the face was torn and pitted hideously with a network of small wounds. Written across the bare chest of the corpse in ink was the name *Grinevetski*.

Even without that name Marie Fedorovna would have recognized before her the portrait of the executed murderer of Alexander II, who had been struck in the face by nails packed in his own bomb. The picture was a photograph of a drawing made on the spot by a well-known artist, which she had already seen in a famous illustrated periodical.

Tania Obolonsky, her favorite lady in waiting, was in her own room when a piercing scream rang out. Marie Fedorovna lay in a faint on the floor by the table. But before she collapsed she must have slammed the album shut to hide the terrible picture. Until the Empress recovered Tania was at a loss to know what had happened to her mistress, and soldiers and policemen were soon scouring the palace in search of a suspected intruder.

General Tscherevin, the new Chief of Secret Police, who also commanded the Ochrana—the personal guard of the Emperor—was instantly summoned from his flat. Tscherevin was a personal friend of the Emperor and Empress, and frequently dined at the Anitchkoff. He was one of the most celebrated among the adoring slaves of the young Empress, and Marie Fedorovna rewarded his devotion by always having him to sit next to her and calling him the most amusing man she knew. While the Ochrana put everybody in the Anitchkoff Palace through a sharp and searching examination Tscherevin busied himself in comforting and reassuring the distressed Empress with the most accomplished grace, although he felt anything but reassured himself. But so gravely did he view the incident that later that evening he drew the Emperor aside, declared to him bluntly that the Nihilists had penetrated into the Anitchkoff, that the picture of Grinevetski must be taken as a threat of vengeance on behalf of one who had died for the Cause, and earnestly advised him to leave the Anitchkoff and make his home in one of the country palaces, near the capital, where security could be made more absolute and where he and the Empress could enjoy greater freedom.

Reluctantly the imperial couple admitted that General Tscherevin was right. They agreed to shut the Anitchkoff, except for those special occasions when their residence in Petersburg would be imperative, and to make their home in Gatchina Palace, which was about a thirty-mile journey by rail from the capital. Tscherevin himself was to leave Petersburg and live with the household at Gatchina, so that the utmost vigilance should be exercised at all times.

Gatchina stood in a park five miles square, the whole of which was enclosed by a high wall. From the day the Emperor and Empress went to live there a brigade of Guard Cavalry was always stationed at Gatchina, apart from the infantry and police guards. A never ending chain of horsemen rode day and night along the outside perimeter of the park wall, the ground here being cleared of all obstacles. In daylight the troopers rode a hundred yards apart, but at night the horse guard was quadrupled and the men rode at twenty-five yard intervals with police lanterns strapped to the browbands of their mounts.

Inside plain-clothes men continually patroled the park, with orders that if they saw the Emperor and Empress taking a walk they were to hide themselves. The reason for this was that the Emperor's violent objection to being "shadowed" soon became known to the police by bitter experience. If the Emperor espied a stranger lurking behind a bush he was liable to burst from the side of the Empress, brandishing a heavy stick, and chase him with roars of indignation; nor was it certain that if he caught up with his quarry his rage would permit him to stop at verbal abuse.

Lady Randolph Churchill during her visit to Russia was the guest of the Emperor and Empress at Gatchina, and has left some interesting impressions, which Lanin, who came to know the Gatchina ménage well, has supplemented with further details.

Lady Churchill describes the hall at Gatchina as

> . . . worthy of an old English country house, full of comfortable writing tables, games and toys; I even spied a swing. In this hall Their Majesties often dine, even when they have guests, and after dinner the table is removed and they pass the remainder of the evening there. The Emperor and the Empress elect to live with the greatest simplicity in the smallest of rooms, which are rather at variance with the Emperor's towering frame.

Lanin is chiefly concerned with the regime observed by the Emperor at Gatchina; but the daily habits of Sasha inevitably affected Marie Fedorovna.

> The Emperor generally rises at 7 a.m. [he says], whereas few noblemen in the capital leave their beds much before midday. He then takes a quiet stroll in the uninteresting, well-watched palace park, returns to early breakfast, and engages in severe manual labor as a preparation for the official work of the day. The latter consists mainly in the reading and signing of enormous piles of edicts, ukases, reports. Upon the margins of these documents he writes his decisions or his impressions with a frankness and abandon which laughs prudence and propriety to scorn. He writes down the thoughts suggested by what he reads just as they occur. They are not always very refined. "They are a set of hogs" is a phrase that occurs more frequently than most. "What a beast he is!" is another. Accounts of famine, crop failure, fire, calamity are almost invariably commented upon in one stereotyped word, "discouraging." After lunch the Emperor takes his recreation in the park, walking with the Empress, with General Tscherevin or an aide. Recreation over, the Emperor gives audience. At 8 p.m. dinner, con-

sisting of four courses, is served with intimate members of the household. After dinner when the Emperor takes tea with the Empress he invariably appears in a checked blouse and leather belt, which would impart a rude shock to the notions of court etiquette prevalent in most European countries. He takes a keen delight in hearing the gossip and scandal of the fashionable world of the capital.

Others have noted the appetite of the "Moujik Emperor" for gossip, scandal and tales of intrigue; but unlike his wife and Tania Obolonsky he only wished to enjoy such items at a distance. It is perhaps appropriate here, after seeing Sasha taking his evening tea in his checked shirt and belt, to record the only kind of social occasions he did enjoy. These were the noted "palace-beer-evenings" described by Felix Volkonsky. "How many a one," says Volkonsky, "in hope of gaining an entrance to these beer-evenings has taken pains to learn an out-of-the-way musical instrument, e.g. the deep bassoon! Art has to serve the ambition of such people: it is not a question of bread and butter." Nobody but the Emperor could invite to a "beer-evening," and he was not likely to invite anbody without a musical instrument. Ladies were not barred, and with them musical instruments were not obligatory. Marie Fedorovna frequently attended with Tania Obolonsky, and the Empress was considered to make a charming informal hostess. It was known that if the Empress wished to forward the career of some young man to whom she had taken a fancy, as she quite often did, she would ask him if he played a musical instrument. If the answer was "No" she would exclaim: "Learn one. When you can play properly I will see that the Emperor asks you to one of his 'beer evenings.'" Like the imperial host, all the men guests were expected to present themselves in gay shirts and belts. Sasha, a competent performer on all band instruments, was for some years after his accession obsessed with the delights of playing the trombone, and it almost seemed that when he blew into his trombone he blew away the fearful burden of worry and anxiety which was his daily lot.

For a period after the assassination of Alexander II the mourning, and the universal undercurrent of fright and suspicion, caused all social activities in the high life of Petersburg to cease. Some may have thought at that time, and with the departure of the imperial couple to Gatchina, that the enchanting Empress had virtually disappeared from the fashionable scenes in which she had shone and reveled as the Tsarevna. They surmised that from then on the unchallenged star of society would be the beautiful, admired, but little-loved Marie Pavlovna, the Grand Duchess Vladimir.

They were mistaken. In the untainted air of Gatchina Marie Fedorovna soon completely regained her poise, and with it the old fascinations of the social whirl once more began to appear delightful. She decided that she wanted to entertain, to be entertained, to display herself in the most magnificent gowns in the Empire, to revive the glories of the Petersburg season and to preside over court entertainments, which should be more magnificent and dazzling than ever before. From that time onward she had her own personal train—in the splendor and embellishment of which she took a childish pleasure—and she would frequently travel into Petersburg unaccompanied by the Emperor and return to Gatchina with the dawn. She entertained lavishly at Gatchina, often using imperial trains to fetch and return her guests, and on such occasions the Emperor was seldom seen. Only on great court occasions in Petersburg was he likely to appear beside her, when his manner was described as "majestic" rather than affable; but at least the scowl of distaste lifted from his brow as he engaged in abrupt conversation with his subjects.

Let us see Marie Fedorovna, the young Empress, through the eyes of two shrewd and worldly contemporaries. In one case, we can have the interesting experience of hearing the same man thirty years later contradict in an important respect his judgment in younger days.

Count Paul "Vassili" was among her most ardent admirers.

She was a charmer in the widest sense of the word [says Vassili]. Her charm was quite indescribable. It exercised a fascination to which it was impossible not to succumb. Her

lovely smile, the gentle look in her eyes—those great lumi-
nous dark eyes that seemed to read into one's soul—brought
more friends to her husband than millions spent on years of
effort would have done.

Adore her, as an exceptionally graceful creature, and do
not look to her for grave intellectual faculties. Say to yourself that she has realized all that could be expected of her;
that, with marvellous intuition, feeling that she had not the
necessary resources to play a great part, she had abstained
from prying into anything outside her circle. Marie Fedorovna has correctly judged herself and acted accordingly,
and it is for this reason that no one can reproach her with
the machinations of certain sovereigns. Few queens have
possessed her gift of mercy, and her desire to be merciful
and kind.

Baron von Samson-Himmelstierna, the German-speaking aris-
tocrat from the Russian Baltic states, is probably more imper-
sonal in his attitude to Marie Fedorovna. As an "Ostsee Junker"
he doubtless had not the advantages of "Vassili" in the Germano-
phobe court circle of the time; but his views upon the Empress
are worth listening to.

Natural vivacity and an optimistic temperament have enabled Marie Fedorovna, in spite of a nervous excitability, to
cheer her husband in the midst of his incessant conflicts
with himself and the world. The Emperor has nothing to
fear from female influence, for hers is never directed to subjects of a political nature. If the Empress now and again
takes a womanly interest in the "lions" of the court balls,
or the admirers of her favorite ladies, it is done in so naïve
and simple a way that no one can well be angry with the
high go-between even in cases of failure.

Because the Emperor is unsociable, he is glad that his
wife finds inexhaustible joy in dancing and amusements,
even though she runs up bills to the goddess of fashion,
which are not seldom as long as those of Josephine, the first
wife of Napoleon, who spent half her life in the dressing
room.

The Empress has the virtue of living peaceably with

everybody (including her brother-in-law and sister-in-law, the Vladimirs) and in threading her way with equal cleverness through the cliques and intrigues which are unavoidable at courts. That she meets the Emperor's occasional outbreaks of violence with extraordinary tact can be easily understood in a woman of so happy and discreet a nature.

Here are the impressions of two aristocrats of Imperial Russia: the former, Count Vassili, writing in French for the outside world in general, Baron Himmelstierna writing in German for Germans beyond the Imperial frontiers. Himmelstierna did not live to revise his opinion upon Marie Fedorovna. Vassilli did so. In 1913, just before his death, he gave his last work to the world, *Behind the Veil at the Russian Court.* For twenty years Marie Fedorovna had been the famous Dowager Empress, a legendary figure talked of with awe throughout Europe.

The aged Vassili reverts to his old love of the 'eighties—the gentle dark-eyed imperial charmer, who seemed to read into men's souls—and repeats most of those words he lavished on her in the old days. But Vassili knew many things which he had not known then; he and Himmelstierna, like everybody else, had been wrong in the 'eighties. In one pregnant sentence he reveals Marie Fedorovna in a new aspect. *"Political influence over the Emperor she possessed to an enormous extent,"* he declares, *"and yet no one ever guessed it, so cleverly did she hide from the world that she ever mixed in politics."*

One criticism of Marie Fedorovna as empress, and only one, does come from Vassili, and for this very reason it is valuable. "Her only weakness lies in the ease with which she will allow people who amuse her to gain her friendship, and for the sake of this one redeeming quality she will pardon many things which are unpardonable." He adds the revealing remark, "This applies in the case of her sister-in-law, the Grand Duchess Vladimir."

Shortly after the accession, the Mistress of the Household, who came to the new sovereigns as part of the legacy of the previous reign, had died. The duties of this aged lady had been more or less nonexistent for some years; but it was now absolutely necessary that the young Empress should find some person of great experience in court affairs and with energy and strength of character who could fulfil this role for her. The Princess Hélène Kotchoubey was a close friend of Queen Louise of Denmark, and it was on the recommendation of her mother that Marie Fedorovna invited her to become her Mistress of the Court.

Nobody knew the age of "the Kotchoubey," as she was usually called. A genuine "old Russian" of fabulous wealth, the famous balls at her palace on the Nevski Prospect rivaled the imperial balls. The Princess was reputed to know the *Almanac de Gotha* from cover to cover, and she was a human encyclopedia of imperial court etiquette. Despite her years this little old lady had the figure and nimbleness of a girl, and Count Vassili thought it "a poem to watch her enter a room. No one who saw her at a state function could ever forget her."

From the first Marie Fedorovna put herself wholeheartedly into the hands of Princess Kotchoubey, and people observed the Empress with amusement as she earnestly studied the Mistress of the Court. But the result was worth a few mischievous smiles: it was from Hélène Kotchoubey that Marie Fedorovna learnt that wonderful regality of manner and bearing, that majestic grace, which one day would make the Dowager Empress so renowned.

Princess Kotchoubey would tell the young Empress what she had to say to each person at a reception, what were their histories, and what she must on no account say to them. If she thought that Marie Fedorovna had carried out her instructions clumsily, she took her to task afterward, showing her how it should have been done. If it was a question of the Empress' guests being seated, then the correct placing of chairs became very important. The Princess set the chairs around the Empress. Then she guided each person to the right chair before he had time to seat himself on the wrong one. She boasted that everybody was always satisfied with the order in which she placed them round the Empress, because they knew this was the right order.

At the proper moment "the Kotchoubey" could be vivacious; but for ceremony she bore an appearance of almost reverential gravity. One look from the Mistress of the Court—and it came frequently—was enough to quell the rising buoyancy of the Empress on an inappropriate occasion. If Marie Fedorovna did not shock old-fashioned Russians by her levity and bubbling spirits, nor involve herself in mild indiscretions, it was because Kotchoubey was always on the watch to save her. Like everybody else the Empress was subject to her sharp tongue, which in the case of Marie Fedorovna sounded all the more awful for the words being cast in a tone of the most exquisite respect and decorum though the meaning was biting.

An amusing episode at a court ball, which took place soon after the mourning had ceased, displays both the "old Russian" implacability of Princess Kotchoubey and the ingenuity of Marie Fedorovna in countering it.

The daughter of the great Baron Alphonse de Rothschild, who was a French subject, had married in Paris a brilliant young Russian Jewish financier named Ephrussi. Ephrussi and his beautiful wife came to Petersburg on behalf of Alphonse de Rothschild to discuss the possibility of an important loan to the Imperial Government. It was desirable that the Ephrussi should receive every attention in the Russian capital.

Marie Fedorovna sent them an invitation to a court ball. Nobody gave the matter another thought until Hélène Kotchoubey, unaware that the invitation to the Ephrussi had been sent out, was opening the letters of acceptance for the Empress in the imperial sitting room. Suddenly Marie Fedorovna saw the Princess jump out of her chair. She was shaking from head to foot and glaring at a letter in her hand. Even the rouge seemed to fade from her wrinkled cheeks and her lips pursed like a thread. She thrust out the letter at the Empress, and Marie Fedorovna realized that it was the acceptance of Madame Ephrussi.

"Monsieur Ephrussi is not eligible to appear at the imperial court. He is a Russian subject!" hissed the Princess. "How can he attend a court ball? On no account may his wife be presented to the Empress. You will have to have them told that they cannot come to the ball."

Marie Fedorovna began to turn white. With her invitation

accepted she perceived the shocking dilemma she was in—more especially because if she accepted the advice of Kotchoubey she would have to face the terrible rage of Sasha, who above all wished to please Baron Rothschild. The voices of the Empress and her Mistress of the Court grew shrill as they faced one another with blazing eyes. Prince Galitzin, Master of the Household the aged male counterpart of Princess Kotchoubey, entered the room on some business. When he understood the nature of the argument he tried to intervene. He called several other members of the household. All declared that under the circumstances the Ephrussis ought to come to the ball. The noise grew worse. Nobody had seen the Princess so angry.

At last Kotchoubey declared: "—Very well. Her Majesty can do as she pleases. But I will not present Madame Ephrussi to her!"

Everybody fell silent. By age-old tradition nobody could present a lady to the Empress but her mistress of the household. They waited breathlessly for the Empress to dismiss the Princess Kotchoubey. They speculated to themselves on the marvelous grace with which the redoubtable old lady would accept her dismissal and sail from the room. But a gleam of amusement lit the eyes of Marie Fedorovna.

"This is what we'll do," she exclaimed. "Don't bring Madame Ephrussi up to me to be presented. You can stand her in a doorway. Then unexpectedly I will come through the door and you can introduce her to me. There is no rule against that at the Russian Court!"

The affair was managed as the Empress suggested. Prince Galitzin, after much painful maneuvering, arrived with the innocent Madame Ephrussi at a position between two double doors from hall to hall, and held her in conversation while he shot frantic glances in the direction of the Empress. Marie Fedorovna disengaged herself at the first opportunity and moved toward the double doors with the sulky Princess Kotchoubey. The introduction took place, followed by a charming conversation with the Empress, and Baron Rothschild was delighted with the attention shown to his daughter.

The venerable and stately Galitzin was a perfect partner for Hélène Kotchoubey, whom he treated with theatrical and exaggerated deference as a worthy colleague in the study of imperial ritual and tradition. Sometimes at the dinner table the brilliant conversation of Tscherevin and the gay chatter of Marie Fedorovna and Tania Obolonsky died away. All were listening with growing delight to Kotchoubey and Galitzin. The two old people, after discussing some matter of court etiquette with a kind of ponderous and tranquil enjoyment, had suddenly found themselves in disagreement and lost their tempers. In their great heat they were completely forgetting their "old Russian" manners. It was usually a bellow of laughter from the Emperor, who rarely spoke at dinner, which brought them back to reality.

Count Vassili, it will be recalled, disapproved of the Empress' showing so much affability to her sister-in-law Grand Duchess Vladimir, saying in this connection that if amused "she [the Empress] will pardon things which are unpardonable." In his opinion Vladimir and Marie Pavlovna wished to take advantage of both Emperor and Empress.

On the morning after the assassination Grand Duke Vladimir received a shock. "The favorite brother," as he was usually called, was seen to leave the new Emperor's study with an agitated expression, while an angry voice roared after him, "Do you understand—I want this done in the way I have said!"

A few days later Sasha growled to his friend Daskov: "As far as I am concerned I believe in the oriental idea that the younger brothers of the sovereign are always the most dangerous troublemakers. Look how my uncles acted toward my father. The Empress must look after my brothers. I don't want them in the council room."

Shortly afterward, the "oriental family policy" took shape with an edict whereby Sasha reduced the incomes, privileges and rights of all members of his family except the Empress and their children.

Nevertheless Vladimir continued to walk in to the imperial study without having himself announced, which was forbidden even for grand dukes, and was a custom observed by the other

Marie Fedorovna, Empress of Russia

Alexander III ("Sasha"), husband of
Marie Fedorovna

Alexander II, assassinated in 1881

Marie Fedorovna, *left,* with her sister Alexandra, who
later became Queen of England

The Imperial Romanoff family in the early 1870's.

L. to r., seated: Emperor Alexander II; Marie Fedorovna, with Grand Duke Nicholas, the last emperor of Russia, on her knee; Empress Alexandra Fedorovna. Standing: Grand Duke Paul; Grand Duke Serge; Grand Duchess Marie; Grand Duke Alexis; Tsarevitch Alexander, later to become Alexander III; Grand Duke Vladimir.

The victims of the Ekaterinburg assassination.
L. to r.: Grand Duchess Olga; Grand Duchess Marie; Nicholas II; Empress Alexandra; Grand Duchess Anastasia; Tsarevitch Alexis; Grand Duchess Tatiana.

Nicholas II, the last emperor of Russia, murdered at Ekaterinburg

Alexandra Fedorovna ("Alicky"), murdered with her
husband Nicholas II

Marie Fedorovna, the Dowager Empress, in exile
in Denmark in 1924

brothers. Sasha, incapable of argument, was thus taken unawares and sometimes had to give way. He was further annoyed because Vladimir treated the Empress with the same lack of ceremony which he had accorded to her as Tsarevna; a matter which did not in the least worry Marie Fedorovna.

The disappointment of Vladimir and Marie Pavlovna inevitably put them into a kind of secret opposition to the throne. In the case of Vladimir this spirit of contrariness certainly did not amount to disloyalty to his brother, to whom he never ceased to be attached. As for Marie Pavlovna, her attitude was more problematical. One form the opposition took was a strong pro-German bias, which challenged the outspokenly anti-German views of the Emperor and Empress. It was the plan of Bismarck's power politics to cultivate the new regime in Russia, which he regarded with profound suspicion—and Marie Pavlovna was an intimate of Bismarck. This led to a scandalous revelation which shook Petersburg.

One day Marie Pavlovna arrived to see the Empress. She could not hide her violent emotion. When questioned by her sister-in-law she spoke out with startling frankness.

Marie Pavlovna disclosed that she had written a letter to Bismarck. One of her husband's aides had found the letter "lying about." He had read it through. Then he had decided without consulting anybody that it was his duty to take the letter to the Emperor. The Emperor had kept it, and the aide had returned and reported his action to Grand Duke Vladimir, with his reasons for so doing. He was immediately dismissed from the grand-ducal palace. Marie Pavlovna's disclosure was a complete surprise to the Empress, for Sasha had said nothing about it to her.

"Was the letter you wrote really so bad?"

"I spoke my mind."

"What did it concern?"

"It was my frank opinion of the Emperor and the people who have the power in this country."

"What do you want me to do?"

"Get me a personal interview with the Emperor now. A member of the imperial family has been insulted by an upstart sub-

ordinate who doesn't know how to behave. The man ought to
be kicked out of the Guard Corps. It might also be of advantage
if my reason for writing the letter to the Baron [Bismarck] was
explained to the Emperor. I must do that myself."

"Galitzin—Daskov—Oblonsky will arrange an interview for
you. They are the proper people. Anything else would upset
him."

"Probably he is very upset already about my letter. I don't
want him to refuse to see me in the presence of Galitzin or anybody else. Even if they haven't heard him raving about it already
and had no idea what it was all about, I'm sure they would be
delighted to turn me away so that they would have a good story
to tell. That's why I want you to arrange an interview. He will
listen to you."

The interview was granted, and the Grand Duchess went in
to her brother-in-law. When she came out, which was not long
afterward, she left immediately for home.

Later that day Sasha had still shown no signs of mentioning
the interview to his wife. At last her curiosity overcame her and
she asked him outright what had happened.

"That woman will be as good as a traitor if she is not careful,"
he growled. "I have punished the pair of them, because Vladimir
is almost as much to blame as she is. I have openly humiliated
them—and, of course, everybody will know of it."

"How?"

"I have made the officer who brought me the letter *my* aide
—and I may not stop at that."

Rumors soon flew about Petersburg that the Grand Duchess,
who had disappeared, was a prisoner in the Fortress of Peter and
Paul. Actually she was in the throes of a nervous breakdown, and
her doctors suggested a long stay abroad.

Scarcely had Grand Duchess Marie Pavlovna returned from
her rest cure and resumed her colorful career in the capital when
she was involved in another resounding scandal of quite a different order, which again brought her before the Emperor's desk.

She was dining in a private room at Cubat's, the famous night
haunt, with a party of grand dukes and duchesses when she dis-

covered that a celebrated French actor whom she favored was entertaining a party in the next room. Judging by the noises which came through the wall the adjoining party was a Bohemian one. Marie Pavlovna sent a summons to the actor to join the grand-ducal party for a drink. Perhaps the Frenchman was drunk when he entered. His behavior irritated the grand dukes, if it amused the ladies. When asked how he was entertaining his guests next door he shook his head and began to laugh in a ribald way.

"If you're afraid to tell us—give us a silent demonstration!" challenged Marie Pavlovna, who prided herself on her daring.

The Frenchman shot her a look of surprise, shrugged his shoulders and muttered, "*Eh bien*." He gripped her round the waist and kissed her passionately, amid an appalled silence. The grand dukes leaped to their feet. Half a minute later the actor was being severely thrashed, and the ladies grew frightened that their menfolk were going to kill him. But rescue was on the way. The roars of the victim brought the wild party next door into the room.

A furious struggle broke out. Dresses were ripped, furniture smashed and bottles and glasses were shattered in all directions. The female intruders gave their attention to the grand duchesses. Cubat, in despair, sent for General Gressor, the dreaded Prefect of Petersburg, who was in the restaurant. Gressor stopped the fight in an instant, and sent them all home. Next morning he reported the affair to the Emperor. Petersburg meanwhile rejoiced over the story, grossly magnifying every facet of it.

Thunder and lightning filled the imperial study as Sasha faced a brother and sister-in-law with black eyes, who had been most reluctant to leave their palace, and told them what he thought of them. The thing was small fry compared to the previous matter; but he well comprehended the rib-shaking that would be taking place at the expense of the imperial family and, worse still, the use which the Nihilist propagandists would make of it. After that interview there was a coldness, which could be broken only by the Emperor, and it was chiefly due to the efforts of Marie Fedorovna that Vladimir and Marie Pavlovna were again seen in the imperial circle and began to regain their old position of power.

The affair of the Holy Band was one which colored the lives of all those involved, between its inception in the late summer of 1881 until the Coronation year, 1883. The Holy Band provided an exciting hobby for the members of the imperial family and the highborn of Petersburg, and enabled them to look at grim and sinister realities almost in the light of an elegant pastime.

By the summer of 1881 the natural ebullience of the Empress had enabled her to regain her high spirits. The mourning still prevented her from taking part in any of those social happenings in which she reveled; but she was ready to be interested and amused. She had reached a point at which she could forget for hours at a time the Russian Bad Man and his icy desert, if there were other things to engage her mind. Yet outside Gatchina things were very bad, and even inside the Gatchina park walls there was the lurking shadow.

Baron Samson-Himmelstierna experienced the nightmarish unrest of that scorching summer.

It was an open secret that the Emperor was not safe for a moment, that the Nihilist conspiracy had followed him to Gatchina, that these phantoms continued to haunt him night and day in this asylum. The slightest rumors were believed —assassins masked in court livery, bombs hidden in the park, threatening letters found on the table—the most ordinary happenings were magnified to tales of horror.

It was ironic that the diversion which offered itself to engage the eager mind of the Empress pertained to the very thing that most terrorized her: Nihilism. One sultry afternoon Grand Duke Vladimir, Count Daskov and some younger members of the Guard of her acquaintance came to her. They asked her to be patron of the Holy Band (*swaschennaya drouzhina*).

The object of the Holy Band was to preserve the life of the Emperor. To this end a number of younger men of the nobility and of the Imperial Guard had banded themselves into a "secret" league—nor had some of them omitted to invite their wives or sisters to join them. If the Secret Police were unable adequately to protect the Emperor and his family, then the nobility would form themselves into a noble secret police, and themselves counter the Nihilist plotters with their own tricks and methods.

Marie Fedorovna gave herself enthusiastically to the Holy Band. Sasha had no objection to the project; but was bluntly skeptical of the ambitious program drawn up by this noble society for his own protection. General Tscherevin, bewitched by the Empress, expressed his belief that state police and the agents of the Holy Band would work side by side in "invaluable co-operation," and hoped to associate himself intimately with the operations of the "drouzhina." Plehve, his right-hand man, a grim and gnarled regular policeman, was sarcastic and resentful, prophesying a "grand mess-up."

As was inevitable in Orthodox Russia, a league with such a name started as a solemn act of dedication, amid clouds of incense and chanting acolytes. Elements of comedy soon began to appear. Young officers had only to whisper in the ear of their commanding officers "swaschennaya drouzhina" to obtain long leave of absence from their duties to carry out a "mission." Young nobles who had started honestly on some desperate trail assigned to them by the committee, or which they themselves had suggested to that august body, ended by enjoying prolonged holidays at the Band's expense all over Europe. Nihilists, who had watched with misgivings the rising clouds of inaugural incense of this secret band of dedicated nobility, ended by laughing, and in some cases offered their own services to the Holy Band. Holy Russia, always a nest of extravagant stories, hearing that the Empress was concerned with the mysterious Band, romantically pictured her lovely form disguised in the dress of a youth and mingling in the dens of Nihilism for the sake of her husband.

An imperial edict had given the accredited agents of the Holy Band the power of arrest, and some noble enthusiasts made full use of it. They shadowed innocent citizens across the face of Russia and finally arrested them. Their suspicious behavior while pursuing their unconscious quarry caught the attention of secret policemen, who made a third party in the trail and finally arrived to seize the amateur detective and his prisoner as joint conspirators.

A state akin to gang warfare reigned between the agents of the Holy Band and the Secret Police. Himmelstierna dryly remarks: "It frequently happened that the agents of the Holy Band and their myrmidons arrested whole sections of the state Secret Police; at other times the reverse happened. These grotesque scenes became the talk of the town."

Jokes and sarcastic references to the Holy Band appeared in the press. There were even veiled gibes about the amateur police work of the Empress herself. The Emperor never saw these, for he never read newspapers—only a daily précis selected for him from all of them. Marie Fedorovna, attending at the central meetings of the Holy Band, heard too often the well-satisfied pronouncements common at such gatherings to believe that she was engaged in anything but a valuable service for the throne.

General Tscherevin was himself beginning to get uneasy; but he had put himself in a false position in his anxiety to please the Empress. At last old Plehve, who could stand no more and who often visited the Emperor with police reports, stood waiting one morning by the imperial desk after his business had been finished. When the Emperor looked up questioningly, because he had not withdrawn, Plehve spoke out.

"I must tell your Majesty about a joke going round among my men, and personally I can't blame them for it after the things that have been happening. One man says to another: 'Have you heard of the latest coup of the Holy Band? Last night the Empress arrested the Emperor for subversive activities against the Throne, and now His Majesty has arrested General Tscherevin for not arresting the Empress for arresting the Emperor.' However silly you think that, I can tell you people are talking about the Holy Band as if it was a league of madmen!"

The Emperor was aroused. A sheaf of police reports about the recent activities of the Holy Band was brought to him the same day. He there and then decided that the Band should be done away with.

Of the many decisive actions taken by Alexander III during his reign the abolition of the Holy Band was probably the only one which was not done with brutal sharpness. It was also the only case in which his wife was involved, which doubtless supplies the explanation. For once, the imperial giant proved that he had tact. The Holy Band, like the old soldiers, was encouraged gently to fade away, and it may be that its originators were happy to see the last of their monster.

CHAPTER VIII

In and Out of Prison With Uncle Sasha

THE PROSPECTS of Coronation Year, 1883, promised blackly for the sovereigns. At Easter, scarcely more than a month before the May Coronation, when they were resting at their Black Sea villa at Livadia they were inspecting the customary gifts of painted and jeweled Easter eggs, which covered a large central table, when Marie Fedorovna espied an especially beautiful one. She picked it out and opened it to find who was the donor. Inside they gazed at a little silver dagger, two carved-ivory death's heads and a gilt-edged card bearing the Easter salutation "Christ is Risen." Underneath was another message, *"You may crush us —but we Nihilists shall rise again!"*

That morning in Moscow the Prefect of Police had received a basket of painted hens' eggs. Several of the eggs were stuffed with dynamite. Nor was a message lacking— *"We have plenty more for the Coronation!"* A few minutes before the Emperor and Empress with their children alighted at the Nicolai station, upon their return to the capital, a mine was discovered under the platform.

At Moscow the Boganovitch plot was exposed. Russian coronations took place at the Kremlin, and this was the stage for the sinister Boganovitch operations.

Boganovitch had secured the contract for wiring the Kremlin with electric light. Russians had been quick to perceive the dramatic possibilities of the new illumination, and the Coronation Committee had planned that at a given moment, when the newly crowned Emperor and Empress proceeded through the vast building, all the lights along their path should suddenly flash on in variegated color, section by section, as the procession moved along.

Boganovitch had wired bombs into his electric circuit to explode when the current was switched into each section. Thus, if the first bomb failed to explode, the second, or at worst the third, was certain to destroy the Emperor and Empress.

The Boganovitch investigations led the police to another discovery in a Moscow attic. This attic was packed from floor to ceiling with high-crowned caps. At a coronation enthusiastic peasants would be expected to toss their caps in the air as the sovereigns passed in the street. Each cap had a bomb fixed inside the crown. The "peasants" wearing these caps were to be human mortars, lobbing their headgear in an arc from the crowd over the heads of the triple line of troops into the processional way.

Cap-throwing was forbidden on pain of serious punishment during the Coronation, and a more elaborate precaution, which lasted till the end of the reign, was adopted as a result of the Boganovitch discovery. From this time on, an eminent scientific man was employed at a princely salary to live at all times with the imperial family. His sole duty was to inspect the palace daily to see that no kind of scientific or mechanical device for causing explosions had been introduced into the building.

But terrifying as these things must have been to the imperial couple, who could not help but expose themselves from time to time in the days ahead, a conviction suddenly began to grow in Moscow—nobody knew how it started, but it proved to be correct—that the Nihilist council had decided in the end to hold their hand during the Coronation rejoicings, having accepted the argument that slaughter on such a sacred occasion would do the cause more harm than good. So strong grew this belief in Moscow that even foreign visitors wrote home about it; so that we may hope it reached Sasha and Marie Fedorovna, for otherwise their ordeal must have been terrible indeed.

It was the ritual for the Emperor and his consort to spend their first night of the Coronation period outside the gates of Moscow at the Petrovsky Palace. From there in the morning the Imperial Procession, said to be the most amazing sight of its kind in the world, set out for the Kremlin.

First in this tremendous procession came an endless column of troops and bands in various uniforms and white sheepskin dress caps. The long clattering mounted section followed after the infantry, hussars and lancers in their historic dress, long-coated Cossacks in tilted kalpaks, the dazzling Garde-à-Cheval in their white uniform, eagle-crowned helms of blazing brass and black gilded breastplates. Then came a gap, which suddenly was filled by a strange and breathtaking spectacle, which none who saw could ever forget.

A dense human and equine kaleidoscope, its colors flowing and mingling in rich tints like an artist's palette, rode forward in solemn disorder with tossing manes and tinkling harness between the lines of troops. The deputies of the vast Asiatic dominions with their massed retinues and floating banners had come to honor the Sacred Emperor: Kalmucks, Khirghans, Khirvans, grim Tartars and Mongols, the denizens of the Kizil Kum and the Kara Kum, dwellers on the banks of the Jaxartes and Oxus, roaming warriors from the far Siberian steppes, the mountain princes of Tscherkasb, the Emir of Bokara and turbaned horsemen of Turkistan, chieftains from Iversk, Kustilnisk, Kabardinsk and Armenia, even a party of Buddhist lamas in golden copes on white ponies.

Alexander III, huge and solitary, striking the contrast in his plain green uniform and his white cap, appeared on a white charger so small that it scarcely seemed as big as he. Strangely, that shapeless figure with heels nearly sweeping the ground surpassed in dignity the magnificent array of grand dukes and foreign princes flooding forward at his back. The golden coaches led by that of the Empress followed in a long line amid scarlet Cossacks of the Escort.

At the Chapel of the Iverski Virgin, the patron saint of Moscow, which stands divided from the Kremlin by the great square outside its walls, the clergy of Moscow in splendid vestments, headed by their high dignitaries in cloth of gold and backed by the mulberry-red ranks of choristers, waited to greet the sovereigns. Beyond in the square before the Kremlin walls the troops of the procession and the Asiatics had formed into massive ranks.

The Emperor arrived at the chapel some distance ahead of the rest. He halted before the clergy and faced toward the roadway, waiting for the coach of the Empress, and signaling to the retinue of princes to form behind at each side of him.

They used to say that the melodious bells of old Moscow were a concert in themselves. That morning, with the sunlight glimmering over the gilded domes and spires of the Kremlin, their music was broken by the endless crashing of guns, the blare of brass, the thud of drums and the frantic cheering as the Empress approached.

The high, heavy golden coach rolled into view drawn by eight white horses. Count Vassili, tensely gripping his field glasses, stood on a balcony opposite Iverski Virgin and watched with emotion the scene which followed below. The Empress, who dazzled him with her loveliness, sat beside her little daughter Zenia and was plainly, serenely visible to thousands, against the white velvet interior of the coach with its glass sides.

The Emperor began to dismount with that ponderous awkwardness so familiar to his intimates. Yet presently he would conduct himself in a manner which astonished them.

The swaying imperial coach trembled to a standstill. The white-and-gold-clad footmen leaped down and made to open the door. An equerry in glittering uniform and plumes ran forward, waved them aside and caught the door handle. But the Emperor himself had now reached the coach. He firmly brushed aside the equerry and opening the coach door helped his wife and daughter to alight. The gesture was knightly, tremendous, and the watchers gasped to see this come from the Russian bear.

Vassili was entranced, utterly approving of such chivalry to his queenly heroine.

> For one moment she stood there dressed all in white, a big diadem of brilliants on her head, innumerable diamonds round her neck and on the bodice of her dress, clothed in cloth of silver and with a cloud of delicate white lace enveloping her graceful figure, the loveliest of smiles playing round her mouth, whilst tears of emotion were glistening in her sweet eyes. With one of those impulses which made her always do the right thing, she turned round and saluted the crowd—staring at her, lost in admiration of her beauty.

Those who understood the cruel burden which the almost solid train imposed upon her frail shoulders, even when borne by the imperial pages, admired her grace as she floated beside the Emperor, holding Zenia by the hand, and advanced to the Metropolitan. She waited with bowed head as he raised his cross to bless them and delivered his homily. Then they slowly climbed the chapel steps and passed through the portal of Iverski Virgin, where some could glimpse them kneeling together in silent prayer. They returned again to the coach with the Emperor holding the hand of his consort, and he himself helped her to her seat and arranged her difficult train. Led by the Emperor and his cortège of princes the line of golden coaches passed before the parade of troops and vanished one by one through a gap in the ancient walls of the Kremlin.

Coronation Day, May 26, was cloudy with gusts of rain. Inside the Kremlin enclosure a broad red carpet ran along a low wooden structure, which crossed the huge outer court diagonally and joined the imperial palace, standing before the belfry of Ivan Weliki, to the little Cathedral of the Assumption, where the crowning was to take place. One end of the mammoth carpet terminated at the top of the grand stairway of the palace, the other at the doors of the cathedral. At each side of the carpet was a sea of eager human faces. A heavy canopy, borne by general officers, had slowly come to rest at the foot of the palace stairs. It was the signal that the sovereigns were about to cross to the cathedral.

A procession of heralds and splendid court dignitaries began to cross along the raised imperial way, and the foreign royalties and the grand dukes and duchesses followed. The great moment had come for those not privileged to enter the cathedral. People near the palace saw the Emperor and Empress descending the stairs between the white Garde à Cheval and the scarlet Cossacks of the Escort.

The ostrich feather canopy was advancing along the carpet with the Emperor and Empress beneath, moving so gently that it scarcely seemed in motion at all. Now the people stood awestruck with bared heads and crossed themselves. Later, when the canopy recrossed the carpet to the palace above the crowned sovereigns, the spectators would fall on their knees, and if there were any Nihilists among them they would forget their cause for that day.

Charles Lowe, sent by *The Times* of London to describe the ceremony for readers who for the most part could not remember a coronation, saw from his place in the cathedral "the Empress arrayed in a sweeping robe of silver, so heavy as to fatigue her," and Alexander III, towering head and shoulders above the tall men around him—"altogether a most uncommon and impressive figure—he looked as if he could with ease bear heavy armor." Lowe watched the Emperor, now clad in the imperial mantle, receive his crown from Monseigneur of Novgorod, "which he himself"—mark that!—*placed upon his own head.*"

For a moment the crowned Emperor sat in motionless isolation on his throne with orb and scepter. Perhaps in that rather foggy mind of his he felt lonely and cut off in the icy Russian desert which he knew lay all around him. His eyes turned to the Empress. He beckoned to her. "The Emperor took off his Crown," says Lowe, "and touched with it the forehead of his Consort, who knelt before him on a crimson velvet cushion; after which he placed upon her head her own crown, topped by a large and lovely sapphire."

But Charles Lowe failed to see the Empress as Count Vassili saw her, "with the folds of her silver dress falling around her, its white shimmer adding brilliancy to her whole figure." Nor did Lowe observe, as did the ecstatic Vassili, how the Emperor crowned her "carefully, with loving movements," or how the crowned Empress lifted her head and "raised her beautiful expressive eyes toward his face."

Lowe must have seen what happened next, for Vassili and a great crowd of others saw it and wiped away a tear, but the British journalist let it pass. Vassili gazed spellbound as the Emperor raised his wife in his arms, and before the assembled glory of Russia and Europe—or forgetful perhaps of the assembly—pressed her to him in a long and fervent embrace.

This was the dramatic climax of the Coronation; but if Charles Lowe undervalued it, he reveals that he was not blind to another and more sinister aspect of the ceremony he was witnessing. Lowe knew Russia and Russians well.

> I myself had reason to know [declares Lowe] there were at the Coronation officials and others, secretly at the orders of the Nihilist party, near enough to the Emperor to have struck a fatal blow if the dread word of command had been given.

✿   ✿   ✿

Imperial Russia has long vanished into the limbo and politically the reign of Alexander III is of small interest today, except in so far as he was the Pan-Slavist Emperor *in excelsis.** He scorned all foreigners and said so bluntly, and thereby often reduced his wife to tears. Expressions of amazement and violent indignation burst from him when somebody suggested the introduction into a Russian palace of a lift manufactured by a foreign firm!

Alexander III was known as the Peacekeeper of Europe, because he played off France against Germany and Austria against

---

* Pan-Slavism: Russia for the Russians—The Slavs for Russia—The World for the Slavs. The Pan-Slavist spirit survived the Revolution and is still active under a different name.

them both, while Britain was always kept guessing. In Russia he was widely loved as the Moujik Emperor. This peasant part appealed to him and he always played up to it. To dissentient minorities in Russia, such as Poles, Finns, Baltic Germans, Jews, and to all religious dissenters he was the Emperor Persecutor, and to some the Second Ivan the Terrible.

He shocked all Europe when he sent Russian army officers to kidnap Alexander of Battenberg, whom his father had made the Prince of Bulgaria, because Alexander stoutly refused to bring Bulgaria in line with Russia's Balkan policy. From that time Queen Victoria, who loved the Battenbergs, called the conduct of the Russian Emperor "unspeakable," and nothing but the close bond between the Princess of Wales and her sister and the obstinate loyalty of the Prince of Wales to his brother-in-law prevented a total break with the Romanoffs.

We know that Alexander III could not argue. None who tried to argue with the Emperor ventured the experiment twice—except Pobedonsteff, and his brother Vladimir. Marie Fedorovna had learned ways of dealing with him; but was several times said to have endangered her life by misjudging the moment to leave the Presence. When he visibly grew enraged in the family circle she swept the children away. To all children but his own he was Uncle Sasha, the beloved buffoon and companion. His own children as they grew older began to fear him, although they too were under his Pied Piper spell and loved him sincerely.

Alexander III was at the same time the biggest blockhead of all Russia's autocrats, and one of the most powerful and respected, inside and outside his dominions. In one sense he was very wise, in that he knew his own limitations. The fearful nervous strain under which he had to live from the first till the last day of his reign had the effect upon him of exaggerating every facet of his personality, making him an enigma, a caricature, a brute, and a lovable child with an almost nostalgic fascination over his intimates.

Such was the husband of Marie Fedorovna from the time he became Emperor of All the Russias. She had known the same qualities in him in the old days; now everything, not merely the increasing weight of his flesh and bone, was on the grand scale.

Strangest of all the stories of Alexander III which circulated in Russia is that of the Gatchina shooting. The Emperor frequently took a nap on the couch in his study at times when he was unoccupied. One afternoon he had gone to the study after luncheon, saying he meant to rest. About half an hour later Marie Fedorovna was startled by the crash of a shot in the study. A heavy thud followed the explosion.

She was petrified with terror, convinced that an intruder had shot Sasha, or that he had shot himself. Nevertheless, she was the first to reach the study.

Her husband sagged in a dazed condition on the edge of the couch. A revolver in his hand was still smoking. His eyes stared fixedly at the floor by his feet. Then she saw that a corpse, with the brains blown out, lay on its back below the couch. It was that of a newly joined aide de camp.

All the Emperor could say—according to the story—was that he awoke to see the man bending over him with his fingers on his throat. He had snatched the revolver from under the cushion and fired in his face.

None knew the explanation of the mystery. The young aide had carried the secret to his grave. Investigations proved him to have no connections with revolutionaries. He came from one of the most loyal of aristocratic families in Russia. It was suggested that he had entered the study with papers, and seeing the Emperor dozing with a constricted look on his face had gently attempted to unhook his tight military collar.

E. A. Brayley Hodgetts, author of a long monograph on the Russian court of the nineteenth century, who had traveled extensively in Imperial Russia, had heard of this killing of an aide by Alexander III, and records it as a fact. It may well be so, for the incident is not out of character and agrees well with the nervous tension at Gatchina.

Two items of a lighter character we may accept without question.

Marie Fedorovna, worried about the health of Tsarevitch Nicky, summoned a celebrated German nerve specialist to examine her eldest son. When the Emperor heard of this he did not object, but he was skeptical at the idea of such newfangled treatment and made it clear that the distinguished German would not be welcome to him at Gatchina.

The specialist presented himself at Gatchina, and the Tsarevitch was brought to him. When the examination was ended the specialist wrote out a frank and comprehensive opinion concerning the Heir Apparent. Although the Empress had called him in the doctor considered that in view of the exalted nature of his patient it was his duty to show his report first to the Emperor. He had himself shown into the study and with an air of importance placed the report before the Emperor on the imperial desk. The Emperor read it through. To him it was an array of nonsense and a gross insult.

He rose to his feet. Rage had seized him; but the German, pompously unaware of this, put out his hand, thinking it was about to be shaken. He received a ferocious box on the ear. Next moment he had been kicked through the study door, and staggered groaning and half dead into the Empress's room for protection.

When Laeken Palace, the Brussels home of the King of the Belgians, was severely damaged by fire, Marie Fedorovna, knowing how careless her husband often was, impressed upon him that he must write a letter of condolence that morning to the Belgian Ambassador. He promised to do so.

About an hour later he wrote with plodding care a letter to the *Netherlands Ambassador*, expressing his deepest sympathy with the Belgian King at the sad accident to his home.

Next morning the Dutch Ambassador arrived at Gatchina. He was the victim of a *gaffe* unique in the history of diplomacy and he was a very unhappy man, for when an ambassador receives a letter from a sovereign he must reply to it. He asked for the Empress, with whom he was on friendly terms. He said he was very worried and told her about the letter. How could he reply to it without making the Emperor look silly? He had hidden the letter carefully, because if any of his staff saw it and talked, it would become the joke of every chancellery in Europe. What did she advise?

She burst out laughing.

"Don't worry yourself," she said. "The Emperor will have forgotten about it by this time. Just forget about it, too—but burn it!"

In the old days Tsarevitch Alexander had been called the "Bullock." He was now known in his household as the "Bull." In the small matters of life he was often troublesome to his wife. The imperial mantle had increased his obstinate incorrigibility. It was necessary for the Empress to inspect his appearance before he showed himself on any kind of official occasion, or before he received foreigners or important Russians. She often sent him back for his valet to re-dress him. He was quite likely at the first showing to have a shabby tunic, stained trousers bagged at the knees, the wrong orders and decorations, a greasy military cap or perhaps some article missing altogether. His valet was far too terrified to argue with him till the Empress took a hand. To press his clothes was a waste of time. He seemed to have a genius for crumpling them.

From time to time Marie Fedorovna tried to persuade him to have his study redecorated and reupholstered. It was the best-known room in Gatchina to a large number of people. The wallpaper was stained and peeling here and there, and the stuffing burst out of slits in the faded upholstery. A thunderous frown greeted such suggestions. He always countered: "It should last a few more years. It's such good quality." Foreign visitors expressed astonishment at the poverty-stricken scene. Marie Fedorovna never consulted him as to renovations in the rest of the palace, but believed in facing him with a *fait accompli*, having the work done behind closed doors room by room. In that way he might never notice the changes.

The first of the official visits abroad took place in August 1885, when the Emperor and Empress of Russia and the Emperor and Empress of Austria met at Kremsier, in Moravia, in the luxurious summer palace of the Archbishop of Olmutz. On this important occasion—far from congenial to Alexander III—Marie Fedorovna was much occupied in keeping her husband in a mood which would not absolutely insult the Emperor of Austria and his officials. Whereas in the Russian court ritual was interpreted in the happy-go-lucky way of highborn Russians and nobody suffered undue discomfort for long, the Court of Vienna was the strictest in Europe. Emperor Franz Josef observed every kind of etiquette with religious devotion. Indeed, but for his flintlike adherence to dusty and inhuman rituals his personality was rather vacant. Franz Josef was always correctly dressed, and despite the most desperate efforts of Marie Fedorovna the appearance of the Russian Emperor plainly filled him with horror and incredulity. Since both the Emperors were taciturn by nature, neither could discover much to say to the other, and the sight of Alexander III loitering in the grounds in peasant shirt and belt, or in an old striped linen jacket, much too tight, of which he was exceptionally fond, left the impeccable Austrian Emperor speechless.

The Kremsier meeting was considered to be politically of high importance, and both sovereigns among their retinues had brought leading ministers and governmental experts. The primary object was to debate the unsettled affairs of Central and Eastern Europe, and the Emperor and Empress of Germany, too, would have been present but for their advanced years. As it was, frequent telegrams reporting the proceedings were querulously awaited in Berlin. Balls, banquets, shooting parties of a fashionable rather than sporting character, and all kinds of entertainments had been devised, and suitable persons brought from the respective capitals to grace them; but if it had not been for Marie Fedorovna and Empress Elizabeth of Austria everything would have been blighted by the two grim-mouthed Emperors, who except in the council room avoided each other as much as possible.

Marie Fedorovna was meeting the celebrated Elizabeth of Austria for the first time. The two fascinating Empresses matched one another in gaiety and levity, and became firm friends.

Empress Elizabeth had long decided that her husband was a bore. She was a beautiful and legendary figure, who spent most of her time traveling abroad, where her conduct was unconventional if not eratic. The two Empresses are said one night to have shocked Franz Josef and his dignified courtiers. They settled an argument on gymnastics after dinner in the drawing-room by practising cartwheels, an art in which Marie Fedorovna, like her sister Alix, was expert from her youth, but in which the eager Empress Elizabeth had something to learn.

Every year Empress Elizabeth went to England for the hunting season to ride with the Quorn and Pytchley, and she drove a trap as if the devil were behind her. When the Sultan of Turkey had visited Austria she took him out driving. The terrified potentate soon decided he could stand no more. *"Achtung!"* he screamed—his only word of German—and then broke into French as the Empress pulled up and he jumped out. *"Vous mourrez seule, Madame!"*

The sovereigns of Russia had to undergo this ordeal at Kremsier. At sight of the fiery Hungarian ponies, Sasha, whose shrinking from horseflesh had grown with his bulk, visibly blanched. He had heard the story of the Sultan.

"Madam, there is only one thing upon which I agree with the Sultan of Turkey," he growled up at the Empress, who was already seated with the whip. "We both hate reckless driving."

Empress Elizabeth laughed, and agreed to drive carefully. She did so to start with. She may have lost control of her Hungarians. Presently the Emperor and Empress of Russia were hurtling through the countryside in scarcely less danger than from their own Nihilists. The top-heavy weight of Sasha threatened to overbalance the frail high trap at any moment. Even the Empress Elizabeth was perturbed by the violent rocking and shouted at him to "keep still," but she seemed unable, or unwilling, to stop the ponies. Sasha caught the reins from her, and with sweat pouring over his face brought the beasts to a standstill by nearly tearing off their heads, making them rear up so that the whole contrivance all but tumbled backward down a steep drop.

Such was the nature of the Kremsier meeting. Things were very different when the Empress of Russia took her husband and the children to visit her father and mother in Denmark. Then it was that they left "prison" behind them; the glorious moment of freedom had come at last. This event happened every year, sometimes at Christmas, but generally in the summer. The Princess of Wales always came to join her sister in Denmark, and everybody was amused to see how the King of Denmark delighted in ordering around his two distinguished daughters, as if they had never left Bernstoff. King Christian treated them much more severely than he did the crowd of grandchildren who attended these great annual family parties, and they seemed perfectly happy to humor their now white-whiskered father, as he strolled rather vaguely about, puffing his endless cigars and frequently arriving on the scene at the wrong moment with a stern look of disapproval, just when Sasha had involved them in some silly prank with the children. They listened to him meekly—in fact were rather frightened and even tried to escape. Mama was also a person to be reckoned with.

The Wales' children generally came with their mother, and the Prince often joined them from some Continental resort. It was Bertie who wrote from Fredensborg to a friend: "We are an immense family gathering—quite a Babel, seven different languages spoken, never sitting down to dinner less than fifty or sixty."

The Greek royal family, King George, Queen Olga, their five stalwart boys and two girls, scarcely ever missed a Fredensborg party, and there were always squads of German relations of all ages.

Every morning at Fredensborg Uncle Sasha led a walk after breakfast through the royal park for everybody under twenty, and for not a few over that age. This was like a school on the move, headed by a gigantic bearded schoolmaster with twinkling eyes; but it was a shockingly badly disciplined school. They came down to the lake. In the summer they would probably seize someone and throw him in with a grand splash, or they might combine to push Uncle Sasha into the water. In winter Uncle Sasha marched solemnly upon the ice so that they could watch it collapse under his weight, and then he stood bellowing with laughter submerged up to his fat knees.

We hear of a summer day when the Empress of Russia and the Princess of Wales, carried away by excitement, join the party led by the Emperor of Russia, which is plundering the big apple tree in the walled garden down the stone steps—sacred to the King of Denmark; and shortly afterward we meet them again, still further steeped in iniquity, hurling apples in through the upper windows of Fredensborg and helping to smash the lights in the unused garrets. But King Christian approaches and they are gone.

We hear the sisters encouraging Sasha to carve his monogram surmounted by the Russian imperial crown on the stems of the big beech trees in the Marble Garden: a practice sternly forbidden to the young. Every minute, as Minnie and Alix stand beside Sasha, their eyes are on the watch for a wisp of cigar smoke above a bush heralding the tall figure of Papa.

The best of all the stories about the two sisters at Copenhagen concerns a day at the Zoological Gardens. They were in the monkey house with a party of nephews and nieces, and the visit being informal the monkey house had not been cleared for the benefit of the royalties. A growing assembly of respectul and curious Danes were forming a little farther back from the cages than the royal party. The curiosity of the spectators was soon to be rewarded.

Marie Fedorovna was wearing a small straw hat, adorned with cherries. This had for some minutes attracted the interest of a small monkey. Suddenly the monkey darted his paw through the bars and gripped the hat. The cherry hat lifted off the Empress' head in the little paw, yet it was still held to the back of her head by a rapidly expanding elastic band. A tug-of-war started with the hat suspended between both parties to the struggle, while the Princess of Wales, apparently convinced that her sister was being dragged into imminent danger, caught her waist and pulled her frantically backwards, the elastic ever stretching the while. The Empress of Russia herself was beginning to grow somewhat disturbed.

The nephews and nieces roared with delight. The ring of

humble Danes stood motionless in shocked and bewildered solemnity.

Suddenly the monkey released the cherry hat. It whipped back to the Empress' head, settling with an absurd tilt over her right ear. "I shall never forget," says their nephew Nicholas of Greece, "Queen Alexandra's uncontrollable mirth—much to the distress of her poor sister."

In the late summer of 1883 when Fredensborg housed a big family gathering, including the Emperor and Empress of Russia and their children, Alfred Tennyson and Mr. Gladstone arrived in Copenhagen harbor in the *Pembroke Castle* on their return from their much-publicized and triumphant cruise in Scandinavian waters. The poems of Tennyson, then in his seventy-fifth year and at the peak of his glory, were acclaimed throughout Europe; for above all poets he had satisfied the lush sentimentalism of the age. Excitement reigned in Copenhagen at this unique invasion, and nowhere was curiosity deeper than at Fredensborg.

Gladstone was a grim figure to be gazed upon with awe, but Tennyson was splendidly colorful: a towering, shaggy, ferocious King Lear with black slouch hat and flowing mantle.

Tennyson, Gladstone and their party accepted an invitation to dine at Fredensborg. Among them was Tennyson's son, Hallam, who has left some details of the Danish visit. At Fredensborg they were evidently surprised both by the number and by the "freedom and unconventionality" of the assembled royalties of all ages.

—We sat down, about eighty, to dinner at a horseshoe table. The King and Queen of Denmark, the Princess of Wales, the Emperor and Empress of Russia, the King and Queen of Greece, the Duchess of Cumberland [Thyra, third daughter of King Christian] and many other notabilities.

Hallam Tennyson omits to mention an incident of the dinner which is heard of from other sources—possibly because it was a happening in which the laugh was against his revered father.

It seems that this was one of those occasions when the great bard was bathed in silence. Perhaps for once he was awed by the unique distinction of the international assembly engulfing him. The entire Fredensborg party had gathered to the meal anticipating the customary magnificent declamation of his own verse with which the bard was wont to regale those who entertained him. But Tennyson ate and drank heartily and held his peace. With the dessert it was becoming obvious that the atmosphere was not right: yet although hints were put out in reverent but audible tones around the great horseshoe table as to the desires and hopes of the company none ventured directly to challenge the glooming bard to give of his riches.

Tennyson sat between Queen Louise, an ardent admirer, and the Princess of Wales. Opposite were the Emperor and Empress of Russia, and several of the Russian suite were nearby. It was the Russians who started a eulogistic argument in English on their favorite Tennysonian pieces. The old poet was watching and listening, obviously flattered. Suddenly Tennyson realized that they were misquoting and stumbling over the lines. They bickered over the title of a poem. Then the Russian Emperor—who evidently had no voice for great poetry in any language—enthusiastically, and deliberately, did the poet but know it, murdered a stanza of "Come into the Garden, Maud." It was horrible. It was Tennyson's favorite poem. These foreigners had no idea how things ought to be spoken.

With startling abruptness the bard roared out, *"NO—it is not like that!"* He had risen to his feet, shaking a little and supporting himself with his hands, but his eyes glowed. *"Come into the Garden, Maud!"* he announced, scanning the table with an eagle glance. Then he gave them his beloved poem in the way that only he knew how to speak it. They listened electrified. When he had finished they stamped their feet and cried out for more. He gave them more. He lost himself in the ecstasy of Tennysonian declamation.

Next day, September 18, a luncheon was given to the royalties aboard the *Pembroke Castle*. A line of boats put out from the shore, each bearing three royal ensigns, those of Denmark, Russia and Greece. Signal flags fluttered up the halyards of the Danish, Russian and Greek warships, gun salutes crashed out and cheering seamen lined the rails. The *Pembroke Castle* was dressed over-all, and Tennyson and Mr. Gladstone waited at the gangway as the glistening boats glided alongside one by one and unloaded the élite of Europe.

Hallam Tennyson describes the luncheon:

> Gladstone proposed the health of the King of Denmark. The Emperor of Russia proposed the health of our Queen; and the King of Denmark that of Mr. and Mrs. Gladstone. Then the Queen of Denmark rose and drank to my father. The Empress of Russia said to him: "What a kind and sympathetic man Mr. Gladstone is! How he stood by little Montenegro!" Everybody was most friendly and everything went without a hitch.

> In the small smoking room after luncheon my father, at the request of the Princess of Wales, read "The Bugle Song" and "The Grandmother." The Empress of Russia paid him some pretty compliment, and he, being very short-sighted, and taking her for a Maid of Honor, patted her on the shoulder and said, "Thank you, my dear."

> The Emperor of Russia observed to my father, "I should like to be King of Denmark!" and in his talk he seemed full of love for the Danes, who are a simple people.

We have heard Alexander III tell Tennyson that he "would like to have been King of Denmark." The sovereigns of Russia were, indeed, very popular with the people of Copenhagen. They moved freely about the Danish capital, surrounded by amiable, kindly faces lacking that strained unnatural fervor which even loyalists seemed to have in Russia, and nobody gave a thought to bombs. Every Sunday during the Fredensborg family parties the citizens of Copenhagen came into the streets to watch the Emperor and Empress of Russia with their children pass; nor did they swirl by to a clatter of urgent hoofbeats in a cloud of shining lances.

Only Protestants attended on Sundays at the palace chapel in Fredensborg. The members of the Greek Church drove through Copenhagen to the Orthodox church in a long line of unguarded carriages, led by the Emperor and Empress of Russia with Nich-

olas, George, Zenia, Michael and—in later years—Olga, with
George and Olga of Greece following with their four eldest sons
and two daughters—all of the royal children being well washed
and starched, sitting solemn, upright and motionless with the
stern eyes of the grownups upon them—a sad contrast to their
usual untidy wildness. Behind came the carriages of the two
suites, which in the case of the Russians were always impressively
numerous and resplendent with priceless jewelry and colorful
uniforms.

> These long processions, at the slow pace of the horses,
> through the streets of Copenhagen [says Prince Nicholas of
> Greece, father of the present Duchess of Kent], must have
> been a source of great pleasure to the inhabitants, judging
> by the number of spectators. Often, after church, we lunched
> on board one of the Emperor's yachts, either the *Polar Star*
> or the *Standart*. They were both fine boats and fitted out
> with great luxury. Lunch was served in a large dining room,
> where about thirty guests could be seated with ease. I do
> not think I need say anything about the quality of the food
> and the wine, for we were at the Emperor's table. . . .

CHAPTER IX

Terror at Borki

THE YEAR 1887 was notable in Russia for a fresh outbreak of Nihilist outrages, following upon a breathing space which had bred a certain complacency both in the authorities and in the imperial household. Still the Emperor and Empress were untroubled at Gatchina, and doubtless refused to let their minds dwell upon the dreadful probability that the menace would soon threaten themselves.

March 13 was the anniversary of the murder of Alexander II, and in accordance with their custom every year since that day, they traveled into Petersburg with their family in the imperial train and drove through the city streets to the Fortress of Peter and Paul, where they attended the commemoration service in the church and went to kneel silently by the tomb of the late Emperor.

Upon their return to the railway station after the service Marie Fedorovna observed her husband in earnest conversation with the Prefect of Police. When all the rest of them had settled in the train he was still engaged with the police official. At last, the Prefect drew himself up and saluted. Sasha turned away and moved slowly toward the train. He looked up toward her and she was startled to find herself gazing, not into a round brown face, but into a set and livid mask, glaring palely above the beard.

Sasha was smiling broadly when he joined her in the saloon. He was so cheerful during the journey down to Gatchina, so talkative with the children, and the big face now looked so robust, that she began to tell herself that the thing she thought she had seen on the platform was a trick played by the light on the glass.

Outside the station at Gatchina a separate carriage was waiting for the family, and the two of them drove off alone. The carriage had begun to cross the park when Sasha started to speak rapidly and in tones which, for him, were subdued. They were lucky—every one of them—to be alive, he told her.

Only a few minutes before their carriage had re-entered the Grand Morskaia on their return from Peter and Paul, the police, mingling in the crowds and working on anonymous information suddenly received, had identified three university students standing in the front rank and carrying books under their arms. The police had pulled them out of the crowd and immediately examined the books. These were hollow and packed with explosives. The student with the largest book, which must have held several pounds of dynamite, had joked defiantly with the policemen, boasting that even if the dynamite had not destroyed the imperial family he would have "finished them all off" just the same. He had 250 hollow pellets filled with strychnine mixed with the powder in the book, and some of those would surely have hit the target.

Charles Lowe, who, as has already been said, was well informed upon current Russian happenings, states that when the imperial carriage reached the palace Marie Fedorovna was quite broken and weeping and had to be helped out of the vehicle. After she had recovered she praised her husband's steadfastness to a friend. She knew that he had been very much terrified and that he was not a man of heroic mold; yet, after he had finished telling her of their narrow escape, he said: "Well, I am ready. I will go on doing my duty to Russia until they kill me!"

Less than a month later one of those mysterious letters from the Nihilist Executive reached the Emperor's desk at Gatchina.

It was brief. It made no demands, it offered no threats. It declared that he was condemned to death, and that fifty sworn comrades had been entrusted with his execution.

All through the summer intense vigilance reigned at Gatchina. The Emperor and Empress were more truly prisoners than ever before.

But the imperial prisoners were determined not to be robbed of their Fredensborg holiday in September. The arguments of worried officialdom were overridden. It was decided that everything should be packed in readiness for the journey and that the Emperor, confiding in nobody beforehand, would suddenly give the order for instant departure, probably under cover of darkness. This ruse initiated a precedent, which henceforth was always followed when the Emperor used his train.

Marie Fedorovna had been in low spirits all through the summer, her physical condition bordering upon illness; for her highly strung nature and her vivid imagination served her badly after moments of severe shock. A few weeks at Fredensborg, however, and she was wonderfully revived, more especially because that year both Alex and Bertie were there. Sasha, too, found relief in unburdening himself to his brother-in-law, who was always so serene and wisely understanding.

That October they had to return home across Germany owing to a breakdown in the imperial yacht, and this necessitated a courtesy call upon the old German Emperor at Berlin. Their instinctive Germanophobia was not lessened when the odious Prince William unexpectedly stopped the imperial train on its way to Berlin at Wittenberg at 3 a.m. and came aboard to call on the Emperor and Empress of Russia and "escort" them to the capital.

A happening at the end of this year illustrates the comical lengths to which Germanophobia could still be carried in the Russian imperial family.

Scientific men in Russia were nearly always of German origin, and every Imperial Astronomer in the records had borne a German name. The old Astronomer died, and the Emperor ordered that the new Astronomer positively must be a real Russian.

One night when the Minister of the Interior dined at Gatchina the Emperor inquired what had been done about the new Imperial Astronomer.

"I have searched the whole of Russia," answered the Minister. "The only pure-blooded Russian I can find, who is an astronomer, is a mere student. In any case, for some reason or other he goes by the name of Kleber."

"Impossible!" snapped the Emperor. "Find somebody with a Russian name."

He looked so indignant that the very mention of a man called Kleber seemed to have insulted him.

The Empress put in, "Do any of the generals with Russian names know anything about astronomy?"

"They know little about anything," said her husband dryly. "Do you think I want to make Russia the laughingstock of Europe!"

"Why don't you make one of the generals Imperial Astronomer," suggested the Empress, "and then if Kleber is really clever make him his secretary? Kleber could be told to compile learned books about the stars and they can be put out as by the Imperial Astronomer."

Everybody was satisfied with this suggestion, and a flattered and bewildered general received his nomination as Imperial Astronomer.

The French Republic was at this time vying with Germany for the favors of Russia, and it was much more blatant and enterprising in its efforts than the Germans. At least one good story emerges here, concerning the Emperor and Empress.

Alexander III had no intention of allying himself with France, but he amiably permitted the Republican Government to expend large sums on an elaborate French Exhibition in Moscow, which he promised to visit with Marie Fedorovna.

We may pass over the fact that on the morning the sovereigns reached Moscow to inspect the French Exhibition four large fused boxes of dynamite were found in one of the pavilions they were to enter. These had nothing to do with the French, who

were deeply horrified and embarrassed, and who managed to
defuse and hide the terrible discovery until the imperial visitors
had departed. Our story begins when the Emperor and Empress
with their ladies and gentlemen approached the art section of the
exhibition.

Old Galitzin, as Marshal of the Court, had been preceding
them by some minutes into each pavilion to ascertain that all was
in order for Their Majesties.

Upon entering the Art Pavilion Galitzin was immediately
faced by a large piece of modern statuary: that of a nude woman.
Perhaps this really bordered on the indelicate in its manner of
execution; perhaps, merely because it was Gallic, the Master of
the Imperial Court was shocked by an association of ideas. He
realized that Their Majesties, as they entered, would, like himself, have no choice but to stand and admire this object. He
could not bear the thought that the Empress and her ladies, before the eyes of many men, would have to group themselves at
the foot of this display of feminine nakedness.

Startled French officials saw the aged Russian suddenly zip
down a curtain and run toward the statue with it. Galitzin was
standing on a chair in the act of winding the curtain round the
statue when the imperial party marched into the pavilion.

After a moment of astonishment all grasped what was taking
place.

The Emperor shouted out in French, "Leave her alone—leave
her alone—take it off her!" Then he turned and winked at Marie
Fedorovna. "I'm not so ignorant that I don't know that the costume this lady wears is the one the French most admire."

The social life of Marie Fedorovna in the last half of the
'eighties, up to the terrible Borki disaster, became more active
than ever before. Even at the time of the worst restrictions and
when her health was poor Gatchina always seemed to be full of
guests, both Russians and foreigners, and dances, dinner parties
and amateur theatricals were the order of the day. In Imperial
Russia, unlike some other lands, it was customary for the royal
hosts on all occasions to remain at their entertainments until the
last guests had departed. This was trying for the Emperor, who,

although one of the greatest autocrats Russia had ever known, had to adapt himself to the social plans of his wife. He took no part in the balls or less formal dances, except that he might be glimpsed playing whist in a side room with some bored old generals, or that, occasionally, he might suddenly be seen sitting among the musicians, playing away at waltzes, polkas and mazurkas with gusto. Yet he had to be standing beside Marie Fedorovna when the guests departed, or went to their beds in the palace, which might be well into the morning hours.

By the late 'eighties he had invented an original method of ending his wife's parties when he decided that he had had enough. He would order the military bandsmen to quietly leave the ballroom one by one. The dancers suddenly became aware that the orchestra had shrunk since they last looked at it. Foreign guests, new to Gatchina, were astonished to see the splendidly uniformed cavalry band change to two or three tired soldiers, struggling to keep the tune going. Russians only laughed when, as sometimes happened, only one musician held his place on the platform for the last dance. They knew that somewhere among the dancing couples Marie Fedorovna was making her round, saying cheerfully, "The Emperor wants us to go to bed!"

✻   ✻   ✻

It was a dark and leaden day of mid-October 1888, with a drizzle of fine rain curtaining the bleak landscape, when the imperial train returning from the Caucasus approached the town of Borki. Groups of muffled peasants bowed low and then straightened themselves to wave to the Moujik Emperor as the train passed. Mile after mile the greatcoated sentries spaced along the line had stood woodenly at the salute till the watchers at the train windows saw the gray figures as they flitted by as mere excrescences of the land.

For an imperial train this one was exceptionally long and its splendor was made awkwardly incongruous by a dim and aged locomotive pulling wheezily in front of the shining imperial engine, and by a faded string of ordinary passenger coaches and luggage cars swaying and rattling behind the imperial coaches.

This was because the Emperor and Empress on their first visit to the Caucasus had taken with them not only all their family, even six-year-old Olga, with attendant nurses, governesses and tutors, but every minister, and generals, admirals, endless ladies and gentlemen of the imperial suite, secretaries, clerks, servants, policemen and Cossack guards. Every important person on the train had brought four times as much baggage as was required.

The imperial train had been traveling slowly, as was usual—obedient to the old order of the late Emperor—but Alexander III had grown impatient that morning. He had ordered the engineer of the line to "put on a good speed."

The long train groaned at 64 versts per hour into a cut some miles east of Borki. In the dining car near the front the imperial family and the suite were at luncheon. Despite the tiresome journey, the rocking train and the depressing weather seen through the windows, spirits were high, and had been ever since they left the Caucasus. The chief reason for this was the animation and gaiety of Marie Fedorovna, who had been touched deeply and almost pathetically delighted by the enthusiastic Cossack acclamation given most especially to herself and the family, during the whole of their triumphant three-week tour of the region. Those broad, sometimes uncouth Cossack faces, beaming with excitement and kindliness, had acted on her like a tonic after the spiritless cheers and the enigmatic expressions so familiar to her among the crowds in western Russia.

The imperial dining car slipped into the shadow of the Borki cut. Suddenly the car swung, shuddered and leaped upward with a mad clashing of buffers and coupling irons. Dust rushed up from the floor, as it split and dropped from under their feet. The walls burst asunder with a rending screech, and the roar of colliding coaches filled the air.

None knew just how it came to happen, but an instant later Emperor Alexander stood on the railway track, with jagged debris up to his knees and the whole central part of the metal roof supported upon his huge shoulders.

There he stood like giant Atlas holding up the sky, blinded by the dust and hearing the screams of his family in the wreckage at his feet, and knowing that they might be crushed if he collapsed under the horrible burden of the roof.

It can scarcely be thought that in the swift moment of crisis he deliberately caught the falling roof on his shoulders in order to save the others, though the story is sometimes so told; but the fact that he landed on his feet and that it dropped upon him probably saved several lives.

When some soldiers came running up the Emperor still held the roof on his shoulders, but he was moaning under the strain. Ignoring the cries which came from the rubble, they seized pieces of wood and shored up one side of the roof, while the Emperor, who had been sinking, let the other side come to rest on the debris.

He struggled dazedly on hands and knees to the side of the cutting, then tottered to his feet. His head and neck were black, but only a small trickle of blood was visible. A look of frantic terror dawned in his eyes and he was about to rush to the wreckage which hid his wife and family, when the cry of a child stopped him. A soldier had picked up little Olga, who had been hurled clear of everything. Olga came rushing to him screaming, "Papa—Papa—now they'll come and murder us all!"

He embraced his small daughter, then turned and started to tear away the wreckage, groaning, "Minnie, Minnie, where are you?"

Meanwhile men and women were tumbling from the shattered carriages, some to collapse against the embankment, endeavoring to staunch their wounds, and others to join the work of rescue. The fine rain continued to fall. The screams of trapped people and the shouts of the rescuers cut into the rushing hiss of steam from the overturned engines, and yet there seemed to be a kind of silence of horror over everything.

The Emperor had found his wife. She was smothered in dirt from head to foot. He was sitting on a stone, clutching her to his breast and crying, "Minnie—Minnie, are you sure you're not hurt?" She was faintly trying to reassure him. Her hands and face were slightly cut and her body bruised, but otherwise she spoke the truth. Soldiers had extricated the rest of the imperial family.

They stood in a group, trembling but unhurt, around their parents. Nobody in the dining car had been badly injured; yet it appeared to have been worse smashed than any other coach. Further along they were carrying the dead and seriously hurt along the line and laying them in a field.

Marie Fedorovna got to her feet. She, too, was trembling so that she could scarcely stand. They set off down the train for the field where the casualties were being taken. The Emperor left them on the way to add his great strength to the search for further victims. When Marie Fedorovna reached the field, twenty-one corpses had been laid in a row, and a court chaplain knelt by them. Nearby, the Emperor's physician, the only doctor on the train, and another priest attempted with rags and handkerchiefs to attend to the seriously injured. Servant girls stood wailing and wringing their hands beside their desperately wounded friends, and many men and women wandered incuriously up and down with blood running over them. No proper aid was in sight, and no provision of any kind had been made on the imperial train for an accident.

> The Empress [says Vassili], forgetful of her own slight contusions, helped the doctor with all the devotion of a real sister of charity. She carried water, made bandages with her own linen, which she tore into strips for the purpose, spoke to the injured, and comforted them with all the sweet words that came to her lips.

Telegraph poles had been torn down and there was no quick method of communicating with Borki. Eventually, five hours later, a relief train arrived.

At Borki the Emperor sent for a local priest, and on the station platform, with the population crowding around them, the survivors of the accident joined in a service of thanksgiving for the living and of memory for the dead. During the service the Emperor and Empress with their family knelt near the priest. They were still begrimed with dirt, with their clothes torn. Tears were seen to be pouring over the Emperor's cheeks. Marie Fedorovna appeared to be perfectly in control of herself, and had one arm around little Olga.

All believed at that time that the catastrophe was the work of revolutionaries who had managed to tamper with the line or had laid a mine. Prince Felix Youssoupoff, who married Marie Fedorovna's granddaughter Irina, was presumably voicing an opinion always current in the imperial family when in 1952 he stated that the Borki disaster was caused by a Nihilist bomb. Vassili, on the other hand, claiming to know persons who conducted the subsequent investigations, declared that it was an accident resulting from rotten railway ties and a top-heavy train. Lowe, writing shortly afterward, had heard that "even the author of the well-planned plot, who was on the train, fell a victim to his own devilish design," but knew also of the official accident theory. "In Russia," he remarks, "it is next to impossible to get at the truth of such things," and he is one of the first among contemporaries to recognize that, whether plot or accident, the effect upon the mind, health and nerves of the Emperor was very serious.

Baron Samson-Himmelstierna alone reveals the result of the shock upon Marie Fedorovna. Her calmness and good sense had been remarkable during the five hours in the rain with the casualties, as had her collected bearing at the service at Borki.

But reaction soon set in.

> For weeks [says Himmelstierna], her highly strung nerves were unable to recover from the impression of those terrible pictures of destruction. The fear that the terrible day would leave permanent traces behind, and necessitate the entrance of the Empress into a hospital has, however, not been realized.

Clearly Himmelstierna can only mean a mental hospital—institutions which in those days were usually referred to by a more horrifying name—so that a nervous breakdown of a very serious kind indeed must have developed before this chronicler, always restrained and serious in his outlook, would suggest the possibility of such a grim future for the Empress of Russia.

However, with the turn of the decade Himmelstierna can declare that all is well with the Empress.

The old breathless rush of society prevails at Gatchina—no spare time for quiet contemplation and reflection—Montenegrin and Greek, Hessian and Mecklenburgian visits, betrothals, marriage schemes, travel and projects of travel, press thick on one another.

CHAPTER X

Marie Fedorovna and Her Children

MARIE FEDOROVNA was possessive over her children. One morning when she was giving a reading lesson to six-year-old Zenia in the day nursery, the Princess Kotchoubey entered to speak to the Empress. The old Princess thought that the child was spoiled and making a fool of her mother, who gave her all her lessons. Nor did the Mistress of the Household consider that the task of a governess was in keeping with the dignity of the imperial consort.

When the Empress left the room for a moment to discuss some item with the Princess, the Kotchoubey remarked dryly that it was time Zenia had a governess.

"Why," exclaimed Marie Fedorovna abruptly, "we *never* had a governess when we were children!"

Marie Fedorovna enjoyed giving lessons to her daughter, and she continued as sole teacher for at least twelve months after that. In the end, the calls on her time made daily attendance upon Zenia so inconvenient that she unwillingly delegated the supervision of her daughter to another.

Nicky was a poor specimen for a Romanoff. The fact grew more obvious every year as his younger brother Georgie developed.

George was a typical Romanoff. He was handsome, he was certainly going to be tall, he was gay, decisive and bright at his lessons. Everybody spoke with enthusiasm of little Grand Duke Georgie. However, it was undeniable that Nicky was *winning*. Perhaps he was more lovable than many small boys, and undoubtedly much kinder.

It was Nicky whom Marie Fedorovna adored. The same kind of bond grew between her and Nicky as grew at Marlborough House and Sandringham between the Princess of Wales and her eldest son, Eddy, the Duke of Clarence. Nicky was the image of his cousin George of Wales, but his character resembled not George's but that of the gentle and uncertain Eddy who loved to be in his mother's company. While Nicky was being spoiled and emotionally overmothered at Gatchina, and thereby the jealousy and misgivings of a vaguely disappointed father were being stirred against him, the same was happening in England, where the Prince of Wales was not happy about his eldest son.

If there was one child whom Alexander III in his colorful role as "Uncle Sasha" at Fredensborg found unresponsive, it was his eldest son. It was Nicky who seemed out in the cold and bewildered when his father was at his antics. It was not his father's fault. He could not break the ice, and it was not much better at home. Nicky persisted in being frightened and sometimes tremblingly terrified of his gigantic father.

Nicky's education as the heir apparent was of the first importance. He was in a narrow sense well educated by tutors, supervised by the aged Pobedonsteff, who year by year grew more like some worn and cantankerous crow. The appearance at the schoolroom door of Pobedonsteff chilled the imperial inmates even before his tight lips broke apart to emit dry and sometimes shriveling phrases. There was no moral structure to be derived from him. Georgie might develop along his own lines. He possessed the character to take care of himself, to formulate his own ideas. Nicky could only have morally developed with the help of his parents. But his father, naturally taciturn and gruff or brutal when he had serious things to say, was uneasy with him and no help at all. From his mother Nicky learned that he was different from other boys and that this entitled him to have anything he wanted. He also knew that she would gently absorb all his troubles and tell him what to do or settle things for him. He had no mind of his own. She told him what he ought to play at. He soon found that it was better not to express the few ideas which came to him to anybody but her, in case he might be snubbed. Life was most comfortable if you agreed with everybody except Mother.

Considering the tremendous task that must one day fall to Nicky—and none understood the burden better than Marie Fedorovna—she was literally destroying Nicky by her love and indulgence.

Yet Nicky was popular, if dimly despised, by boys who were his contemporaries. Since he inherited the nostalgic charm of his mother—having none of the sourness of many spoiled children—his quiet, smiling manner and his eagerness to agree or admire earned him true friends, who in later years tended to feel protective towards him. Some would also know how to take advantage of his shortcomings.

A loyal friend to Nicky was his robust cousin the Grand Duke Alexander, son of the Grand Duke Michael, who was two years his senior and afterward his brother-in-law. Much information concerning the last of the Romanoffs comes from this long-suffering friend, who was so intimately associated with him throughout his tragic career.

Michael, the third son in the imperial family, was seven years younger than George, and of necessity received his grand-ducal education on his own, which was probably not to his advantage. All that is necessary to be said about him at the present juncture is contained in some words of Count Vassili upon Michael in early manhood, for it reveals all. "A meek young man, one of those indifferent beings who are sorry to be put in responsible positions." Michael would in due course play his sensational part in the family history and a sadly ineffectual one in the collapse of Imperial Russia.

Olga, born four years after Michael, had likewise to grow up on her own. Where Michael emerged from this process as a highborn nonentity with a vacant, affable smile, Olga stepped forth as an individual in her own right. It was Olga who was the companion of her mother in the years of trouble and heartbreak, and Olga who came to be spoken of as the most popular and the most natural of the last generation of reigning Romanoffs, and she who as a wife and mother most happily adapted herself to the exile which was the lot of the survivors.

It was in the early summer of 1884, when Nicky was just sixteen, that an event of great significance happened in his life. There arrived in Petersburg a Hessian princess of twelve with golden hair and bright blue eyes, whose rather solemn features gave promise of great beauty. She was destined to be his future wife, the woman who, alongside the notorious Gregori Rasputin, has been most generally accused of being the Doom of the Romanoffs.

She was Princess Alix—Alicky—the third daughter of Grand Duke Louis of Hesse-Darmstadt. Her mother, Princess Alice of Great Britain, Queen Victoria's adored second daughter, had died a few years before of diphtheria while nursing her family through that ailment. Alicky had come with her father to attend the wedding of her sister Elizabeth to Grand Duke Serge, the brother of the Emperor. It was an exciting year for Alicky, for that April her eldest sister Victoria * had married in Darmstadt Prince Louis of Battenberg, who was in the British Navy, and had gone to live in England.

The Emperor and Empress had taken up residence at the Winter Palace for the wedding festivities, and Grand Duke Louis of Hesse and his daughters were also lodged there. It was at the Winter Palace that Nicky made the acquaintance of Alicky.

None of the grownups took to Alicky. They thought her haughty, self-centered and rude. They even spoke of her uncouthness—not of appearance but of manner—and deplored that the poor child lacked a mother. Alicky in her turn would slip away into some side hall of the Winter Palace, if she could, to avoid an approaching adult of the family, whom she knew she ought

* Later 1st Marchioness of Milford Haven and mother of Earl Mountbatten of Burma.

to have greeted with a smile or even a curtsy. The truth was that Alicky was a slave to her own shyness. She was also dreamy, and a lot of people jarred on her.

But for Alicky, Nicky the Tsarevitch was different. The manner in which this sulky twelve-year-old adopted Nicky was quite remarkable. It was almost on people's lips to say that the child was a shocking hussy. But Alicky had only found something in Nicky that she found in nobody else. They would talk and laugh together for hours and lose themselves in the Winter Palace. Indeed, according to Miss Muriel Buchanan, who knew the Hesse-Darmstadt family well, Princess Alicky and the Tsarevitch were seen playing hide-and-seek together all through the vastnesses of the tremendous building.

Alicky departed with her father after the wedding. There is no record that she and Nicky corresponded, and it is unlikely, as boy and girl liaisons were not then encouraged. But they never forgot each other.

In May 1886 Nicky began his military career as an ensign in the Probajansky Guards in Petersburg. This meant a parting from his mother, and it was a moment of deep sadness for them. She came into Petersburg and herself arranged two smallish rooms at the Anitchkoff for him—meager apartments which he and Alicky were destined to occupy all too soon in their first months as Emperor and Empress.

But Marie Fedorovna had a strong sense of duty, and her loneliness without her eldest son did not prevent her, when she met his colonel, from advising that officer to "keep Nicky up to the mark," because he was lazy, and also to see that the drill sergeants did not spare him when he did his drills with the recruits. She wanted her eldest son to become a distinguished officer. It was perhaps to be symbolic of Nicky's natural meekness that in twenty-three years as Autocrat of Russia, even when he was Commander-in-Chief of Russia's wartime armies, he always insisted on wearing the epaulets of a lieutenant colonel, the highest military distinction he achieved.

Nicky's mind was broadened by his brother officers in the Probajansky. It was not long before at some night haunt in the capital the handsome young Tsarevitch was singled out from a party of his comrades by a beautiful Polish dancer of the State Ballet. She had soon so arranged matters that he could entertain her to a champagne supper in a private room. But she had no idea who the little Guards ensign was until he had fallen madly in love with her, a process which was achieved in about an hour. When she realized that he was the Tsarevitch she willingly became his mistress.

The Probajansky mess approved of the liaison. It was the right thing for a young officer to do, and when the Emperor heard of it, which was very soon, he had no objection and was pleased that Nicky had that much initiative. Even when some time later he heard that a son had been born and that another child was on the way, he was, though surprised at such carelessness and put a little uncomfortably in mind of his father's impassioned affair with Catherine Yourievsky, reluctant to tell Marie Fedorovna, who he knew would be upset by such news of her favorite son.

It may be that if Alexander III had been on easier terms with his eldest son he could have comprehended that Nicky was not of the kind lightly to occupy himself with an affair of the emotions, and to emerge with elegant indifference before he was singed. As it was, the Emperor had reached a point where he found the presence of Nicky extremely irritating. The silent and unquestioning agreement of his heir with every word he uttered, and his permanent attitude of exquisitely polite awe was unsatisfactory to the Bull. The Emperor had taken to ignoring Nicky. It was better to do that than to box his ears soundly and tell him to show some spirit, which would have mortally wounded his mother.

Some idea of the awe in which the Tsarevitch held his father can be gauged from a story which passed among his young brother-officers. Nicky himself had told them of the happening. It was he himself who had startled them.

They had always envisaged a very easygoing parent-and-children relationship in the imperial family. The regiment was at the time at the Peterhof maneuvers. Nicky had returned wearily to his quarters after a grueling day. He told them that he had pulled off his boots and tunic and thrown himself on his bed. He was dozing when his father walked into the room. None of the listeners could conceive what was coming—some fearful row between father and son, some crazy prank of the Moujik Emperor?

"—Imagine my *terror*," snickered the Tsarevitch, "when I saw the Emperor watching me and I had *no boots on!*"

In a way Nicky was in awe of his mother, too. He was not of that nature which when spoiled bullies and scorns the spoiler. He never shrank from bringing her his troubles and his needs, because he had never met resistance here; but he admired and respected her as the most wonderful woman in Russia. Indeed, she must be, for how else could she conduct herself so confidently with his father? Circumstances were to increase Nicky's awe of his mother as things of greater magnitude put him more helplessly into her hands, till it amounted to a fear of displeasing her at any point.

The Russian Tsarevitch was becoming as he attained manhood a figure of interest to all Europe; for Russia had not been so universally respected and suspected during the century as she was under Alexander III, and eyes were looking to the future.

A London *Daily News* correspondent reported that the young Tsarevitch was "in all respects the Empress' child," and rightly predicted that "she is likely to retain, when he comes to the throne, the influence she has been in the habit of exercising."

Since the Emperor was still in his forties, the apparent assumption of an early demise is striking.

The *Kölnische Zeitung*—the celebrated *Cologne Gazette*—had evidently taken note of Nicky's habit of swallowing without protest or argument every word of his father:

> Seeing everything through his father's eyes, he has learned to look down upon all nations without exception. It may be pretty positively affirmed that he will tread in his father's footsteps when he comes to the throne. One must reckon with one factor—the Tsarevitch is very easily influenced.

Both forecasts were correct; but the *Daily News* was shrewder than the other. Nicky would dutifully decide to scorn all foreigners; but the influence of the mother would exorcise the shade of the father to the extent that one country, at least, he would agree not to despise: Great Britain. Through this weak instrument the lifelong ambition of Marie Fedorovna and her sister Alix of Wales could be achieved—the true bond between Britain and Russia.

During the Petersburg season of 1888-89, Nicky met Alicky of Hesse for the second time. She was now a beautiful young woman, who had "come out" in Hesse-Darmstadt in the previous year, and since that time she had been acting as hostess for her father. She was admired but not liked in Hesse-Darmstadt. She had served her father well, and all her social arrangements had been efficient; but she was cold. True, her smile lighted up her face when she did smile, but that was seldom. People felt she looked forward to the moment when they came to say good-bye, and they were right. Alicky did not think she was too good for them. It was the old shyness. When she arrived with her father to stay with her sister, Grand Duchess Serge, at the Serge Palace on the Nevski Prospect, the Petersburgers felt the same way about her as did the Darmstadters. They praised her loveliness, and left it at that. But Alicky was not cold to the Tsarevitch, and naturally this fact was noticed.

The Emperor and Empress resided for a part of the season at the Anitchkoff, which was just across the thoroughfare from the Serge Palace, and Nicky, being on the friendliest terms with his fascinating aunt-in-law "Titinka," the Grand Duchess Serge, was able to find endless daily excuses for slipping across the road to be with her younger sister. Nicky and Alicky were falling in love.

This season was long famous for one unique feature. Marie Fedorovna gave several brilliant balls at the Anitchkoff; but several days before the first of these, when preparations were in full swing, with the Empress in her element, the Mistress of the Household informed her that it must be canceled. Some aged Austrian archduke had suddenly expired of heart failure in

Vienna. By the custom of the time Russian court mourning must be observed. In dismay Marie Fedorovna agreed, and notices of cancellation reached the guests that evening.

But next morning the guests were surprised to receive a second invitation card: the ball would take place. The Empress ordered that it was to be known as the *Bal Noir*, and that all ladies were to wear black gowns, without colored trimmings, but with as much jewelry as they pleased.

Marie Fedorovna had suddenly recollected an occasion, not so long before, when the Court of Vienna had ignored a Russian court mourning, about which there had been some bitterness at the time—of which the Viennese had not been left in ignorance.

Nothing could have been more convenient at the present crisis. The *Bal Noir* should be the Russian retaliation. "At least," she commented as she happily resumed preparations, "we are going to be politer than the Austrians!" The magnificent display of gems against the black velvet and satin dresses and the brilliant uniforms made the *Bal Noir* an unforgettable spectacle.

At the same time as the Tsarevitch with a lively air was passing to and fro between the Anitchkoff and the Serge, he was a regularly recognized figure in a respectable middle-class section of the city, where the highborn were rarely met with except on clandestine business. Here was the abode of his Polish mistress and their family, and here when Nicky passed over the threshold he was fond, gentle and positively a domesticated bourgeois. He had all the makings of a good little husband, and sometimes startled his highly-contented Polish ballerina by seeming to reveal shame that they were not really married.

Alicky and her father returned to Hesse-Darmstadt, and not long afterward Grand Duke Louis was told in a letter from his daughter Elizabeth, the Grand Duchess Serge, that she was sure the Tsarevitch was in love with Alicky and that sooner or later he would make some move. Louis was deeply disturbed, declaring that he would not have another daughter of his renouncing her faith and joining the Greek Church. News about Nicky and Alicky evidently at this point also reached Queen Victoria, who perhaps because Alicky bore the same name as her dead mother was in the habit of talking of her as her "favorite German grand-daughter." Vague as everything was, the Queen let it be known that she strongly disapproved of Alicky accepting such a danger-ous position as the wife of a future Emperor of Russia. It looked rather as if Alicky learned of her father's sentiments, for as far as she was concerned the matter absolutely dropped until his death three years later.

But on December 21, 1889, Nicky wrote in his diary, "My dream is to marry Alix of Hesse." He was, needless to state, fondly continuing his life with his Polish ballerina.

Then, in the following summer the most staggering story shook the mess of the Probajansky. The Tsarevitch had confided to some of his cronies that the only woman for him was his Polish mistress. She was really a good woman, and it was up to him to make her an honest one. *He would marry nobody else.* He seemed to be inflamed by a kind of knightly romanticism. Noth-ing so naïve as this had ever been heard of in the annals of the Russian imperial grand dukes, nor in the Probajansky. They as-sured him he was in the hands of a clever "gold digger." On the contrary, he replied, the lady was deeply upset at the suggestion, and was strongly advising him to do nothing so mad.

The Emperor was soon warned about this. Now, indeed, the shade of his father rushed up before Alexander III. He was hor-rified. In his dismay, he went to tell Marie Fedorovna. He hardly ever spoke to the boy. He could not tackle this. He felt like strangling the fool. It was she, who had always been so near to him, who must deal with him now.

Marie Fedorovna, hearing of the affair for the first time, broke down. Illogically, she was sorely wounded that Nicky, whom she counted on to tell her everything, had not informed her about his mistress and their family. But it was the jealousy of an emo-tional mother which made it impossible for her to tackle Nicky about this. For once, without resort to finesse, she turned on her husband. On this occasion she knew she would cow him, and she did so.

"It must be stopped—for his own sake—for Russia's sake. You are the Emperor. He is the Tsarevitch. You must deal with it!"

Dogged and ferocious, the Emperor blundered to his study and instantly summoned the Tsarevitch from the barracks.

The nature of Alexander III permitted him to deal with difficulties in only one way. He had to be brief, terrible and brutal.

Nicky stood stiffly at attention before the imperial desk and hardly opened his mouth. He listened to a direct order never to see his mistress or her family again. He promised to do so, and saluting his Emperor returned to the barracks.

During the remainder of that year various eligible princesses appeared at Gatchina when Nicky was there, but his parents were disappointed; neither the two superb daughters of the King of Montenegro, then being schooled in Petersburg, upon whom great hopes were placed by the Emperor, nor the daughter of the Comte de Paris, a Catholic but much favored by the Empress, moved him at all. Both at home and in the regiment Nicky was mooning about like the tragic and lovesick Hamlet. Bailey-Hodgetts mentions a Turkish military attaché who, when dining with the Probajansky, watched the Tsarevitch sitting in glum silence while the other young officers sang lustily and played pranks. He saw the Tsarevitch, "without provocation or warning, angrily throw some object, such as a matchbox, across the room, evidently in a fit of despair or rage."

Nicky's peculiar conduct was frightening his mother. People were beginning to talk, saying that the Emperor had done something to him. Then friends of the family suggested that a long overseas tour might freshen up the Tsarevitch and improve his mind. The plan was enthusiasticaly adopted, and Nicky himself seemed pleased with the idea. It was decided that his friend and cousin, Prince George of Greece, the arch-buffoon of Fredensborg holidays, was the best person to wake him up, and his brother Georgie was also to accompany him on a voyage to India, China and Japan.

George of Greece proceeded to play his part well—too well for the more staid members of the Russian suite who sailed with the Tsarevitch. George turned the ship into a madhouse. Nicky responded with gusto. Unfortunately, his brother Georgie, who had not been well for some time, took a bad tumble. He appeared to be very ill, and was shipped home.

No sooner had Georgie reached home in December 1890 than the doctors informed his dazed parents that he had developed tuberculosis of both lungs, which must long have been latent in his system.

The shock was terrible to Marie Fedorovna, recalling that awful day when her first fiancé, Tsarevitch Nicholas, had died after his accident. She started to blame herself for neglecting Georgie, who should always have been treated with the greatest care.

Sadly the mother departed with her sick son to Cannes: to the imperial villa where she had knelt before the dying Nicholas holding the hand of Sasha. It must have seemed horrible to Marie Fedorovna to enter that place with her son, who was almost certainly doomed; but the doctors had ordered the South at once. Georgie could not bear the thought of hotels, and at Cannes was the only imperial residence.

Late in the spring of 1891 they left Cannes for Abbas Touman, near Kazbet, in the foothills of the Caucasus. Georgie did not want to be exiled from Russia, and the Caucasian foothills offered the ideal climate for him. A wooden villa had been building there for Georgie, and it was ready when they arrived. The house suggested no imperial spaciousness, but it was picturesque, with a long veranda overlooking the valleys, and Georgie seemed to be pleased. She settled him in, and then, promising to return as soon as she could, she left him. The thought of his lonely lot filled her with despair.

Meanwhile in Japan Nicky had been attacked and almost killed by a fanatical Japanese policeman, who had somehow been angered by the exuberant imperial party. Only the strong walking-stick of George of Greece had saved Nicky from a fatal sword stroke. As it was, the severe wound he received on the head seemed to have served to clear it. His demeanor upon his return was more reassuring to his parents.

Time passed, the New Year of 1893 came, and still, where princesses were concerned, Nicky appeared amiably listless. He would be twenty-four in a few months. It was high time he found a wife. Louis of Hesse-Darmstadt had died in the previous spring, and Nicky may have been aware that with his death went the religious barrier which had shut off Alicky from him. When in this New Year his father sent for him and declared brusquely that he ought to find himself a wife, as the matter was now becoming one of concern to the state, Nicky, for perhaps the only time in his life, answered the Emperor with decisive sharpness.

"It's Alicky of Hesse—or nobody—for me!"

This did not please the Emperor. He thought Alicky "too German altogether." Marie Fedorovna, though receiving this declaration sympathetically, was disturbed. She considered Alicky quite the wrong type for Nicky. She was shy, haughty, difficult and probably temperamentally incapable of filling the role of a Russian empress. Moreover, from what she had heard she suspected that the girl was hysterical, and that sort of thing always grew worse.

Nothing more was said: Nicky was left in the air. But the parents were nonplussed, and their worries became common talk amongst the far-flung family. It was said to have been Nicky's aunt, the Duchess of Edinburgh, and Alicky's two sisters, Victoria of Battenberg and Elizabeth, Grand Duchess Serge, who espoused her cause and prevailed upon Queen Victoria to favor the Russian match for her "favorite granddaughter." The Emperor and Empress were impressed when the backing of Queen Victoria was understood. Nicky himself sensed the change of wind. But he bided his time throughout that year to let his parents grow more desperate. He had learned from his young Aunt "Titinka" that her sister had admitted to her that she loved him. But there was an unexpected obstacle. Alicky, who was now acting as hostess at Darmstadt for her brother Ernst, the new Grand Duke, had, upon discovering that Ernst had no scruples for her over a change of faith, developed scruples for herself. Nicky thought that her religious qualms might be overcome if he could see her.

In February 1894 it was decided that the Tsarevitch should

represent his parents at the April wedding of Grand Duke Ernst of Hesse to Victoria Melita, daughter of the Duke and Duchess of Edinburgh, at Coburg. It seemed to Nicky that the moment had arrived to tackle Alicky. He approached his mother, who told him that his father would almost certainly give his consent. This the Emperor gave Nicky, with an uncommon show of affability and emotion.

The Russian Tsarevitch was a noticeable figure at the great Coburg wedding: a handsome young bearded Red Hussar, with elegantly flapping furred dolman. The beard was an improvement, for it hid his weak mouth and chin. Queen Victoria, who was present, was startled by his extraordinary resemblance to George of Wales. She was also "quite thunderstruck," according to her journal, when Nicky and Alicky, the former triumphant, the latter smiling through tears, came to her hand in hand to announce their engagement. Apparently, the Queen had heard that the religious scruples were very strong. "I knew that Nicky much wished it, I thought that Alicky was not sure of her mind."

It had not been easy for Nicky. He had embarked on his interview with Alicky directly after dinner on April 20. At midnight she gave her consent. "The poor thing cried a great deal," runs his diary; but, at last, his fate was decided, "a beautiful, unforgettable day." There had, indeed, been one material factor which had pushed Alicky in the direction of Nicky. From the moment of her brother's marriage she would become *de trop* in Darmstadt. Moreover, she disliked her brother's choice. Violet-eyed Victoria Melita of Edinburgh was bold, wild and too sure of herself, and was making a fool of her brother even before they were married. She knew there would be trouble if she stayed in Darmstadt.

Alicky was invited to make a long stay in Britain. Queen Victoria had much to say to her favorite granddaughter before she became the wife of the Tsarevitch. Nicky, also, was to come to Britain for a month. Alicky arrived there before him. First there was a short stay at Windsor, and some quiet talks with the Queen. Then she went to Harrogate for the cure. Already she was showing symptoms of those imaginative and hysterical ailments which afterward played no mean part in the course of Russian history.

Nicky landed on English soil, very debonair with a Homburg hat tipped at a truly grand-ducal angle, and accompanied by a hirsute Orthodox chaplain, who was to remain after his departure to prepare Alicky for her change of faith.

From Balmoral, Nicky wrote to his mother, telling her how astonished he was that even Queen Victoria allowed him to drive out alone with Alicky or go for walks with her. During the few days which he had spent at Sandringham he had been shocked by the extraordinary company Uncle Bertie entertained there—financiers, flashy racing men, horse dealers, people who never entered Petersburg palaces, and his English cousins had mocked at his "efforts to keep away from these queer guests to avoid talking to them." Aunt Alix had assured him that she had no idea who some of them were, and she did not seem to care. He was getting on well with Queen Victoria, and she let him call her "Grannie."

Nicky, with his gentle and elegant courtesy, his constant anxiety to please, must have been a figure of intense curiosity to the Queen, who not long before had called his father "a barbaric, tyrannical Asiatic" about whom "I cannot trust myself to write." Now the future Emperor of Russia paced reverently beside her pony carriage, dressed like some fashionable stroller at a Continental beach, and she could not imagine the need of ever having to express such opinions about *him*.

Nicky was entirely under the spell of "Grannie." He informed his mother that he had refused a dinner invitation to the Guards Mess at Windsor, "because Grannie loves me so, and doesn't like me missing dinner."

July came, and Nicky set out for Petersburg, to be present at the wedding of his sister Zenia to his cousin Grand Duke Alexander. He was to join Alicky at Darmstadt in the autumn. Their own wedding was planned for the spring. But such were Alicky's religious scruples once her lover had left her that some have doubted if the wedding would have taken place even then if destiny had not taken a sudden hand. Father Yanisheff, her adroit Orthodox instructor, confessed afterward that she had faced him with abstruse theological problems, which set him "scratching like a cat" to find her an answer.

At Petersburg the engagement of Zenia had not been accomplished without difficulties set up by Marie Fedorovna, and Alexander has left an amusing record of the way in which the Empress' objections were finally overcome.

Zenia was nineteen, and she had been a firm friend of Alexander ever since she was five years old, when Grand Duke Michael had brought his five sons back from the Caucasus. Alexander—known to the family as Sandro—was now a naval officer and for years everybody had known that he and Zenia planned to marry.

Marie Fedorovna had come greatly to enjoy the companionship of her eldest daughter, and she had invariably countered all approaches to the subject of marriage by saying that Zenia was much too young to marry. At first there had been some excuse for this opinion, although grand duchesses often married on the young side; but in 1894 Zenia would reach her mother's age of marriage, and still Alexander felt that years might elapse before the Empress withdrew this argument.

Soon after the New Year, Alexander, summoning his courage, had sought an interview with his uncle the Emperor. He was cordially received in the study. He was listened to with a look of sympathy. His hopes rose high.

"Well, of course, my boy, it's a matter for her mother to decide. I wish you luck!" exclaimed the Emperor with a bland smile and a pat on the back.

It was later that January and the season was in full swing, with the imperial family in residence at the Anitchkoff, when Grand Duke Michael, who had heard of his son's despair, sent for Alexander.

"Sandro, it's time this affair of Zenia was settled one way or the other. If you can't do anything I shall go to the Empress myself," he told his son decisively.

Grand Duke Michael set off, there and then, for the Anitchkoff. He was as good an ambassador as any, because he was an intimate friend of Marie Fedorovna, and always spoke to her very frankly. But Alexander was frightened. "I knew the Empress. She hated to be contradicted or rushed—she might say 'no' in a manner precluding any further attempts on my part."

After some time had passed with Alexander in a fever of anxiety, his heart suddenly began to throb violently, for he heard the familiar footsteps of his father returning. Grand Duke Michael had gone to his study. A bell rang. An aide appeared and summoned Alexander.

The door was open. His father rushed at him and embraced him.

"Everything is arranged. Go and see Zenia at half-past four this afternoon!"

When the first transports of jubilation were over, Alexander asked if the Empress was very angry.

"Furious. The word is too mild to describe her rage. She abused me in the most disgraceful manner. She said I was trying to break her happiness. That I had no right to steal her daughter. That she would never speak to me again—"

Alexander set off for the Anitchkoff. Becoming engaged when the lady was forewarned and waiting for him was soon accomplished in a satisfactory manner. Zenia suggested that now they had settled everything they had better find her father and mother.

"Be careful with Mother. She is still furious. She wanted to annihilate your father for forcing her to consent."

Alexander was not quite reassured by the expression on Marie Fedorovna's face as they entered. It might be that of real anger. He smiled nervously. But she kissed him before she spoke.

"I know I should not kiss you for stealing my daughter, but what can I do? Please tell your father not to dare to come near me for at least a year!"

The Emperor, who had anticipated the rejoicings by secretly telephoning a few minutes before to Grand Duke Michael to come at once, winked broadly at Alexander. Then he rang for his aide and issued a summons for all members of the imperial family to attend dinner at the Anitchkoff that night.

CHAPTER XI

Sudden Change

WHEN THE Princess of Wales with her daughters Victoria and Maud arrived at Gatchina in July 1894 to attend the August wedding of Zenia and Alexander, she was horrified by the appearance of her brother-in-law, the Emperor. For a long time he had looked much more than his age. He was forty-nine in this year. At Fredensborg in the previous summer Sasha had seemed jovial and robust, but now his face was putty-colored and unsmiling. His broad cheeks had sunk into hollows. His great body seemed to have slipped away from the shoulders, so that it looked like a sack bulging at the bottom and with little at the top. He walked as a man moving beneath a heavy weight.

Minnie in her letters had not told her that Sasha was ill. Alix knew he had had a bad attack of influenza in the winter, but that was all.

Marie Fedorovna had secretly suspected for a long time that something was wrong with her husband; but she had refused to admit it to herself. She could date the change in him to several years back, soon after the Borki disaster.

Since the influenza Sasha had been complaining of pains in his back. The doctors had said that his trouble was overwork and nervous strain, and suggested "change and fresh air." The annual excursion to Finnish waters in the *Polar Star* was therefore advanced to June.

During the voyage, which he seemed not to enjoy at all, it became obvious that one of his troubles was a kidney complaint. Even so, the medical opinion was unanimous, but for one dissentient, that rest and simple treatment would clear this up. The dissentient was a young doctor, new and of little account in the suite. He alone made an analysis. He was aghast at what he found: the Emperor was suffering from advanced and acute albuminuria, considered in those days to be almost fatal.

The young doctor said nothing to the Emperor; but he went to the Empress. At first she refused to believe him when the nature of the complaint had been explained to her. Eventually, when the senior doctors, after examining the sample, admitted reluctantly that their colleague was right, she grew terrified. She begged them to say nothing to her husband for the present—at least until after the wedding of Zenia. She was still possessed with a vague, desperate hope that with Sasha the thing might right itself.

Upon their return the Emperor was expected to visit the great summer camp of the Imperial Guard on the plains of Krasnoe Selo, and since he was not to be told of his serious illness there seemed to be no pretext by which he could be stopped from doing so.

The Krasnoe Selo Camp was a permanent one: a huge circle of brightly painted wooden huts, messrooms, storehouses, stables, halls and officers' villas surrounded a big artificial mound—the Emperor's Mound—where the sovereign sometimes dined in state with multitudes of officers in a fantastic pavilion. Krasnoe Selo was a camp of ceremony, unique in Europe, a spectacle which foreigners liked to describe as truly Russian and barbaric. There, the maneuvers of troops were of less account than the excellence of vast warlike choruses and of massed bands, than the purity of white military shirts or the gleaming coats of cavalry chargers. The Imperial Petersburg Ballet performed nightly in the Krasnoe Selo theater. Carriages full of highborn ladies passed to and fro through the lines amidst the crop-headed clusters of guardsmen. Vestmented priests and clouds of incense seemed as much a part of Krasnoe Selo as the uniforms. Such an occasion demanded much of the Emperor, who must traditionally pose as the idol of the Guard, constantly in the saddle, constantly addressing the regiments and moving among them. It was bound to wear him out.

The Emperor had not shown himself to the Imperial Guard for some time, a matter which had not been allowed to pass without grumbling. When, one afternoon, he rode on his black charger into Krasnoe Selo Camp, followed by a vast staff and by a train of open carriages bearing the Empress, the grand duchesses, the Princess of Wales, the Queen of Greece and the ladies of the households, the eyes of many thousands of soldiers followed with bewildered amazement the pitiful progress of the sagging giant who led the procession through their midst. This had been an eagerly anticipated moment for the Guard, and now the cheers almost died on their lips.

That evening after the sunset rocket had shrieked skyward the Guard gathered again to study their Emperor, as he stood wearily before the imperial party in the light of the setting sun, while an old sergeant, who had advanced from the ranks, read the Lord's Prayer facing him. They looked to see the Emperor bear himself with proud solemnity as the massed bands boomed out the stirring notes of the imperial anthem. They saw an old crumpled officer, who did not appear to hear it.

When the lights of Krasnoe Selo began to twinkle over the plain, the camp traditionaly turned into a great fairground. The air became alive with the music of concertinas and the earth shook with the rapid padding of jackboots. That night there was an air of restraint in the revelry. The men were discussing the Moujik Emperor, who must be very sick.

Soon rumors from Krasnoe Selo were flying all over Russia and reached the outside world. The frequent appearance of the Emperor among the men in the days which followed did nothing to dispel the first impression.

As the weeks passed since the truth had been revealed to Marie Fedorovna, she herself began to disbelieve in the gravity of Sasha's condition. She was afraid to believe in it. After the wedding at Peterhof, she prevailed on the doctors to give her husband only a vague idea of his dangerous plight. As long as they persuaded him to accept the proper treatment, all that was necessary was being done. But now the family was going off to Poland on a shooting expedition, and he was excited like a boy, as was usual with him on such occasions.

At the imperial hunting lodge at Belovége in the dark Polish forests the party consisted of the Emperor and the Empress, Nicky, Olga, Michael, the Grand Duke Vladimir and Marie Pavlovna, and the Emperor's nephews, the Grand Duke Nicholas and Prince Nicholas of Greece. It had been the intention of Nicky to join Alicky of Hesse at Darmstadt after Zenia's wedding, but warned perhaps by the doctors and the ministers he had declared that his mind was changed: he was coming to Belovége.

In the days of September extraordinary and ill-advised efforts were made for political reasons to hide the sickness of the Emperor, with the result that the most fantastically sinister rumors began to grow: the Emperor had been spirited away into the remote forests, where he was being secretly poisoned by members of his own family—nothing was too strange and terrible for Russia in those days.

At Belovége a division of Guard Infantry had been collected as beaters and roadmakers, and the bison shoot began. Nicholas of Greece noticed that his Uncle Sasha was constantly restless. He always wanted to be moving somewhere else in the forest. He missed with every shot he fired. At the lodge there was no fun in him.

Before a fortnight had gone, and contrary to arrangements, the party had left Belovége by the Emperor's order. On September 15 they settled into the Spala Palace near Warsaw. By the Emperor's wish the stag-shooting was to begin the next morning. After the first day of the shoot, during which he had hit nothing, he was perfectly exhausted. He did not sleep all night, and came down to breakfast wearing his military top boots and his old striped jacket. When asked why he wore his top boots, he answered, "All my other boots feel too tight!" His legs were beginning to swell—the first signs of virulent dropsy.

There was to be no shooting. The Emperor mooned about all day lighting cigarette after cigarette and tossing them away unsmoked. As usual the servants placed huge helpings of food before him. He sent away plate after plate indignantly. There was shooting on the next morning. Again the Emperor missed everything, and returned to Spala almost in tears. Marie Fedorovna, seeing Sasha's disappointment, quietly wept for him when he was not looking in her direction.

On the following day the Emperor was obviously in a state of agitation. Nobody knew why. In the study he ordered the secretary to telegraph to Georgie to leave Abbas Touman immediately and come to Spala. Sasha told Marie Fedorovna what he had done only after the telegram had gone. She burst into tears, imploring him to cancel the summons to Georgie. She had visited the Caucasus with Zenia and Alexander in the spring, and she knew how ill Georgie was, how dangerous a sudden change of climate might be for him. But it was not only that. She was frightened by Sasha sitting there silently and ordering his sick son to rush across more than a thousand miles of territory to come to him.

All that Sasha would answer was: "I want Georgie with me for the present. He has a command from the Emperor, so, of course, he will come."

Somebody told Marie Fedorovna that Dr. Leydon, the famous Berlin specialist, was then in Warsaw. She sent for him and then, when he had arrived at Spala, went to her husband to tell him that Leydon was waiting to examine him.

He was furious. He almost flew into one of his fits. It looked to her as if he might box Leydon's ears, as had happened with that other German specialist in the old days. In a way she was delighted to see him so frantic. It had roused him. But he soon slumped back in his chair, and said that Leydon was to come in. Then she saw Sasha's eyes, and she knew how scared he was of what he was going to hear.

After the examination Leydon gave his diagnosis to Dr. Zacharin, whose duty it would be to inform the Emperor.

Zacharin was shown into the study.

"I have to inform your Majesty that your malady is incurable. With proper attention your valuable life may be saved for some months. It is useless to hide that no remedy can prevail beyond a certain period."

Following a brief silence, the Emperor gently thanked him for his frankness and then rose and shook his hand. He asked that all members of the family, including the Empress, should be gathered in an adjoining room, when he would come to them.

When informed that they were waiting he came in. He simply said, "Zacharin has just told me there is no hope." His voice broke with the last words. He began to weep quietly, standing before them. It was a terrible moment, which none who were there could ever forget.

That evening he was cheerful and ate a good dinner. A telegram had arrived that Georgie was on his way.

The news had to be given to members of the family everywhere, but in confidence. Leydon had suggested a warmer climate for the Emperor than Gatchina in winter could offer, and Queen Olga of Greece, his cousin, who had been staying in Petersburg with her daughter Marie since the wedding, at once telegraphed that Mon Repos, the Greek royal summer villa on Corfu, was at his disposal. Her offer was gratefully accepted. The Emperor seemed boyishly pleased, almost as if he was about to start on a holiday. His brother-in-law, the Greek King, began to have elaborate preparations made at Mon Repos as soon as the Emperor's acceptance reached him. It was decided that the imperial party should move to Livadia, the imperial villa on the Black Sea, as the first stage toward Corfu.

Meanwhile, Georgie arrived at Spala. His appearance was not reassuring; but he was clearly rousing himself to be as spirited as possible when in his father's company.

On the following morning the Emperor announced that he and Georgie were going duck-shooting along the marshes. Marie Fedorovna protested, for it was a chill windy day; but it was difficult for her to express her feelings without upsetting the two very sick men. With a sensation of foreboding she watched father and son set off with their guns and luncheon.

Late in the afternoon they had not returned. The dusk began to draw over the landscape. Her anxiety grew. The Polish marshes were notoriously treacherous. Just as a party was setting out to look for them, they staggered up arm in arm. Black shining slime plastered them up to the hair. Georgie had sunk in the bog. His father had eventually dragged him out.

Georgie's eyes were on fire, and there was no doubt that he was already in a high fever. He was coughing and fighting for breath. The Emperor was shivering and tired out, but appeared in better shape.

Georgie was immediately given a hot bath and put to bed and the doctors were summoned. He was very unwell, but Zacharin declared that it was less likely to do him any permanent harm than might be the case with the Emperor. Marie Fedorovna insisted that her husband also go to bed, although after a bath he had wanted to join the party for the evening. Zacharin had warned her that the great danger for him was a chill on the diseased kidneys.

Spala was a large building, full of drafty corridors. The Emperor's bedroom was in the middle of the palace and that of Georgie on the same floor but at the end of a distant wing. As the Emperor lay in bed his anxiety about Georgie grew, and several times he told Marie Fedorovna, as she sat talking beside his bed, that he wanted to go and visit him. She sternly forbade him to move. He did not protest. At about 10 p.m. he was dozing, and soon after Marie Fedorovna, imagining him in a deep sleep, went to her room. His eyes opened directly the door closed behind her.

When all was quiet, but for the noise of the gale shaking the windows, he got out of bed, put on his dressing gown and slippers, and set off down the long, deserted corridors. It was no night for a thinly clad invalid to be traversing unheated passages. Georgie was awake, but he did not stay long with him. When he had decided for himself that his son was not as ill as his mother had made out, he returned.

For several days afterward the Emperor kept to his bed. The doctors declared that his complaint had taken a more acute form. When they discovered what he had done, they feared he might have shortened his life by several months.

They set out for Livadia, completing the journey by sea. When the *Polar Star* steamed into Yalta on October 10, while salutes from the warships echoed across the roads, a reception party and a great crowd awaited the Emperor and Empress on the quay-side. The people of Yalta had no idea of the gravity of the Emperor's illness.

The onlookers saw the Emperor struggling down the gangway, helped by the Empress. Once on the way he paused to gaze at a new Russian warship and made some remark to his wife, and then he was on the quay, tottering urgently toward his carriage as if nobody were there. For a moment there was almost a gap in the cheering caused by the universal amazement. "He looked like a ghost," says Vassili, "with the saddest of smiles upon his lips." Marie Fedorovno acknowledged all about her in her usual enchanting manner, as she appeared almost to push the Emperor onward, murmuring that he was "very tired but much better."

The imperial carriages started at speed for Livadia, the long white palace-villa, with its square-topped towers, arched verandas and terraced gardens on the edge of the Black Sea.

Desperate rumors had flown about the region after the people's sight of the Emperor at the landing; but the next afternoon he was seen driving out alone with the Empress in an open carriage at Massandra, returning through Yalta. He seemed happy and pleased to be greeted along the roads, and the rumors were lulled. At Livadia he spent his days in the beautiful gardens. All the members of the imperial family began to arrive before they had been sent for, making various excuses to cover the true reason for their visit. The Emperor watched their arrival with fury and misery. At Yalta, when he had paused on the gangway to examine his new warship, he had exclaimed to Marie Fedorovna that he must pay it a long visit as soon as he was better.

But now, to show the gathering relations that he would have no truck with their nonsense, he began to speak to them openly of what was to happen after he was dead. If his wife appeared at these painful moments, he would smile and act as if he were in good spirits.

One afternoon in the garden he told Nicky that he might as well cancel the Corfu trip, or at least warn the Greeks, because he knew he would never leave Livadia alive. Later the same day Nicky secretly telegraphed in code to Alicky at Darmstadt. He begged her to set out for the Crimea at once, and suggested that when she arrived they should be married before his father in the private chapel at Livadia.

When Nicky received a reply that Alicky was on her way, he confessed to the Emperor what he had done. Count Vassili declares that the Emperor seemed deeply annoyed that Alicky had been invited without consulting him. He spoke out sharply about the project of a private wedding.

"As for a wedding here—I forbid that. It must be celebrated with proper pomp and ceremony in Petersburg to please the people."

Nicky was now going about with a look of desperation. Sometimes his eyes seemed to be imploring his father not to die. His friends, knowing how unready he was to become the Autocrat of All the Russias, were sorry for him. Nor could they restrain uneasy feelings about the future. His uncles, on the other hand, especially the two most forceful ones, the Grand Dukes Vladimir and Serge, observed him with curiosity, which was not unamiable or unsympathetic, but was tinged with contempt.

Dr. Leydon reached Livadia on October 16, with the intention of accompanying the Emperor to Corfu. That evening he placed in the hands of Marie Fedorovna the bulletin he had prepared for issue. "The disease of the kidneys shows no improvement. His Majesty's strength has diminished."

All idea of Corfu was abandoned. Marie Fedorovna, who had up to then acted with perfect self-control at all times, began to be beside herself with grief. Only in her husband's presence was she still calm and smiling. She would sit up with him for hours, holding his hand and talking quietly. Sometimes he grew very agitated. He had always been religious in a primitive, unquestioning fashion; now he was spiritually bewildered and apprehensive.

One day when some relations entered the room the Emperor looked up and, taking Marie Fedorovna's hand, said, "Even before my death I have come to know an angel!" Whenever he could manage it he was on his feet, and wandering from place to place; but Leydon had ordered him to keep to his bed in the mornings. Two days later Zacharin came upon him in the garden before breakfast, looking wistfully at a spade which had been left sticking in the ground.

"Which doctor counseled your Majesty to be out so early?" Zacharin demanded sternly.

"*No* doctor," came the answer. "I'm doing it in obedience to the Emperor's own command!"

The Grand Duchess Constantine was one of the last to arrive at Livadia. She had delayed in order to bring with her the famous Father Ivan of Kronstadt, the miracle-worker. This aged priest traveled all over Russia at the summons of rich people and was reputed to make many astonishing cures by his prayers. He handled great sums of money, almost all of which he distributed among the poor, so that he was shabby and owned practically nothing. That evening Father Ivan prayed with the Emperor. He passed the first peaceful night for a long time, and awoke late in the morning.

Alicky came to Livadia in the evening of October 22. At the Russian border she had sent a telegram to Nicky, written in a private code arranged between them—originally as a joke—declaring that she had decided to join the Orthodox Church upon her arrival.

That day had been a bad one for the Emperor. He was beginning to suffer from a sense of suffocation. Zacharin advised him to stay in bed, but he insisted that he would dress and await Alicky in his room. In the past he had shown little enthusiasm for her, and had usually turned silent at mention of her name. In the morning, however, he had wakened very early, and had been so agitated and excited ever since at the idea of seeing her that, by the late afternoon, the doctors were seriously troubled lest her actual appearance should affect his heart.

When she entered his room with Nicky, he blessed them both with shining eyes. Then he told Nicky to leave her with him. He talked with her alone for a long time. Nobody ever knew what he said to her.

After she left him, he seemed greatly exhausted, but overjoyed —perhaps because she was going to enter the Orthodox Church— and he was sleeping peacefully when Alicky, with the Empress and Nicky beside her and the imperial family behind her, took part in a service of Intercession for the Emperor's life in the chapel. It was the first Orthodox ceremony she had ever attended.

The condition of the Emperor was visibly worsening. He had begun to spit blood. Dying in bed made him groan with discomfort. He began to spend the night sitting in his big armchair. In the afternoons, clad in the old striped jacket, which had once amused his friends but now seemed a mockery, he would have himself wheeled to the open window, or sometimes, if the day was exceptionally fine, to the terrace overlooking the sea. Everybody began to fear that if things went on much longer as they were, Marie Fedorovna would break down completely, or perhaps temporarily lose her reason. The Emperor had no idea of the agony of her distress; but the others knew that every time she came out of her room she had emerged from a terrible paroxysm of grief.

On October 29 Marie Fedorovna felt she could bear no more without the presence of her sister Alix, and she telegraphed to Sandringham. The answer reached her next day that both the Prince and the Princess of Wales were on their way. In the evening she broke the news to Sasha that they were coming. He was delighted for her sake, and seemed quite roused at the idea of seeing Bertie. Perhaps he also felt that the sturdy presence and cool wisdom of the Prince of Wales would give some strength to Nicky in the ordeal he was about to face.

November 1 dawned bleakly, and all night the Emperor had

sat awake and wrapped in blankets in the armchair. Marie Fedorovna had not left his side. He was restless, but had scarcely spoken. At about 8 a.m. he stirred out of a doze and gazed at his wife.

"I feel that the end is approaching. Be calm. I am quite calm."

He spoke with difficulty and his breathing was hard. He asked for a pencil and paper, and after writing folded the paper.

"Give this to Alix of Wales if she arrives after I am gone."

Father Ivan of Kronstadt came to him, and he asked him to repeat the prayer of the dying, repeating the words after the priest in a voice which grew weaker and weaker. The children were summoned; first Nicky and then Georgie, Zenia, Michael and Olga came up to the chair one by one. The Emperor blessed each one, but he scarcely said a word to any of them, even Nicky, who was so soon to succeed to the imperial throne. His eyes were dull, but once he looked at Marie Fedorovna and seemed suddenly stirred by emotion. "Poor Minnie," he murmured, and the tears trickled down his cheeks.

The Emperor had gone into a dream when the door opened and all the relations crowded silently into the room, and crossing themselves stood gazing at the still figure in the chair. They waited, almost without movement, for a long time—perhaps an hour—and then the Livadia clock struck three. The Emperor must have heard it. He began to revive, and demanded that the striped jacket should be put on him and the chair wheeled up to the window.

"Throw it wide open," he ordered in quite a clear voice.

The sound of the waves crashing on the beach and the painful breathing of the Emperor alone broke the silence. For a moment hope had stirred that by some miracle he was about to recover. But Marie Fedorovna and Father Ivan perceived that this was not the case. She knelt down on one side of the armchair and the priest on the other.

Marie Fedorovna put her arm round Sasha's massive shoulders, and his head slipped sideways and rested on her cheek. One long sigh came from his lips and he was dead. His wife remained immovable beside the corpse, with her arm still about it. Her face was calm and she looked across at Nicky.

Father Ivan rose and crossed the room to the door. He opened it, revealing the household and the servants kneeling and praying fervently. In clear and ringing tones he announced:

"God has called his servant to Him."

Father Ivan beckoned them to enter the death chamber. They rose and without a word being spoken they filed through the door one by one and up to the chair at the window. This was their last farewell, not only to the dead Emperor, but to Marie Fedorovna as Empress, too. First they kissed the hand of the corpse and then the hand of the Empress. Many, who had wept as they kissed the dead Emperor, broke down when they kissed Marie Fedorovna. Then they turned to kiss the hand of the new Emperor. Nicky stood before them perfectly stunned. He did not offer his hand. They had to lift it to kiss it. If they had not realized he was numbed by the shock of grief, they would have talked of his strange behavior among themselves afterwards.

A quarter of an hour later, while the guns of the warships boomed, the garrison of Livadia stood bareheaded and unarmed in the courtyard surrounding Nicky, his mother the Dowager Empress, Alicky, the grand dukes and duchesses and the imperial household. All, including Marie Fedorovna, raised their arms aloft and swore the Oath of Allegiance to Emperor Nicholas II. The dead Emperor, meanwhile, remained sitting in the armchair by the open window. And there they left him until the evening, when his brothers, his sons and his nephew Nicholas of Greece lifted the huge form and laid it on the bed.

On the morning of November 3 the Grand Duke Alexis met the Prince and Princess of Wales at Sebastopol. Alix of Wales ran toward him.

"Are we in time?" she cried urgently.

He shook his head, and she burst into tears. When Marie Fedorovna was told that the carriage of the Prince and Princess of Wales was approaching Livadia she came quickly down to meet them. She had been entirely composed before the others ever since the Emperor's death, but now she threw herself into her sister's arms with loud sobs. "Her agony was piteous to behold," says Vassili. Alix of Wales led her sister away, but for a long time she was unable to stem her bitter tears.

Both Grand Duke Alexander and Nicholas of Greece bear witness to the terror and distress of their cousin Nicky at this time. His brother-in-law Alexander recalls an occasion when "for the first and last occasion I saw tears in his blue eyes."

It was on the evening of the Emperor's death, and Nicky had caught Alexander's arm at the top of the stairs and led him to his room. There, Alexander confesses, he was so moved with pity for Nicky that he wept in sympathy with him, holding the new Emperor in his arms.

"Sandro, what is going to happen to you, to me, to Zenia, to Alicky, to Mother, to all Russia?" Nicky had moaned. "I am not prepared—I know nothing of the business of ruling. I have no idea even of how to speak to the ministers. Will you help me, Sandro?"

Nicholas of Greece, though a foreigner, had much the same kind of experience with his cousin Nicholas II, when, "walking with him in the garden at Livadia a few days after his father's death—he was telling me how much he dreaded being Emperor. The odds against him were terrible. It is little short of a tragedy to ask a man of Nicholas II's character to become an autocrat."

Nicky seems to have shunned giving orders and instructions in the first days after his father's death, and it was a time when many decisions were expected to be taken immediately by the new Emperor. Since it was impossible for the uncles and brothers of the Autocrat to take upon themselves to act for the Autocrat, it was the Prince of Wales, according to Count Vassili, who at this crisis became the voice of Russia. It was he who fixed the dates in the various acts of the tremendous funeral which had to take place; he who was ready to be consulted on all kinds of problems, and most especially he who decided that the Emperor must marry Alicky as soon as the funeral was ended, and who fixed the date, November 26.

On the fifth night after the Emperor's death the body, embalmed and placed in a magnificent coffin with the face exposed, was taken from the palace to the small Byzantine church on the cypress-clad slopes of Livadia, for the first Lying-in-State. That weird moonlight procession, moving slowly across the hillside with blazing torches, was described by all who witnessed it as the most impressive hour in the long obsequies of Alexander III. The night was still, the moon had just risen from a bank of black clouds and the treetops were sharply silhouetted along the heights, as they set out. Four sounds impressed themselves on the ear: the beat of muffled bells, the measured thump of military boots, the crackling and hissing of the torches and the sad notes of a military band, rising and falling. The dancing light played over the white face of the dead Emperor, borne aloft by Terek Cossacks, on brazen helmets, bayonets and the white straps of the infantry. The ghostly vestments of the priests shone below the moving coffin. Behind it walked Nicholas II holding the hand of his mother, who was covered by a long drooping veil, and following came the grand dukes and duchesses, Alicky, and the Prince and Princess of Wales.

A few days later the imperial coffin in slow-footed procession traveled along a cypress-strewn highway to the sea, where the cruiser *Pamiat Merkuria*—that new warship which had caught the interest of the dying Emperor on the gangway at Yalta—bore the body and the mourners to Sebastopol. The imperial funeral train stood in the station—a black, forbidding monster of barbaric nightmare—waiting to carry them slowly for thirteen hundred miles to the capital, and all the principal mourners, including the Prince and Princess of Wales, boarded it after the coffin had been laid in the funeral car.

Marie Fedorovna, now that her sister was with her, was entirely in control of herself. The appalling spectacle of the funeral train had at first sight seemed to grip all of them by the throat except the widow. Even the measured chugging of the big locomotive sounded funereal as they crawled out of the sunlight of the Crimea into an endless flat landscape misted with rain and roofed with dark clouds, while for mile upon mile peasants knelt weeping beside the line.

Even the mournful services held on the station platforms of

big town after big town did not outwardly disturb the calm of
the widow. At times Marie Fedorovna was almost cheerful, with
that feverish liveliness which sometimes takes hold of the bitterly bereaved. She seemed almost excited about the new life
before her. She remarked that she had never known a Dowager
Empress during her time in Russia; but had heard they were
awe-inspiring and venerable, more deferred to than anybody else
in the land. Having had no model to shape herself on, she would
have to create a dowager empress according to her own ideas.
She did not speak entirely in jest; in Russia a dowager empress
ranked above the reigning empress, and traditionally required
reverence and even obedience from the Autocrat himself.

The train drew into a silent capital, draped in black. There
was no sign of revolutionary activity, and none was expected.
Once again the Nihilists were looking hopefully to a new Emperor. The daily requiems began in the cathedral, with the whole
imperial family mounting the steps to the magnificent catafalque
each morning to kiss the brow of the corpse. We may pass to
that final day, November 19, when Alexander III was to be carried over the Neva and left with his ancestors in the Fortress
of Peter and Paul.

The foreign correspondent of the London *Chronicle* has de-
picted the breath-taking scene at the last requiem in the cathedral, before the removal of the body, in vivid words:

> The Requiem was commenced with a magnificent chant, at
> whose opening notes all the congregation fell to their knees
> and noiselessly lighted their tapers by passing one swiftly
> from hand to hand. When all rose from their knees, the
> Cathedral was, for the first time, lighted through its whole
> extent, with an effect which baffles description. A thousand
> glimmering candles were reflected in the silver wreaths, the
> majestic brocade of the canopy, and the star-spangled
> breasts of the uniforms, producing a scene of such splendor
> as is seldom witnessed.

Charles Lowe, who eleven years earlier had witnessed the
glories of the Coronation, was present at the entombment. He
saw the young Emperor standing by the coffin as the lid was

fastened down. He saw him spread the imperial mantle of his father over the lid; then Nicholas II was joined by his brothers and uncles, and together they lifted the coffin and moved solemnly with it on their shoulders to the mouth of the vault.

While the bellowing guns of the Fortress shook the building and the coffin rested beside the open grave, Marie Fedorovna fell on her knees before it, with the Princess of Wales at her side and the grand duchess behind her. The grand dukes fell to their knees on the other side of the coffin and Nicholas II joined his mother.

Then the Metropolitan, in a strangely hollow, resonant voice, began that weird speech, spoken as from the mouth of the corpse, which caused a freezing of the flesh in foreign mourners.

". . . *Yesterday I spake with you, and suddenly on me came the dread hour of death. But come ye all that love me and kiss me with the final kiss, for never shall I go with you again, or further hold converse with you. For I depart unto the judge where no respect of persons is, where slave and lord together stand. . . . I beg you all and entreat all unceasingly to pray Christ-God for me, that I be not bidden into the place of torments, but that He may appoint my lot where is the light of life.*"

As these words were heard Lowe observed that

. . . the new Emperor and his mother were completely overwhelmed by their emotions; and as soon as the Metropolitan had uttered the last words of the Burial Service, with its thrice-repeated, "May thy memory endure for ever, O our brother, who are worthy to be blest, and to be had in remembrance!" the Palace Grenadiers and the Sergeant-Majors representing the regiments of which Alexander III was chief, lowered the coffin into its vault, while the thunder of cannon, the crash of musketry, the acclaiming shouts of the soldiery as they greeted their new Emperor, the rolling away of the carriages through the vast multitudes outside, and the bursting out of the bands into lively tunes as the troops marched away to barracks—all proclaimed, *urbi et orbi,* with a sense of relief that Alexander III had at last been laid to his everlasting rest.

The last tragic reign in the story of Imperial Russia had truly begun. Emperor Nicholas II stood beside his mother and his future bride surveying bitterly the cheering throngs below him before descending the steps to the imperial carriage. If Marie Fedorovna looked ahead with lesser misgivings than many others on that day, it can only have been because she trusted that her eldest son, strengthened by her guidance and experience, and by the favor of Heaven, might prove adequate to face the imperial task. As for Alicky, she understood none of these things. She did not even understand herself.

CHAPTER XII

The "Old Empress" and the "Young Empress"

ON THE MORNING OF November 26 the Dowager Empress drove from the Anitchkoff to the Serge Palace to attend the final stages of the robing of the Emperor's bride, after which she was to bring Alicky to the Winter Palace, where the wedding was to take place in the chapel. No widow's weeds hid Marie Fedorovna that day. She was dressed in white. The Dowager Empress was almost gay as she alighted from her carriage outside the Serge Palace. She had received such a wonderful ovation along the crowded streets that if she had shed a tear as she traveled it was because she was touched with joy. She looked so young and so lovely, her upright little figure was so supple that she might have been the bride instead of the dowager empress. Marie Fedorovna was forty-seven.

When the Dowager Empress reached the robing room of the bride she was astounded by what she saw: there sat Alicky before the big mirror in a dressing gown with her hair down. The Grand Duchess Elizabeth appeared to be in tears and Alicky leaned back in the chair as if in a state of collapse. A scene of panic reigned around her.

A rush was made toward the Dowager Empress, and the tale of woe poured in her ear. The famous coiffeur who was to put the traditional ringlets in Alicky's hair had not arrived. They had telephoned his shop. He had left for the palace hours ago. He had vanished. The last of the guests would soon be taking their places in the Winter Palace chapel and presently Grand Duke Ernst of Hesse would be descending the stairs to meet his sister at the main entrance. It was a moment for decisive action. Even had Marie Fedorovna been broken and ill with grief that morning, she would have had to bestir herself. Everybody else seemed nonplussed. It was no use for them to declare wildly that the coiffeur had been kidnapped out of spite by Nihilists, or that he had been run over or committed suicide. The coiffeur had to be found.

Marie Fedorovna suspected a simpler explanation: a slip-up in the elaborate security arrangements might have diverted the coiffeur to the wrong place. She began by sending servants running in all directions through the Serge Palace. The coiffeur was found by a valet. He was sitting in a state of agitated bewilderment in a room off the guardroom. Something was amiss with the pass issued to him and an officious noncom had detained him. A message sent upstairs had in passing from mouth to mouth dissolved into thin air.

The ceremony was naturally very late, and as was certain to happen in Russia, strange whispers began passing through the Chapel. When the bride at last made her appearance she looked lovely and, to her friends, surprisingly composed, which by that time was not the case with the bridegroom. The entrance of the Dowager Empress in her white dress, with the magnificent imperial jewels gleaming upon her, caused a deeper stir than the bride. Many, expecting a black, veiled figure, were moved by this gracious gesture to the young couple.

It was not until the Dowager Empress saw the marriage ceremony beginning before her in the crowded chapel that the lightness of spirit aroused in her by the wearing of a beautiful dress and splendid jewels, by the affectionate and admiring acclamations of the street crowds, and by the excitement over the missing coiffeur, suddenly deserted her. She looked down at her gleaming white dress. It was a mockery. She saw her eldest son standing beside Alicky, and he was wearing a Red Hussar uniform as Sasha had done when he had stood beside her at their wedding so many years ago. She found herself a lone spectator watching her own wedding over again. But there was no Sasha now. It was all horrible. She was a widow! She was standing near the bridal couple holding the arm of her father, King Christian. It was another heartbreaking link. She had held her father's arm when he brought her to Sasha in the chapel.

The King of Denmark became aware of the increasing pressure of his daughter's arm upon his. Her weight was dragging at him; he thought her about to faint. A loud sob was heard, and then followed sob upon bitter sob. She had lost control. Count Vassili sorrowfully watched. "Her eyes were red with weeping, her whole appearance was one of complete dejection, she was quite broken down. Her father in vain did his best to comfort her. It was a touching sight seeing the old man trying to sustain her." The agitation of Nicky visibly grew with the distress of his mother. Alicky was very still with her head bowed.

But when the time arrived for the nuptial crown to be placed on the head of the bride the Dowager Empress, who had crumpled against her father, straightened herself and, taking the crown, floated forward in the white dress with a matchless grace which stunned the congregation. Smiling through her tears she set it gently and firmly upon Alicky's head and retired to her place.

At last the marriage service was ended. The Emperor and the new Empress turned and faced the chapel. Marie Fedorovna rushed to her son and caught him in a fierce embrace. Then she folded Alicky in her arms; and at that moment nothing but affection stirred in her for her daughter-in-law.

The chapel emptied and everybody proceeded to the Malachite Drawing Room, where an elaborate buffet luncheon was set. The chapel being comparatively small, many guests for whom a place at the service could not be found had been invited to the wedding reception. All expected to be informally presented to the young Empress.

It soon became clear to a large number of people that the bride of the Emperor was either painfully shy or extremely haughty. She nodded woodenly, without the flicker of a smile, at those who were led up to her. Some were not absolutely certain that she saw them at all. She had nothing to say, and silence followed the introduction. She could not be expected to be fluent in the Russian language; but every well-bred Russian thought that all educated Europeans should speak French with fluency. When the Empress said a few words now and then in schoolroom French, making several mistakes, they were shocked. Some went away and tittered.

It was true that Alicky was tired out by the weight of her silver train, especially since the chamberlains had ceased to hold it up. At one point her brother, Grand Duke Ernst of Hesse, noticed his sister standing alone in the middle of the room. She was swaying, with her body perfectly rigid, and he thought she was about to drop to the floor. He went and asked her what was the matter.

"I don't think I can move," she gasped. "I'm pinned to the ground. What can I do? I can't bear the weight any longer!"

Grand Duke Ernst sought out Marie Fedorovna, who was always so kind and understanding with everybody. She was looking ill and wretched, not at all herself. She did not hear him as sympathetically as he expected when he told her about Alicky.

"Yes, I know how heavy it all is," she nodded. "But I'm afraid that it's only one of the lesser weights which need to be borne by a Russian empress."

Then her good nature got the better of her. She signaled to two chamberlains, and told them to hold up the train of the Empress as she walked round the room. She remarked dryly to Grand Duke Ernst that it was quite untraditional for the Empress to have her train held up for such an occasion as this. The Dowager Empress was the first to leave the reception, and many thought that under the circumstances she would have been wiser not to appear. It was noticed that she had spoken little to her daughter-in-law.

Marie Fedorovna had decided to settle at the Anitchkoff, which henceforth was generally spoken of as the Dowager Empress' Palace. When deliberations were being held after the death of Alexander III it had been decided that it would be sound policy if the Emperor and Empress were once again to make the Winter Palace their home in the capital, and to reside there a good part of the year. But the Winter Palace was not fit to receive them until considerable alterations had been made, and in the meanwhile they were to reside with the Dowager Empress at the Anitchkoff.

On December 10 Alicky wrote a letter from the Anitchkoff to her sister, Victoria of Battenberg, with whom apparently she had not communicated since the wedding. Portions are interesting for the light they throw on the regime at the Anitchkoff. She first refers to the wedding day.

> . . . One's feelings you can imagine. One day in deepest mourning, lamenting a beloved one, the next in smartest clothes being married. There cannot be a greater contrast, but it drew us more together, if possible. Aunt Minnie [the Dowager Empress] is so sweet and patient in her grief. She touches one with her gentleness. . . . Here we get out but little, as Nicky sees people all day and then has to read through his papers and to write. Only tea we have together, all the other meals upstairs with the rest [the Dowager Empress and the household]. . . . The rooms are quite comfortable. We chose Nicky's old ones and two others with nice light furniture and chintzes. . . . It was horrid saying goodbye to the dear ones when they left again for home. But one must not think of that. For Nicky's sake I must be good, so as to cheer him up. . . . If only I could find words to tell you of my happiness. Never can I thank God enough for having given me such a treasure. He is too good, dear, loving and kind, and his affection for his mother is touching, and how he looks after her, so quietly and tenderly.

According to Vassili it had been Alicky herself who had interrupted the family councils at Livadia to suggest that Nicky and she should live with Marie Fedorovna at the Anitchkoff until the Winter Palace was ready, saying, "this is not the time when 'Mama' ought to be left with another empty place at her dinner-table." Evidently that was one of the stories circulating in Petersburg about the young Empress—spoken of as Alexandra Fedorovna—in early days when generous indulgence was given to shortcomings, of which many very soon had personal experience. It may well be true; for nobody has denied that at first Alicky made most earnest efforts to be attentive to her mother-in-law.

Certainly the conditions under which Alicky had to live at the Anitchkoff would not have contented many quite humble brides. They had Nicky's two old bachelor rooms and two others. One room, their sitting room, was also Nicky's study, the place in which he interviewed people a good part of the day and from which the Autocrat of All the Russias ruled his vast domains. It was not a big room. The room adjoining it had to be used as a waiting room. All kinds of queer people were in and out of it, or dozing on sofas at all hours. It was no use to Alicky. What the third room was used for we do not know—perhaps as a pantry or bathroom—but we do know from Baroness Sophie Buxhoeveden that the fourth room, the bedroom, was the only room in which Alicky could sit when the Emperor was receiving visitors. Ministers coming to make a report to the Emperor saw the young Empress rise with her book or her needlework and vanish into the bedroom. Baroness Buxhoeveden, who for years was lady in waiting to Empress Alexandra Fedorovna, always understood that she had been quite happy living largely in her bedroom, and that she would have much preferred to have her meals there alone with Nicky.

"So dutiful was the Emperor to his mother," says Baroness Buxhoeveden, "so fearful of hurting her feelings by any change, that at first they even went to her apartments for breakfast." This plan was soon abandoned, and although Nicky often slipped up to his mother in the daytime—there were many things about which to consult her—he and Alicky together joined her only for dinner. After dinner Nicky usually had to return downstairs and work on papers until at least 10 p.m., and the Dowager Empress with her daughter-in-law went to her private sitting room. For the first month the gap between dinner and the arrival of Nicky upstairs for tea was cheerful and easy, because Alix of Wales stayed on to be with her sister after Bertie had returned to England. After that, mother-in-law and daughter-in-law were not happy or spontaneous in each other's company.

It was not their fault. They had almost nothing in common. Alicky was dreamy, thoughtful, soaring into colorful flights of imagination, lacking in humor, not easily tempted even to smile. Marie Fedorovna was effervescent, practical, quick, very much down to earth all the time. Baroness Buxhoeveden suggests that "without actually clashing they seemed fundamentally unable to understand one another." At first there was no need to "clash." Later, between such contrary personalities, there were bound to be constant concealed clashes, and sometimes an uprush of flame that could not be blanketed.

There were various items concerning the Dowager Empress which soon secretly disturbed Alicky. Even in the days of mourning certain subdued court occasions had to be observed. It was a profound shock to the pride of the young Empress to discover that her mother-in-law held precedence over her. Always the Dowager Empress walked first, holding the hand or the arm of Nicky. Alicky, humiliated and also burning with jealousy to see Nicky ahead with a woman more radiant than herself, had to be contented with an uncle-in-law, the senior prince present. She was equally upset to learn that the Dowager Empress would retain all the crown jewels allotted to the Empress, while she must content herself with those ornaments of inferior glory which were normally worn by the Tsarevna. This was perfectly in accord with tradition. Nevertheless, no rule existed to prevent Marie Fedorovna from being more generous than she actually was; she was so abundantly supplied with treasures that she might have passed a share to the Empress. All she gave Alicky was two outmoded tiaras of Catherine II. These were very heavy and she had never worn them. After Alicky had worn one of the tiaras for the first time, Marie Fedorovna quite innocently asked her how she liked it. The piece, if out of date, was certainly very beautiful.

"It's so heavy it ought to be worn by a giantess," answered Alicky. "I have a violent headache. I should think the other is just as bad. I shan't risk wearing either again!"

It was scarcely a "clash," but it was the first time the young Empress was heard to use a sharp tone to the Dowager Empress.

The truth of this matter was that Marie Fedorovna could not bear to part with the jewels she had worn with such magical effect. They were part of her delicious enchantment, which she had exercised with such enjoyment for so long over everybody; and in this fact can be found a more complex aspect of the relationship between the "young Empress" and the "old Empress." Marie Fedorovna was *too young* to be a dowager empress. She would have instinctively resented as a usurper any woman—no matter how well she personally liked her—who put her from her place as the young and ravishing Empress. She was, in fact, middle-aged. But by force of habit all had gone on thinking of her as young—until the death of Emperor Alexander. She thought, she felt, she looked and she acted like a woman more than ten years younger than her age. It might turn out to be exciting, entrancing, to act the part of a majestic dowager empress or, at least, she might make it so; but it was also mortifying.

The young Empress had to have a household appointed to her, even while she was at the Anitchkoff, and inevitably it was the Dowager Empress who selected these individuals. First in importance came the Mistress of the Household. Hers was the task of grooming and guiding a raw Empress, who was sadly in need of both. It would be unjust to suggest that Marie Fedorovna deliberately chose for this post a woman who could be relied upon to carry out her duties so badly that in the future people would inevitably be tempted to draw regretful and unkind comparisons between the *gaucherie* of the Empress and the wonderful graciousness and bearing of the Dowager Empress. But this in effect was the result. Indeed, the very appearance of the new Mistress of the Imperial Household, who was always to be seen with the Empress in public, was no ornament to Alicky. By her proximity she even made the Empress look a little ridiculous.

The Princess Marie Mikhailovna was very aged, and she was also in her ideas the oldest of "old Russians." She invariably wore a poke-bonnet of the kind fashionable in the 'forties, because these had looked very charming on her as a girl. On important occasions she decorated her bonnets with an elaborate assortment of feathers. The result was singular and striking.

When the old Princess was first brought to Alicky by the Dowager Empress she was wearing her feathers. The young Empress watched Princess Mikhailovna with fascination when she was in another part of the room. Then she turned to her mother-in-law and was heard to ask her with perfect seriousness if that quaint headgear was the traditional hat of a Mistress of the Imperial Household.

Princess Mikhailovna was extremely lazy. Once at a reception the Empress, who always felt horribly wanting on such occasions, complained to the Princess: "I wish you would *tell* me something about these people. Then I would *know* what to talk to them about."

"What does it matter what you say to them?" snapped the Princess. "It is honor enough that they are meeting the Empress!"

But the ultimate crime of Princess Mikhailovna in the mind of Alicky was that she was frequently closeted for long periods with the Empress Dowager. She imagined these visits consisted of long conversations about herself. She may not have been right. The Dowager Empress liked the caustic-tongued old Princess. She was a mine of amusing gossip. It was in all probability simply because she favored her that she had given her the post. Vassili, it will be recalled, admitted the readiness of Marie Fedorovna to favor people who amused her.

Even Count Vassili, always on the lookout to eulogize Marie Fedorovna, cannot overlook that if things were becoming amiss between herself and her daughter-in-law, she was partly to blame. She was not helping her.

"She did not like to play second fiddle where she had reigned for a number of years. She thrust her daughter-in-law aside in a most unceremonious manner, and instead of drawing the latter's attention to her mistakes she magnified them and used them to keep hold of both authority and position."

Vassili recounts one rather remarkable story about the first court ball after the mourning. The young Empress was inclined to be a prude. It was always the Empress who issued the invitations to the court balls, and in the previous reign it had never occurred to Marie Fedorovna to question the reputations of the people she invited, although many of them had decidedly colorful tales told about them.

The young Empress, however, having listened to the gossip of her young ladies in waiting and others, secretly made notes about people of both sexes whose conduct was supposed to be scandalous. When the lists of persons eligible for invitations were brought to her, she stunned her secretary by the number of names she instantly struck out. "The result was disastrous. Only a few elderly ladies were present." In recording this obvious exaggeration, Count Vassili seems almost to be voicing personal disappointment; but the first court ball was a sensational failure. It aroused a storm of anger and bitter laughter in Petersburg. All the ladies and gentlemen who had been struck off were soon aware of the fact. A revolution in high life and personal insults to the Empress were threatened. Some went about boasting that even if they were invited to the second court ball they would refuse.

It was clear that something would have to be done to stop the Empress from behaving in the same way before the second ball. Even Nicky was upset, although he dare not say anything to his wife for fear of hurting her, or perhaps because he was already aware of a terrifying flame which might flicker up in Alicky. Nicky went to his mother. She promised to deal with Alicky, and in order to calm hot tempers in Petersburg she let it be known around the capital that in future she was taking over the matter of invitations. She firmly, but not unkindly, told her daughter-in-law that owing to her perfectly natural inexperience certain unfortunate omissions in the first batch of invitations had caused misunderstandings, and that the Emperor felt it was wiser for her to settle the invitation lists for the present. Alicky, who had not yet ventured any open disagreement with the Dowager Empress, submitted.

The second court ball was a success. Quite spontaneously the guests treated the Dowager Empress, not the Empress, as the central figure of the ball; and if she herself responded to the fervent hand-clapping and looks of adoration thrown in her direction she can hardly be blamed.

In certain small, but important, respects, the young Empress was laying herself open to criticism. Whenever she received anybody she thrust out her hand to be kissed. The gesture was not graciously executed—it was almost aggressive. Marie Fedorovna had scarcely ever required her hand to be kissed. She simply shook hands. When the young Empress received people she expected them to stay on their feet until she dismissed them—which she had no idea of doing in an elegant manner. In Russia it was the custom for those who were presented to the Empress to be given a place in a circle of chairs around her. The Empress was expected to treat elderly persons with the greatest respect and consideration. Old ladies—real "old Russians"—almost fell backwards with incredulous amazement when they saw the young Empress hold up her hand and keep it there till they kissed it. Their indignation was intense when no chair was provided for them.

One further factor which had some potency in stirring feeling in Alicky against her mother-in-law is disclosed by Baroness Buxhoeveden; but in this case no blame attached to the Dowager Empress. "If the Emperor spoke of the political situation and of the difficulties of government, it was not to his young and inexperienced wife, but to his mother, whose advice on general questions he had always been accustomed to seek." Although Nicky's conduct was quite reasonable here, it was nevertheless only human that his proud and jealous bride should resent it. Alicky was highly intelligent, and time would prove her to be politically ambitious, though this was not then apparent.

All these things led up to that state of affairs spoken of as the rivalry between the courts of the "old Empress" and the "young

Empress." The tussle was a personal one, rather than a court feud; but the legend that a perpetual court combat was in being gave foreign visitors to Petersburg a colorful and unsavory impression of imperial circles. The conjecture that in one of those dazzling palace processions, in which the magnificent Dowager Empress with her court formed a solemn vanguard to the Empress and her court, the beautiful imperial mother-in-law and daughter-in-law were both burning to seize each other's throats and exhort their bejeweled Amazons to battle, called up a thrilling and intriguing picture, which was visualized in many corners of Europe.

One feature of the new reign which soon became apparent was the absence of the Empress from time to time at certain traditional functions, such as the New Year Presentations and Rewards, and similar great occasions when Russians expected to see her. It was the Dowager Empress who stood in all her glory beside Emperor Nicholas II, and who occasionally appeared to prompt her son the Emperor. The Empress had stayed at home. She was the victim of a violent headache. True it certainly was that at this period Alicky was engaged in the normal pursuit of a young Empress, endeavoring to produce an heir apparent; but the notable absences did not usually coincide with the last days of pregnancy. The cruel headaches, which occurred so conveniently, were almost certainly the first ominous signs of the development of that latent hysteria which Marie Fedorovna had suspected in her.

It was not until late October 1895, on the eve of the birth of Alicky's first baby, that she and Nicky left the Anitchkoff for homes of their own. The alterations had at last been completed. Their official home was to be the Winter Palace; but the huge country palace of Tsarkoe Selo, outside the capital, was to be used in the spring after the season, or at other times when opportunity offered. They were to move to Tsarkoe Selo for the accouchement, and the Dowager Empress and Alicky's sister Elizabeth, Grand Duchess Serge, accompanied them.

In Russia the birth of an imperial grand duke was signaled by the firing of three hundred guns, and the birth of a grand duchess by 101 guns. On the morning of November 15 all Petersburg knew that the Empress' child was on the way even before the guns started. Many thousands stood in the cold, silent streets counting the reverberating detonations in audible tones, and every eye shone with excited anticipation. Everything depended on shot 102! At shot 101 the crowds began to cheer and stamp their feet: the vital shot was coming! In the messrooms of the Guard officers raised their glasses aloft to drink to the new Tsarevitch. But the guns had stopped. It was a grand duchess. Foreigners among the crowd heard the people groaning.

The little girl was christened Olga. Nicky, in the kindness of his heart, smiled through his disappointment, declaring that it was sure to be a boy next time. Marie Fedorovna had felt so confident that a son was to be born, and had expressed her convictions so openly, that quite unintentionally the imperial grandmother was now by her very presence a reproach to the mother of Olga. It was hard for Alicky to hold back the tears when she looked at Olga in the cot beside her. For Alicky the birth of this girl child was a personal tragedy. If only she could have given Russia a Tsarevitch.

When they left her alone she became bitterly upset. She knew how unpopular she was, and she knew from passages she had read in the newspapers that all Russia had been expecting a Tsarevitch. Instead of pleasing the stony-hearted Russians she had let them down. She had not one friend among them, and she never would have till she had a son. She would soon have to go through all this again; but next time she would be haunted from the first minute by the dread that she would bear another daughter. Now she would have to face the terrors of the Coronation next spring, and the people would not even cheer her, because she had not presented them with a Tsarevitch. She had had it all carefully planned. While she passed smiling through the streets of Moscow, a baby Tsarevitch would be lying in the nursery at home, and the wild acclamations of the crowds would deafen her.

Five months later the Coronation was upon them. The cere-

mony of May 1896 was the same as that of 1883; but in detail
there were notable differences.

When that splendid procession of the Entrance to Moscow
moved through the city it was seen that in the first of the long
line of golden coaches, following the massive entourage of Nicholas II, sat the Dowager Empress. Surmounting her coach was
a large crown, signifying that here came one already crowned.
She was alone in the coach and she was weeping bitterly, overcome once more by the sorrowful memories which had assailed
her in the Winter Palace chapel. All along the way the cheers
swelled to a thunderous roar as the crowned coach drew level.
Hat-throwing was forbidden, yet hats stormed into the air.
Women flapped their handkerchiefs frantically and wailed in
sympathy with the adored Marie Fedorovna. Even with her face
mottled with grief this Dowager Empress looked startlingly
young and appealing, and foreign visitors believed they were
cheering the young Empress.

Then, as the coach drew by, the shouts quite suddenly seemed
to die away. The second golden coach was coming up. There
was no crown above it. Inside, very still and upright, sat another
beautiful woman, the Empress Alexandra Fedorovna. The figure
exuded a chill loneliness, which was felt by the crowd. "A dread
silence greeted her," says Vassili.

In one aspect, this Coronation procession was observed by
Count Vassili to differ strongly from the last: except when the
Dowager Empress appeared he never once heard the people
"hurrah from the heart."

This time, at the famous Iverski Chapel outside the Kremlin
walls, the Emperor stood awaiting the arrival of two empresses.
First he helped his mother to alight while the air vibrated with
acclamation; then, as the clamor died, he did the same for his
young wife. Placing himself between them, he took the hand of
each and led them toward the Chapel.

On the day of the crowning one happening was witnessed
which was declared by almost every Russian who saw it and,
indeed, by nearly all who heard of it, to be an omen of grim import. At one point in the ceremony the Emperor, while walking

in his immense mantle of state and his top-heavy crown, was seen to stumble. The crown slipped awry, the scepter crashed on the floor, and Nicholas II, with beads of perspiration on his brow and cheeks white as paper, sought support from an attendant. The Emperor, looking so much smaller and weaker than most of the men around him, was led aside and given a glass of water.

Only a few days later came the first of those disasters which shadowed the reign of Nicholas II, and which, however unjustly, was always to the end identified in the Russian mind as the work of the Autocrat himself. It came to be called the Massacre of Khodinka Field.

It was the custom at coronations for deputations of men and women, with their children, to come from all parts of the Empire to Moscow for the great occasion. These people, all peasants, were treated to a vast open-air entertainment by the Emperor after the Coronation on the Khodinka Field which lay about two miles out of Moscow. Whole herds of sheep and oxen were slaughtered for the banquet, hundreds of barrels of wine were carted out to the field, and tables were spread to accommodate at least half a million people. Brightly painted booths were set up with sideshows, and in one section hundreds of stands were piled with pyramids of metal goblets, enameled with the imperial arms. These were to be distributed to all the men, while head scarves bearing the imperial device were given to all the women. Khodinka presented the spectacle of a great fairground. It was one of those massive, barbaric occasions, to be seen only in Imperial Russia. Yet the Khodinka Field, large as it was, appeared to strangers a small space in which to entertain such an excited multitude. A gaily decorated pavilion, overlooking the scene, awaited the Emperor, all the imperial family, the diplomatic corps and the foreign Coronation guests.

The police arrangements demanded by the Khodinka Field assembly were traditionally the nightmare of Moscow's governors, but none of them had ever failed in their duty in this respect. The new Governor of Moscow was Grand Duke Serge. He was a man in appearance remarkably like his father Alexander II, and was noted for his arrogance, for his ready self-confidence and for his ability to make enemies, both inside his family as well as out of it.

On the sunny morning when this celebrated occasion was to take place, the first of the various imperial processions to make its way out to Khodinka was that of the Dowager Empress. Her carriage was open and she could see all around her.

She had not long left the outskirts of the city when she was surprised to see that the road ahead was not clear, as was to be expected when the imperial processions started to approach. A line of big unhooded military commissariat wagons was moving toward the city down the side of the wide road and this rattling column stretched as far as the eye could see without a break. She looked at the soldiers slumped on the boxes of the wagons. They neither straightened themselves nor turned in her direction. Their crumpled white military shirts were dark with stains. The wagons bore heavy loads covered with tarpaulins. Something strange in the faces of the passing soldiers caught her interest, and she turned as one of the wagons went by.

The tarpaulin cover was small for the load. Marie Fedorovna saw a thing so horrible that, at first, she told herself this was a hallucination. She dared not turn her head. Another wagon passed. This time she was left without doubt. Thrusting out from under the cover at the back, vibrating with the wagon, were human legs and arms, embroidered skirts, red boots, lace petticoats, baggy trousers and top boots, all the articles of peasant finery mounded together. Further wagons passed displaying here and there the same nightmarish spectacle. It was incredible; hundreds of corpses were being carried from the direction of the Khodinka Field. Some of the wagons were uncovered, and people moved in them. There were small children with faces covered with blood. But most of the wagons were covered. Behind, other imperial processions were coming up the road, with the occupants gazing in horror at the passing vehicles. An officer cantered down the column, shouting at the drivers, who began to whip the horses. He was giving an order that the road was to be cleared before the coming of the Emperor.

All the previous night an army of peasants had dozed, danced and sung on the borders of the Khodinka Field. Before sunrise the crowd had increased to six hundred thousand strong. White ropes, stretched along posts, separated them from the field, guarded by a thin line of policemen, while a bored squadron of Cossacks patrolled up and down the line. Stronger groups of police stood by various wooden gates in the flimsy fence; but at dawn the main body of police and mounted men had still to arrive.

Some said that revolutionaries had appeared in the excited throng, spreading the tale that the Emperor had provided not nearly enough gifts to go round, and that only early-comers would get either gifts or food.

Suddenly—the sun had just begun to shine over the scene—a roar went up from the multitude. The mass heaved all along the edge of the field. The fence collapsed. The police were engulfed. Cossacks, spurring their horses, charged headlong into the human flood, cracking their whirling nagaikas. Horses and men rose bodily in the air on the heads of the people. Others were torn to pieces by frantic hands gripping at them for support. The vast wave surged forward toward the pyramids of goblets and the gift tables. Men, women, children in the front ranks vanished under the feet of those behind. Even so, the disaster might not have been catastrophic; but a fearful obstacle ran athwart the path of the advancing mob—a network of six-foot trenches. Khodinka Field had been used as a practice ground by an engineer regiment. The fieldworks had not been filled in; only wooden planks here and there bridged the trench system. Soon the trenches were piled to the top with dead and injured, and still the crowd stamped over them.

For hours the most horrible confusion had reigned in Khodinka Field. The scene was like a battlefield. Bewildered troops, rushed from their barracks in carts, were launched into the melee, without clear instructions as to what they were to do. A combat raged round the gift section. The officials in charge of the pyramids of goblets, terrified that they would be thrown down and crushed, started to hurl these into the crowd. The weaker were collapsing in all directions.

When at last order was restored, five thousand corpses and nearly double that number of injured lay in various parts of Khodinka Field. Orders were given by the terrified Moscow Police Superintendent that the field had to be cleared before the arrival of the Emperor. He then galloped off to report to the Grand Duke Serge.

The Grand Duke Serge was awakened by the arrival of this official, to whom he had left all the arrangements. He accompanied him back to Khodinka Field, saw the magnitude of the disaster, and with an unruffled countenance declared that he would go to the Emperor to ask if he wished the ceremony to go forward.

Vassili believes that when the Grand Duke Serge reached his nephew and made his report, he gave him a very imperfect idea of the magnitude of the tragedy, hoping that things could be concealed as far as possible. His calm demeanor doubtless had its effect on Nicholas II. Nevertheless, he did ask if the occasion was to be canceled, and the Emperor could not have failed to understand that the casualties were serious.

"I see no reason to cancel Khodinka Field because some people have been crushed to death," he declared. "With such a crowd these things are likely to happen."

Several people were in the room when he gave this decision. It was not long before his words became known all over Russia. Loyalists might seek to excuse him on the grounds of ignorance, but the words were never forgotten.

It soon became apparent to the authorities on the Khodinka Field that it was going to be impossible to clear the area of all its grim sights before the arrival of the Emperor and Empress. Several hundred corpses were hastily hidden under the imperial grandstand by the troops, and many more were pushed back into the trenches and covered with brushwood and shovelfuls of earth. This was naturally unknown to the sovereigns when they took their seats in the grandstand amid feeble cheers; nor were they aware when they left the field several hours later that a charnel house had been beneath them. But it was noised about in Russia by the revolutionary elements that the young Emperor and Empress had not turned a hair when informed that they were sitting on the corpses of their own subjects.

That night the French Ambassador was giving a ball in honor of the Coronation. France was at that time doing her utmost to identify herself with Russia, and rumor had said this was going to be the most splendid ball of the Moscow celebration. The French Ambassador came to the Emperor and suggested that under the circumstances the ball had better be canceled. He, like all the foreigners, was perfectly aware of the ghastly tragedy that had taken place, and there had been great amazement among strangers that the Emperor and Empress had appeared as if for a celebration at Khodinka Field. Still greater amazement was expressed everywhere when it was learned that the ball was to take place.

If the Emperor still did not know the full facts, he must have been much more fully informed than in the morning. All other members of the imperial family seem to have known the details. His brother-in-law, Sandro, who was his intimate friend, declared that he himself and his brothers were so disgusted by the decision to let the ball go on that they decided to boycott it. For the sake of courtesy they presented themselves to the French Ambassador at the beginning of the ball. After a few words with their host and hostess, and without paying their respects to the Emperor and Empress, they walked out of the building. Their protest did not go unobserved, nor unmarked. A further painful sensation was caused when the Emperor and Empress were seen to dance every dance.

Marie Fedorovna did not attend the French Ball. Vassili informs us that she was visiting the crowded Moscow hospitals. "While her son and daughter-in-law were dancing and smiling, she was consoling the wounded. Once again an angel of mercy, she brought sunshine to desolate hearts and bereaved homes."

The terrible tragedy of Khodinka Field had set the Romanoffs at variance among themselves. The Michaelovitchi, as Alexander and his stalwart brothers were called, went together to their

cousin Nicky and demanded the dismissal of their Uncle Serge
from the Governorship of Moscow for gross negligence and in-
efficiency. The uncles—Vladimir, Alexis and Paul—rallied round
their brother Serge, accusing the nephews of being "friends of
the Revolution." When the Michaelovitchi had walked out at
the French Ball, their Uncle Alexis had declared venomously,
"There go the Imperial followers of Robespierre!"

Nicky, who according to Alexander "spent the first ten years
of his reign sitting behind a desk listening with near-awe to the
well-rehearsed bellowings of his towering uncles," submitted, as
his cousins expected, to the demands of the elders, and Serge retained the governorship of Moscow.

The months passed, and the first painful sensation aroused in
Russia over the affair of Khodinka Field faded away. Once again
the news spread that the Empress expected a baby. On June 10,
1897, Petersburg listened breathlessly to the sound of the saluting guns. Once again gun 101 boomed out, and silence fell. The
child was christened Tatiana.

In September 1898 Marie Fedorovna was at Fredensborg. She
had come on a holiday and Alix of Wales was there, as well as a
number of others. But it was not one of the grand old family
gatherings. Since the death of "Uncle Sasha" the heart had gone
out of Fredensborg holidays. Besides, King Christian and Queen
Louise were now very aged. Louise was eighty. Her daughters
had not realized how near the end she was until they reached
Fredensborg that year.

They still wheeled her out in her Bath chair into her favorite
rose garden on every fine day. She dozed most of the time, wak-
ing up occasionally to issue orders to whoever was nearest to
her. The doctors told them she was dying. She would "go out
like a candle." The sisters knew that once she was gone they
would just visit Papa quietly every year. They would not want
even the pretense of a party; it would be too full of memories
which hurt them. They would arrange to come to Fredensborg
at the same time, because this was one of the only excuses they
could find for regularly meeting one another.

On September 29 Queen Louise died in her sleep, and a trainload of mourners of many nationalities traveled with the royal coffin to the small town of Roskilde, where the kings and queens of Denmark and their children are laid to rest in the ancient cathedral.

June 1899 came; once more Petersburg was in a mood of expectancy. At Tsarkoe Selo all was in readiness for the third accouchement of the Empress. The Dowager Empress arrived, and Elizabeth came to be with her sister, as she had done at her two previous confinements. If as yet a surface coldness was rarely perceptible between the Dowager Empress and her daughter-in-law, both were almost surely beginning to freeze in their hearts when they came together, which was still with considerable frequency. Marie Fedorovna always joined the family at Christmas and Easter and at birthdays. She was as deep in the councils of Nicky as she had ever been, a fact which with the passing of time preyed more bitterly on the frustrated Alicky. It was, for instance, known to Alicky's ladies in waiting that she thought the Dowager Empress exercised a most unfair monopoly over all the notable Russian charities. "As there don't seem any good works left for me to do," she had once been heard to grumble, "I shall have to invent some for myself."

On the fifteenth of the month the saluting guns were heard— 99, 100, 101. Silence. The baby was christened Marie.

A fortnight later terrible news came by telegram to the Anitchkoff from the Caucasus. Georgie was dead. There was a strangeness in the wording of the telegram. Something horrible had happened. Marie Fedorovna had visited him that spring at Abbas Touman. He had certainly seemed no worse. He had become a very keen cyclist and went for long rides by himself whenever the weather was good. She had suggested that he come back and spend the summer in Russia, as he had sometimes done before; but he had refused. She knew of the story current in Russia that he was secretly married to some woman at Abbas Touman. But she did not believe it.

So far as the end of Georgie could ever be known this was what had happened. One evening he did not return from a cycle ride, and the staff at his villa had set out to look for him. They met an old peasant woman, who told them that several miles away an officer was lying unconscious in a ditch beside a bicycle. He was bleeding from the mouth. Georgie was dead when they reached him. He had probably died of a sudden hemorrhage. But the most sinister rumors flew about Russia, and people spoke of it knowingly as a shocking mystery about which the true facts were being withheld.

With Georgie's death Russia was without a Tsarevitch. The Empress persisted in producing girl children; but as yet, though there were many who were beginning to become uneasy, none would admit that she might never bear a male child. It was therefore decided, since the Empress would doubtless soon be pregnant again, that the Emperor's brother Michael—Mischa— should be declared Heir Presumptive, but that no Tsarevitch should be nominated.

Some months later Nicky fell dangerously ill with an attack of typhoid fever in the Crimea. It was believed that he might be on his deathbed. Panic broke out in governmental circles, since Russia—the land of autocracy—could call into play no such machine as a council of state. If the Emperor suddenly died the kingdom might go rudderless unless there was an acknowledged Tsarevitch, who could instantly assume the vacant place of the Autocrat. This could give the Nihilist elements a chance to create a state of chaos and overthrow the regime.

It was the Dowager Empress who, following the advice of Count Witte, the Prime Minister, persuaded the sick Emperor to declare Michael to be the Tsarevitch. By doing this she crossed the wishes of Alicky, who believed herself to be again pregnant, and was urging upon Nicky that as he was bound to recover such action was unnecessary. Alicky seemed obsessed with a feeling that to appoint a new Tsarevitch would be a kind of bad omen for her own hopes of shortly providing Russia with a Tsarevitch. When Michael was duly proclaimed as Tsarevitch, she was said to have regarded the action of the Dowager Empress in the light of a personal rebuff—a lack of confidence in her ability to bear a son. Further, she left on others the impression that she thought the Dowager had interfered in the affair because she favored her son Mischa, whom she was reputed to overmother, and would like to see him on the throne if Nicky died. There was, in fact, no reason to suppose that Marie Fedorovna had been moved by any motive but expediency.

This did not create an open break—the point of impact was avoided; but for the first time the views of Alicky emerged in direct opposition to those of her mother-in-law.

The affair in itself turned out to be of no importance, because Nicky made a good recovery; but an odd repercussion of this event was that it gave an excuse for the first rancorous words which the "young Empress" is recorded as having addressed to the "old Empress."

On an occasion when the Dowager Empress was visiting the Winter Palace some time afterward and taking tea with her daughter-in-law and several others, the conversation turned to Tsarevitch Michael. He was in his twenty-first year and some well-meaning lady declared that no doubt he would be starting to look around for a Tsarevna.

At this remark the Empress looked sharply at the Dowager Empress.

"Well, I can tell you one thing," announced Alicky with an acid smile, "when Mischa has found himself a Tsarevna, the *Empress* will have to appear in public without any jewelry at all. Mischa's wife will get every bit of mine because it belongs to the Tsarevna, and the Dowager Empress cannot spare any of the rest."

For a moment Marie Fedorovna was taken aback. Then she smiled, and her smile was not acid but sweet.

"Your *son* will soon set that matter right, my dear," she exclaimed. "He won't want a Tsarevna for years!"

Alicky turned pale. It was clear that she was deeply hurt and enraged, believing that her mother-in-law had spoken ironically. But those who heard this verbal exchange were convinced that the Dowager Empress, who was always quick at repartee, simply came out with what seemed to her the obvious answer. She was still confident that Alicky would soon have a son.

CHAPTER XIII

Grandchild of Doom—
Springtime for Rasputin

"OUR EMPEROR is an Oriental—a hundred per cent Byzantine! We talked for two solid hours. He shook my hands. He embraced me. He wished me all the luck in the world. I returned home beside myself with happiness and found his written order for my dismissal on the desk." Thus Count Witte describes the moment of his dismissal by Nicholas II.

"I suppose Nicky was the politest man in Europe!" writes his cousin Alexander, who lived with Zenia in the Winter Palace in apartments adjoining those of the Emperor and Empress. Or again, Alexander sorrowfully depicts the last Autocrat of Russia when faced with making a decision. "Nicky walked up and down. He was pale. He said nothing. And, of course, he lit a cigarette."

Alexander remembered times when Nicky, having surrendered to the ferocious demands of one of his uncles, was faced next day by the indignant bellowings of another uncle, demanding the exact contrary. On such occasions the original decision had always been reversed, and the first uncle had to hasten back to the palace to win a second victory.

Count Witte recalls the affair of the Siberian Railway. Seventeen times in seventeen days the Emperor reversed his decision as to whether the civil power or the Army should control the new railway. The two contestants were Witte himself and General Kourapatkin, the irate Commander in Chief. Witte won the last round, but Kourapatkin had previously secured the Siberian Railway on every alternate day.

It is important to get these sidelights on Nicholas II, for without them it is impossible to understand how things went as they did with the imperial Romanoffs in the twentieth century. Fate played a grim hand, and the chief ally of fate was a feeble Emperor.

Everybody wanted to advise Emperor Nicky, some out of pity and some for selfish ends, and he in his turn had to listen to and appease everybody. With him the strongest and most persistent won. For ten years his mother was close in his councils, and none knew what words she addressed to him, only that she constantly besought her son, and indeed all those of her friends who she thought might prevail with him, to smooth out the ancient misunderstanding between Russia and Great Britain, and bring the two great empires into alliance. That Marie Fedorovna was herself sometimes the tool of clever favorites in her approaches to Nicky is almost certain, for we know that favoritism toward those who "amused her" was her weakness. Till the painful march of events made the balance swing, and the baneful influence of Empress Alexandra Fedorovna replaced that of the Emperor's mother, the Dowager Empress was, in the eyes of Europe, the power behind the Russian throne; while to Russians her majestic presence, her readiness to deputize in public for her shrinking daughter-in-law and her striking appearance of youth made her seem to be more truly their empress than the young Empress herself.

Old Pobedonsteff, still squinting across his "icy desert," was yet behind the scenes—as much revered, as set in his heartless convictions, and much more terrible to the new Emperor than he had been to his father.

Let us see one scene enacted between Pobedonsteff and Nicholas II in the imperial study in the Winter Palace, as recounted by the troubled young monarch himself to his cousin Sandro. Grand Duke Alexander had a name for Pobedonsteff—*Mephistopheles*. This odd dialogue spoken in the early years of this century is most revealing when set against future events in Russia. The problem at issue was the appointment of a minister.

"Whom do you recommend for this post, Mr. Pobedonsteff?"

"—Plehve or Sipyagin. Plehve is a scoundrel. Sipyagin is a fool. Either will do."

"Why?"—uttered in a tone of astonishment.

"Because the imperial regime depends on keeping Russia in a frozen state. A warm breath of air and all will rot. You need men like Plehve or Sipyagin to serve you."

It was on June 18, 1901, that the Empress gave birth to her fourth daughter. The baby was christened Anastasia. When Nicky heard the news he was in the presence of his mother and Grand Duchess Elizabeth. For the first time he betrayed his distress. He said nothing, but turned on his heel and went for a long solitary walk through the park at Tsarkoe Selo.

Probably Marie Fedorovna was not surprised when not long after the birth of Anastasia she was informed that the Empress had taken up with the mystics. There had always been a mystical set in Russian high life, and the leading exponents at that time were the Emperor's cousin the Grand Duke Nicholas and his wife, and the two "Montenegrins"—Militza, the Grand Duchess Peter, and Stana, the Duchess of Leuchtenberg, the two tall, dark and sensationally beautiful daughters of the King of Montenegro.

Marie Fedorovna, who had never patronized this set, must have felt even less attuned to her daughter-in-law than before upon making this discovery, but she no doubt found some excuse for Alicky in that the state of nervous hysteria produced in her by continued failure to bear a son had left her in just that condition in which the desperate turn to such things for solace.

But when, some weeks later, Alicky declared that she was expecting another child, and at the same time it was disclosed to the Dowager Empress by a third party that her daughter-in-law, with the full agreement of Nicky, had placed herself entirely in the hands of the mysterious Dr. Philippe of Paris, who was then amassing a fortune in Petersburg, she was horrified and extremely angry. Philippe was known as the modern Cagliostro, and was supposed to have hinted darkly that he was the original Cagliostro and that he held the secret of eternal life. The mystics had introduced him to the Empress. The whole of Petersburg soon knew that Dr. Philippe was a regular caller at the Winter Palace and that he was putting the Empress into hypnotic trances. Many of those who themselves had consulted the modern Cagliostro were scandalized when they heard that he was attending the Empress.

Dr. Philippe was a little man, voluble, exquisitely dressed and with a natural attraction for women, who constituted most of his patients; but the thing which especially drew Alicky to him was his claim that he could not only tell the sex of an unborn infant, *he could alter its sex* in the womb by his system of hypnotism.

The French Ambassador, who was a friend of the Dowager Empress, came to her in perturbation. He had received a report about Philippe from the Paris police, who had become aware that he was in the confidence of the Emperor and Empress. Philippe was a criminal, an impostor who had never even posed as a medical man in Paris. He was quite unscrupulous and might do serious harm to the Empress.

"What ought I to do?" asked the Ambassador.

"Go to the Emperor," said Marie Fedorovna. "Give him the report. You will make a stronger impression on them. If I did it my daughter-in-law would say I was interfering. I shall go to Nicky, but after you."

The Ambassador sought an audience with the Emperor. When he disclosed his business the Emperor appeared shocked—but not, the Ambassador thought, by the criminal record of Philippe. Rather, he seemed to be horrified that he was faced with breaking the news to the Empress. His manner was curt, almost rude, as if the Frenchman had tried to harm him. He was certainly not grateful.

When the Dowager Empress herself came to her son, he was uneasy and unhappy. He fidgeted and tried to evade the object of her visit. She began to be stern with him, which usually worked.

At first he paced up and down, saying nothing. Then he muttered that famous remark, heard then for the first time by his mother, but later to be uttered in other contexts to many who were almost strangers.

"I would rather have Dr. Philippe *than put up with the perpetual tantrums of Alicky.*"

A scene followed between mother and son. After all, argued Nicky, the French police had offered nothing to prove that Philippe did not have supernormal powers. Protests were a waste of time. Marie Fedorovna realized that she was not really arguing with Nicky; she was arguing with Alicky, who was lying down with a headache and would not see her.

Dr. Philippe continued his attendances at the Winter Palace. After some months of treatment he assured the Empress that she was certainly going to have a son. Naturally this news leaked out of the palace. Everybody was whispering that thanks to the miracle man Russia was going to get a Tsarevitch this time.

The period arrived when the Empress had the appearance of a woman very near her time. Yet the court doctors, who had to attend her on such an important occasion, were puzzled. Alicky herself was in a state of exalted happiness. Even Marie Fedorovna was impressed by the change in her daughter-in-law, and began to hope that there really might be something in Philippe.

The usual assembly at Tsarkoe Selo took place. Russia was waiting; the Continental newspapers reported the coming event. The expected day passed. A fortnight went by. The doctors examining the Empress believed that they saw the signs of pregnancy vanishing. A few days later no doubt remained: the Empress was the victim of that hysterical condition of false pregnancy which sometimes develops when frustrated women are obsessed with the desire for motherhood.

The truth had to be told to Alicky. Everybody knew that an appalling scene would follow, and it came: fits of hysterical grief and shame and a complete nervous breakdown. The last person who should have been with Alicky at that moment was her mother-in-law. The genuine sympathy of the Dowager Empress made Alicky's hysterical abandon worse. Marie Fedorovna herself could see that; but Nicky needed her in this hour of distress and she had to stay. Poor tragic Alicky had made an absolute fool of herself, and she could not forgive the Dowager Empress for having seen it all.

In the summer of 1902 Marie Fedorovna bade farewell to her second daughter. Olga was just twenty, and she had been the constant companion of her mother in the last few years. She had become very popular in general society, because by nature she had nothing of the aloof air which distinguished some other members of the imperial family. Olga was in features reminiscent of her father, tall and with a smile which reminded people of "Uncle Sasha" in his spirited moods, and that no doubt was one reason why her mother was so attached to her.

Petersburg Society said that Marie Fedorovna had positively *given* Olga away, and declared that it must be a case of the lesser of evils: if Olga did not marry her Russian cousin, Prince Peter of Oldenburg, she would almost certainly before long have married some German prince and gone to live abroad. With Prince Peter she would live for much of the year in Petersburg, and then her mother could see a great deal of her. There was another alleged reason for the match: Marie Fedorovna had been an intimate friend for years of Peter's mother, Eugenie of Oldenburg, and everybody knew how Marie Fedorovna was influenced by her friends.

These things would not have mattered if Olga had been more than lukewarm in her love for Peter, or he for her. Moreover, Peter suffered from a chronic disease for which no cure could be expected—a fact which according to Vassili was well known throughout Petersburg, if not to Olga's mother. This marriage therefore aroused surprise and much discussion in the capital.

The eighteen months following this event, which ended with the Russo-Japanese War, were uneventful ones in the lives of the imperial Romanoffs. Marie Fedorovna, by virtue of the very fact that she had so unsatisfactory a daughter-in-law, grew in popular esteem and influence. To any minister or official concerned with high affairs, the idea of listening to an opinion of Empress Alexandra Fedorovna would have seemed fantastic, absurd; but they listened reverently to anything that the Dowager Empress had to say. Her dominion over the Emperor at this period was considered to be the more absolute, because her daughter-in-law spent much of her time as a nervous invalid and confined herself to her beloved sitting room.

Marie Fedorovna was frequently with the imperial family, for she was beginning to take a warm interest in her three eldest granddaughters, Olga, Tatiana and Marie. Olga was eight, Tatiana six and Marie four, and the little girls, who all promised to be very good-looking, would eagerly anticipate the lively visits of Grannie Empress.

The presence of the children eased the delicate relations between the two women, and while Alicky rested with her feet up on her sofa in a corner—surrounded, almost submerged, by overloaded tables and shelves with knicknacks and souvenirs, books, portfolios of prints and photographs, and the tools of her various artistic pursuits—the Dowager Empress amused herself with the children. It was a surface tranquillity, and as Alicky with her dark-ringed eyes lay watching her mother-in-law, who she knew would presently ask if Nicky was free, she was probably telling herself that she was biding her time, though as yet she could not tell for what.

1903 was the year in which King Edward VII, the last British monarch to play a decisive personal part in European politics, came to the conclusion that, after the splendidly successful *entente* he had achieved with France, he might do something with Russia.

There were grave differences to be smoothed out, and the process of accord could only come slowly, but he thought he detected a friendlier feeling toward Britain among certain important Russian statesmen than of old.

The tedious development of the Anglo-Russian accord, in which personal and family contacts played such a quiet but de-

cisive part, is of scant interest today in its details; but the ultimate result was that the French-British-Russian alliance saved
Europe in the first desperate days of World War I. The painful
process of alignment can be studied by the political student in
Sir Sidney Lee's monumental life of King Edward VII.

At the same time in Russia another process was under way in
1903. This was a campaign of relentless provocation to Japan
over Russo-Japanese interests in Manchuria and Korea. In Russia
there were two parties who believed that a war could be bene-
ficial to the Empire—a war in which resounding victories could
be won quickly and easily. One of these parties consisted of
those in high places, who were convinced and loyal supporters
of the imperial regime in its autocratic form, and the other party
were the generals and the admirals. Both parties wanted such
a war for the same reason. There was grave discontent throughout the nation against the sovereigns and against the weak and
corrupt system of government, and police reports showed that
the forces of revolution were growing, although as yet their
activities were mainly underground. Nothing could so well pop-
ularize the Autocrat and all he stood for as triumphant successes
by his soldiers and sailors, coupled with small losses and ter-
ritorial gains.

The Dowager Empress, the entire imperial family, who all had
things to lose by the decay of the old order, inevitably came into
this camp; yet Marie Fedorovna must have been divided in her
views, for a break with Japan ran counter to the course of Anglo-
Russian friendship. Britain had just entered into alliance with
Japan, and although this would not bring her into the war
against Russia in the Far East, the British interests in that region
and the natural sympathy of Britons toward an acknowledged
ally might raise grave complications.

War broke out in February 1904, and Russia sped the depart-
ing warriors with an outbreak of patriotic and religious fervor.
The Emperor stood on his balcony listening to deafening cheers.
It was an unfamiliar sound to his ears.

Things went badly for Russia from the start. The generals had
been badly misinformed about the Japanese. News of each new

defeat followed hard on the last. If the Russian soldier was proving his traditional courage, the Russian war machine was proving
its rottenness. All the old bogeys were in the field, from cork-
screwing bayonets to paper boots. Masses of men died who
should not have died. The Japanese generals were more than a
match for the indolent and ignorant Russian commanders. The
landslide of disasters was a tremendous shock to the people at
home, and the masses, far from rushing together to acclaim the
triumphant Autocrat, grew more and more indignant and dis-
contented month by month, as fresh casualty lists and worse
tales of administrative corruption followed new defeats.

But in the sixth month of the war Russia ceased for a space to
think of happenings at the front. An "event" was expected at
Tsarkoe Selo—could any optimist dare to set the word "happy"
before it this time? Nevertheless, recalling the Philippe scandal,
Russia was interested.

It can be imagined what unkind jokes and cruel remarks about
the Empress were heard in the streets, in the public houses, in
the cafés. There would be hoots and jeers this time when the
guns stopped at 101, and because the people were in an ugly
mood there would be something much more dangerous in their
hearts than mockery. In any case, the guns might not be heard
at all.

On August 12 the dazed crowds were still listening to the guns
when they had reached 110 before the truth really dawned on
them. A scene of dementia filled the streets of Petersburg, and
there were similar wild outbreaks of joy all over Russia as telegrams brought the news. But the public jubilation was not as
great as the jubilation of Alicky as she lay in blissful exhaustion
in her bedroom at Tsarkoe Selo, with the Tsarevitch beside her
in his cot. The boy was to be christened Alexis. He was of good
size, and the doctors prophesied that he would be extremely
healthy.

From the hour of the birth of Tsarevitch Alexis Nichaelovitch
a change came in Alicky, and the first outward manifestation of
this change was a startling one. At that time there were several
committees of ladies in Petersburg which met regularly to pre-

pare and pack bandages for transmission to the front. Among
the most prominent and fashionable of these committees were
two: one consisting of the court of the Empress and their circle,
and the other of the court of the Dowager Empress and her
friends.

Almost from the start of the war there had been rivalry between these two distinguished assemblies as to which could
turn out the most work, and it had not been entirely a friendly
rivalry. The atmosphere between them had been worsened by
the fact that the Emperor had visited the large hall in which
his mother's committee worked, but he had not appeared at the
Empress' workrooms—probably because he considered that she
was deputizing for him.

It is not known what the subject of conversation in the Empress' workrooms happened to be which gave rise to a strange
incident soon after the birth of the Tsarevitch, when she had
returned to her Red Cross activities in Petersburg. This must in
some way have concerned the Emperor or the Dowager Empress.

The Empress, who sat at the head of the long worktable, was
seen to be drawing on a sheet of paper with a pencil. She signed
her name at the bottom of the paper, and then without a flicker
of a smile passed her drawing down the table.

There could not be the smallest doubt what the drawing de-
picted: a little bearded man wearing a crown and holding a
scepter was sitting in a baby's high chair, with a bib tied round
his neck. It was her husband. A woman, also crowned, was standing over him in a scolding attitude and feeding him from a bowl
with a spoon. Equally unmistakably, this figure was the Dowager Empress.

The ladies stared at the sketch dumfounded, and then pushed
it on hastily as if it were a piece of red-hot coal. They did not
know where to look. They thought the Empress must have gone
mad. Someone let out a loud titter, which ended in a kind of
hysterical squeal. In a minute the whole room was in fits of
laughter. The shock caused several to weep with uncontrollable
mirth. The sketch returned to the Empress, who had been sitting

like a statue observing the effect of her handiwork. With a
faintly mischievous gleam lighting the usually sad expression in
her rather lifeless blue eyes, she tore up the sketch. One or two
elderly ladies were so horrified that when they came to their
senses they invented excuses to leave almost immediately.

Alicky had declared war on her mother-in-law, and the campaign was one which in her new confidence she felt sure she
could win—for the main assault was to be delivered against a
weak fortress, *her husband.*

Inevitably this happening was soon the sensation of the capital, and the story must have reached members of the court of
the Dowager Empress. History does not relate whether or not
it was told to Marie Fedorovna, but Petersburg was so full of
ardent mischief-makers that it seems quite probable.

However that may be, the Dowager Empress joined her son
and daughter-in-law for the family Christmas at Tsarkoe Selo.
It was a gloomy and threatening time and the palace guards
were doubled. The police reports at home were very disturbing,
and at the front the armies were dying by thousands in nightmare retreats through snow and icy winds. Even the birth of the
Tsarevitch was beginning to be forgotten by the disillusioned
masses, among whom revolutionary agitators were appearing in
all directions.

They were back in Petersburg soon after the New Year. There
was no Petersburg season, but in spite of the black news from
the front the ceremony of the Blessing of the Waters had to take
place on the Neva, with all its usual pomp. This year, however,
there was to be one unexpected feature. It was a sign of the
times.

The religious ceremony on the ice was ending; above at a
large window stood the Empress, the Dowager Empress and the
ladies of their courts. Across the Neva the saluting guns opened
fire from the Fortress of Peter and Paul. For a split second there
came a sharp, terrifying rushing of air. A crash followed, and
smoke and dust blotted out the imperial window. They stood
dazedly with glass falling at their feet and the biting air in their
faces. A shell had exploded against the wall under their window.

Nobody was injured, for the shell had struck the wall between two stories. Since only saluting cartridges were stored at the fortress, there could be no doubt that there must be revolutionary elements among the Guard artillery.

Shortly after the Blessing of the Waters it became known that the factory workers at Petersburg were about to march on the Winter Palace. Panic reigned among the highborn in the capital, and many prepared to leave the city. The wildest rumors were afloat. Some declared that the workers were going to attack the palace and depose the Emperor; others that they meant to force him to make immediate peace.

In actuality, the demands of the Petersburg workers were to be in the nature of a mass petition presented in person to the Emperor. Revolutionary agents were undoubtedly at their head; but they were coming with their wives and children, dressed in their best clothes, confident that the Emperor would come out to greet them and listen to their troubles. They were asking, in fact, for some quite minor reforms which would improve their own hard lot.

At this crisis "the Dowager Empress was the only person who kept cool, and would not give way to terror," declared Count Vassili.

When a note from Nicky reached her at the Anitchkoff on January 21, the eve of the march, telling her to leave Petersburg at once and go to Gatchina, she was furious. She declared to her household that she had no intention of doing so. On the contrary, she intended to join her son and stand beside him when he met the people. She believed her presence would have a good effect on the crowd. She telephoned Nicky and informed him of her intention. He begged her to go, and sounded in a fearful state of agitation. She said she would come round to the Winter Palace to see him. He answered that he could not meet her, that he was fully occupied with the authorities and must ring off. She would hear from him again presently. Another note arrived from Nicky. It was terse: a direct command from the Emperor to leave the capital. She respected that. She left for Gatchina in the evening, with her thoughts sorely troubled by the picture of Nicky facing the mob alone in the morning.

But Nicky had no such intention. Perhaps it was less that his personal courage had failed than that the hysterical terror of Alicky had overwhelmed him. She had insisted that they should leave Petersburg—she would not go alone. He had to consider the safety of the Tsarevitch first. There were plenty of people who could deal with the mob for him.

The Grand Dukes Vladimir and Nicholas were to be left at the Winter Palace. These two, considered the men of action of the family, had no doubts as to how to act if the marchers were "turbulent." But at the council of war held in the palace on the evening before the march, somebody asked what they were expected to do if the crowd were "not turbulent." According to Vassili, the Emperor answered without hesitation, "Treat them as if they are so!"

Darkness had fallen when the Empress stumbled into the study, "crying violently, her son in her arms." Nicky put a cloak round her and they ran down to their carriage. Few knew they had left the palace. All the Emperor's papers had been abandoned in the study. Alicky had nothing, not even "clothes and linen."

When the column of factory workers spread into the Winter Palace Square next morning, singing the national anthem and headed by a huge picture of the Emperor borne aloft on poles, a field gun and two regiments of Cossacks, many dismounted with rifles in their hands, awaited them.

The great crowd flooded forward expectantly to within a short distance of the troops, with their eyes on the palace, where they looked for the Emperor to appear. Women and children had handkerchiefs and small flags in their hands to wave to him.

They refused to believe the police, who told them the Emperor was not in the palace. They stood patiently crying for him to come out, and repeatedly singing the national anthem. Only a few young men showed impatience. It was nothing.

The Cossacks raised their rifles. A volley of shot tore into the crowd, and then another. Men, women, children dropped and the air was full of screams. The terrified mass broke and fled down the Nevski Prospect with Cossack horsemen riding them down and thrashing into them with their steel-shod whips. A trumpet recalled the cavalry, and the field gun opened fire down the broad street.

The citizens of Petersburg watched silently from their windows as municipal rubbish carts went by packed with dead and wounded. Ninety had died and more than three times that number were carried to the hospitals, while many injured were brought home by their friends.

In February trouble broke out in Moscow. On the seventeenth of the month Grand Duke Serge was blown to pieces by a bomb while crossing the square before his palace. Grand Duchess Elizabeth was with a Red Cross working party in a room overlooking the square and rushed out, guessing what had taken place. It was she who collected the remnants of her husband in a box when the police shrank back from the horrible task, and carried the box into the palace. The frenzied assassin, pinioned by policemen, had laughed at her as she knelt in the bloodstained snow amid dead horses and the splintered carriage; yet she pleaded with the Emperor to spare his life and, when her intercession was ignored, visited the man in prison to tell him of her forgiveness.

Not long afterward Grand Duchess Elizabeth became a nun, forming her own religious Order of Mary and Martha, the only body of working nuns in Russia. Grand Duchess Elizabeth was childless, but when Alexandra the Grand Duchess Paul had died in childbirth in the early nineties she had offered to act as mother to Marie and Dmitri Pavlovitch to help their grief-stricken father. Now Marie and Dmitri became wards of the Emperor and Empress and made their home with the imperial family; a development which in the case of Dmitri was destined to have a grim repercussion in the last days of the Romanoffs.

That summer a domestic scandal shook the whole imperial family and set them in two camps. Victoria Melita of Edinburgh, who had married Alicky's brother, Ernst of Hesse-Darmstadt, had separated from her husband in 1901. They had never got on

together, and only the fear of Queen Victoria had kept her beside her husband for six years. All the time she had been secretly
in love with her cousin, Grand Duke Cyril of Russia, the eldest
son of Grand Duke Vladimir and Marie Pavlovna. Alicky, who
had always disliked Victoria Melita, and who had been moved
in her decision to abandon Hesse-Darmstadt by her desire to
avoid her, declared a deadly hatred for her after 1901, openly
abusing her for treating her brother disgracefully. In 1905 Victoria Melita obtained her divorce from Grand Duke Ernst—an
unheard-of action for a royalty of the period—and shortly afterward Grand Duke Cyril announced to the family that he was
going to marry her.

Alicky was beside herself with fury and indignation. Nicky,
who liked his cousin Cyril, was ready to treat the matter with
moderation—an official reprimand from the Emperor and perhaps
a few years' residence abroad—till Alicky turned her anger upon
him. He summoned Cyril and forbade him to marry Victoria
Melita. Cyril refused to obey his order. He was deprived of his
imperial title and the whole of his imperial allowance, and was
banished indefinitely from Russia.

When Cyril's father, the redoubtable Vladimir, heard of this
he instantly set off for Tsarkoe Selo. Finding that the Emperor
was in the study, he burst in without warning. His nephew happened to be alone. Shouts of rage and the stamping of feet was
heard through the partly closed door. The aides were tempted
to enter, fearing violence to the Emperor, and hovered outside.
But Nicky was inspired with strength by his terror of Alicky.
When his uncle rushed out of the room, slamming the door violently, it was seen that the mass of medals was missing from his
chest. The Emperor, deathly white and shaking, stood puffing at
a cigarette with the medals at his feet. His uncle had ripped
them off and hurled them at his head.

The Dowager Empress sided with her old friend Vladimir and
with Marie Pavlovna, who was deeply upset by the harsh treatment of her son, and she went to Nicky. But she quickly saw
how the land lay: Nicky had given the order, the decision had
been made by Alicky. Yet, since the Empress did not officially

come into the matter at all, in an affair of grand-ducal misbe-
havior, the Dowager Empress could not approach her daughter-
in-law without admitting that it was she who ruled Nicky, and
this she still refused to recognize even to herself.

Cyril and his wife went into exile, and attention returned
once more to the last catastrophic stages of the war. In September a peace, arranged through the good offices of the President
of the United States, was signed at Baltimore.

Marie Fedorovna was slowly becoming more isolated from her
eldest son and his family. They had lived at Tsarkoe Selo since
the January massacres, and did not intend to return to Petersburg. At her first visit to Tsarkoe Selo after that terrible event
the mother did not feel that her son was at perfect ease with her.
Was there a kind of veiled defiance and impatience? Later in the
year, after the affair of Cyril, she experienced this sensation more
strongly, and since it was not in her nature to keep things tightly
to herself, her friends became vaguely aware of what was
troubling her. It was as if Nicky was pleased and frightened to
see her at the same time—but not frightened of her. She guessed
he was afraid, when he saw her, that she had come to stir up
something which would get him into very hot water in another
quarter. She pitied Nicky, and jealousy sometimes flamed in her,
as she felt her way along a blank wall. Yet she could perceive
that the more she tried to bring him back to his old place the
more she harmed him and made his life miserable. It would not
be long before her son-in-law, Alexander, who was always devoted to her, would be noting the "loneliness" of the Dowager
Empress.

There was a saying of Nicholas II which was very familiar to
members of his Household— "That is for Her Majesty to decide."
At first this had always referred to some domestic or nursery
matter, which might be considered her province. Perhaps he did
not now use the words with quite the same expression of un-
concern which he had once used. Perhaps he was using them
more often, or perhaps he now sometimes implied the words by
a furtive look when he did not actually utter them, and when a

matter of wider import was involved. The phrase, at all events, stirred irritation in some hearers.

One day Marie Fedorovna after a return from Tsarkoe Selo was sitting in her room when she let out a sigh and murmured to an intimate, "If Nicky is not careful he will one day be saying, 'That is for Her Majesty to decide!' to one of his ministers." Her remark was more than shrewd. It was a true prophecy.

Yet the depression of spirits in Marie Fedorovna, which was not, indeed, an uncommon phenomenon in the winter of 1905-6, did not prevent her from vying with her old social rival, Marie Pavlovna, to make the first Petersburg season after the war a brilliant one. The Emperor and Empress were scarcely seen and remained at Tsarkoe Selo.

Never had Pobedonsteff's saying—"Outside the imperial palaces lies the icy desert of the Bad Man"—been truer from the viewpoint of the Romanoffs than that winter in Russia.

In November, Moscow, the *conservative city*, had been in a state of open rebellion, and the Semenoffsky Guard Regiment had fought its way from barricade to barricade through the narrow streets.

The Emperor had been afraid to recall the demoralized regiments from the seat of war, because he could not trust them at home. Yet every month that they rotted in the Far East they grew more dangerous. Meanwhile their wives and mothers cried out for their return. It was a nightmare. His perplexity in this dilemma had at last forced him, upon the urgent advice of his ministers, to grant Russia a constitution before the return of the armies. This he had done with a very bad grace, and that Christmas he was in a state of mind in which he spoke of the elected representatives from all the provinces, who were to come to the first Russian Duma in the spring, as if they were his personal enemies.

The opening of the first Duma on April 27, 1906, was an event such as Imperial Russia had never seen. To the mind of a Romanoff it was almost equivalent to the celebration of a revolution.

In a great hall of the Winter Palace ranks of chairs faced one another across a wide central space. On one side sat the ladies of the courts in their shimmering headdresses and the ladies of high society wearing their finest jewels and gowns, with an imposing array of uniformed and frock-coated escorts. On the other side the elected representatives of the nation filed sluggishly to their chairs. How could the average Russian know how an elected representative should conduct himself? Count Vassili observed the scene with sardonic amusement: the ladies tittering, chattering, pointing rudely at anything that amused them, earned angry glances from the embarrassed deputies. Here came a bewildered country group in peasant caftans and top boots, who seemed to be worried as to whether they had come to the wrong place. Provincial lawyers and tradesmen, who had surpassed the peak of their ambition, strutted scornfully to their places. Socialists with flaming eyes sneered, snarled, almost spat at the lovely rows of fine ladies. Every human expression from low greed or unconcealed ferocity to intense patriotism and awe showed in the faces of the motley mass when all were in their places.

Trumpets sounded and the doors swung open. The splendid procession of Old Russia moved down the hall: heralds; chamberlains with wands; pages of the Imperial Cadet Corps with their black horsehair crests, dozens of them; white Gardes-aux-Chevaux; tottering old gilded courtiers; young scornful courtiers; the Emperor, irritable impatience in his blue eyes, fingering his white uniform gloves; the Empress, the Dowager Empress, side by side, wonderfully beautiful both of them, with their ladies walking in their traditional magnificence behind them. The peasants had bowed their heads in wonder, some of the Socialists were laughing and others glared murderously at the pageant. The bourgeois bent pompously from their waists, and the ladies opposite curtsied and unconcernedly resumed their conversations.

Vassili thought the Empress "cold, bored more than anything else." The Dowager Empress was acknowledging the bowing deputies with her usual grace. Yet she was "extremely moved and agitated. Her eyes were red, and she kept putting up her handkerchief as if to wipe away tears. She keenly observed the assembly, as if trying to read their countenances, to guess what lay behind them. The Socialist group attracted her attention quite particularly, and she watched it the whole time, with something akin to anxiety in her lovely dark eyes, which then wandered toward her son, resting on him with passionate yearning and sadness. Her countenance was perfectly dignified, and yet a whole tragedy lurked in her figure as it bent under the blessing of the Metropolitan."

Such was the inauguration of the ill-fated and short-lived first Duma.

In July Marie Fedorovna was a guest at Marlborough House and Sandringham. She had not seen London for more than twenty-five years. Last time she and Alix had had great fun startling the Londoners by always dressing alike. Life had been gayer then—neither of them had worn a crown. What a lot had happened since those days—more to her than to Alix. It was less surprising that Alix still managed to look so young at sixty-one, than that she herself was able to do so at fifty-eight. Marie Fedorovna could walk about the London streets and into the wonderful shops without anybody bothering about her, and she took a childish delight in these expeditions. Life seemed so easy in England, even for royalty.

We hear of her one afternoon when she went with Queen Alexandra to have tea with the young Duke of Teck (the future Queen Mary's brother), who was commanding the King's Lifeguard at Whitehall. To be able to sit at the open window of the officer's room, and to look down on the passers-by just below her and at the flow of traffic in Whitehall, seemed to fascinate her. Anybody who looked up could see her, but it never occurred to them to shoot at her with a revolver, and they would not have known where to find a bomb to lob in at the window. It was so tranquil after Russia, and she spent an enraptured hour gazing out, almost silent and a little sad. Perhaps the thought crossed her mind that if poor Nicky's heritage had been Great Britain instead of Russia he might have got along very well.

While Marie Fedorovna was still in England, a terrible happening had taken place at Tsarkoe Selo. Little Tsarevitch Alexis was growing very active. While tottering about he had tumbled several times, and his mother had noticed the large swollen bruises which quickly came up on him. She had said nothing, but the sight had made her heart stand still. She knew that hemophilia was inherent in her family. She knew that two of her uncles, who had died of the dread disease, had suffered from large bruises at every slight knock, that for them every scratch had been a nightmare. Then, in July, Alexis fell out of his pram. It was not a bad tumble. He did not even cut himself. But when his mother saw the huge swollen blue mound rising under her son's skin and heard his cries of pain, she was stricken with terror. Weeping bitterly, she flew to her husband. She told him what was the matter with Alexis before the doctors came to confirm it. A bruise was almost as dangerous as a cut, for since the mass of escaping blood under the skin could not be released by the lancet for fear of fatal bleeding, blood poisoning and convulsions were liable to follow.

As the swelling grew the child's agony increased. The doctors had no remedy. It was in this moment of despair that the Grand Duchesses Militza and Stana, who had previously sent the ruffian Philippe to the Empress, begged her to summon a holy man or *Staretz*, who had recently appeared in Petersburg and was said to have made some miraculous cures by prayer and the laying-on of hands.

The manner and behavior of this man had been causing a sensation among the wealthy set, who were devoted to mysticism. He had a growing following. Yet some strange and revolting stories were widely spread about him. Nicky, having heard of these things and mindful of the Philippe scandal, called into consultation his two confessors and Archbishop Theophane. All three agreed that the miracle-worker was at times possessed by a spirit of terrible evil, but declared that they knew he suffered such agonies of contrition for his sins that he became "as pure as a child washed in the waters of baptism." He had become very holy—"chosen of God"—and Baroness Buxhoeveden quotes the Archbishop as saying, "I would all but guarantee his eternal salvation."

A man more than six feet high appeared at Tsarkoe Selo, dark and swarthy, with the long hair and unclipped beard of a *Staretz*. Behind his black eyes a red-hot furnace seemed to burn perpetually. The heavy face peering from the uncombed beard was wildly handsome, and a thick and richly sensuous lower lip quivered faintly when he spoke. He wore a black frock coat, open over a slightly soiled white caftan, under which his huge shiny peasant boots trod forward with catlike lightness. A walking-stick was in one hand and a bruised and rounded gray felt hat in the other. He was not an aged man, as they had expected; he was perhaps forty-five years old. The voice boomed, hoarse, breathless, ugly, and his manner to the agitated sovereigns alternated cool insolence with peasant respectfulness.

This was Grigori Rasputin—the destined doom of the imperial Romanoffs. His real name was Effimovitch, but he preferred the nickname *Rasputin*, meaning highwayman, which was said to denote the pattern of his early manhood. He was neither monk nor in holy orders, as is often affirmed, but a *Staretz*, a holy pilgrim and lay preacher among peasants, who had "come to town." Many were the inspired miracle-workers and holy fortune tellers of Russia, but Grigori Rasputin was, of his kind, a genius. One day, even his bitterest enemies would wonder if he was supernatural. In him the power of God and the power of Satan were alike dynamic forces.

As yet the crazy boozings and lecheries of Rasputin, for which he repented so passionately, were confined to the lower quarters of the city. His journey was only beginning.

On that first visit Rasputin came and knelt by the cot of Tsarevitch Alexis, who appeared in the last stages of exhaustion. The *Staretz* prayed till his large body seemed convulsed with devotional fervor, and the Empress stood watching him. The *Staretz* rose, his coarse yellow hands tensed before him abruptly, and the finger-tips, with black unclipped nails, gently brushed the Tsarevitch. "He will recover," he said. "I shall come again when you need me."

Nothing of this was known to the Dowager Empress when she returned to Russia, except that a new misfortune had befallen her family, and that her grandson's life was declared by Nicky and Alicky to have been saved by some peasant miracle-worker sent to them by the mystics.

That autumn Marie Fedorovna left Russia again, for Denmark, where Queen Alexandra awaited her. In the summer they had been negotiating for the purchase of a villa called *Hvidore*, on the coast near their old Bernstoff home, within sight of the place where, as children, they had all driven down to bathe on summer afternoons with Papa and Mama in the big, jolting, box-like family wagon. Old King Christian had died that January at the age of eighty-seven, and he had been so worn and tired before the end that none of them had felt that death was anything but a blessing to him, or that it was an occasion for long and deep mourning. The two of them had felt that they wanted a home of their own in Denmark, to which they could slip away for some time in each year and live together quietly and without the fuss and decorum which had occupied so much of their lives.

CHAPTER XIV

On the Eve—Donkeys, Umbrellas and Stones

IN THE SPRING of 1907 the Dowager Empress wrote to her daughter Zenia, who with her husband and family were at Biarritz, complaining of "lonesomeness," and Zenia and Sandro urged her to join them at the Villa Espoir for a long stay.

Edward VII and Queen Alexandra were at Biarritz that spring, so that the Dowager Empress would be bound to find congenial company when she arrived. Everybody at Biarritz knew King Edward, although he seemed to avoid the society of the place for the seclusion of the Hôtel du Palais, or for tours through the countryside in his magnificent car, which announced its approach by a bugle-horn blown by an attendant.

The splendor of the Dowager Empress' luxurious train roused a sensation when it arrived at Biarritz, and the crowds watched fascinated as an army of colorful Russian servants and body-guards poured out of it. The awe with which Marie Fedorovna had been met by the French President at Paris, and by lesser lights at other stations, not to mention the respectful welcome of the top-hatted municipality of Biarritz, filled her with surprise and sad amusement, for she could not help reflecting that she was now more valued abroad than she was at home. She had not quite realized what a Continental reputation she had, and it was delightful. She began to revive.

The drama and majesty of her arrival had put her brother-in-law King Edward in the shade, and it was expected that she would only appear as a glamorous local figurehead, who lived in regal exclusiveness; but she soon showed that, unlike the King of England, she was going to mix enthusiastically in the rather raffish and polyglot society of Biarritz. Newcomers to the resort were amazed when the famous Dowager Empress was pointed out to them in all kinds of ordinary and sometimes notoriously extraordinary company. They had heard of her as a sort of Queen Victoria of the mainland of Europe, but she seemed to be quite a young woman, who danced and behaved in rather an unseemly way. Even Sandro and Zenia had wondered if Marie Fedorovna would deign to meet some of their friends.

Grand Duke Alexander had always adored his mother-in-law, and now he was delighted with the way in which she was ready for anything. "Although I called her 'mother,'" he says, "and was well aware of her age, I considered her as my pal and associate when it came to going out to a party or to arranging a party." The Dowager Empress was frequently to be seen driving out in a huge Delaunay-Belleville car, built especially for Grand Duke Alexander and designed to carry himself, Zenia, their six children, governesses, nursemaids, an aide and a few more.

In June they all returned to Russia in state on the imperial train, which on its return received the same honored reception—until it passed the Russian border, when a blight descended on their high spirits.

The summer was notable for one outstanding event, which gave great joy to the Dowager Empress. Russia and Britain settled their century-old differences in the Middle East by a treaty in which all points at issue were amicably resolved.

A year later, in June 1908, this full alliance was finally to be cemented at the famous meeting at Reval in the Baltic between the Emperor of Russia and King Edward VII. There, two imperial Russian yachts, the *Standart*, bearing the Emperor and the

Empress, and the *Polar Star,* with the Dowager Empress and her sister-in-law Olga, Queen of Greece, awaited the *Victoria and Albert,* coming through the Kiel Canal with King Edward and Queen Alexandra aboard.

There was only one incident of the Reval meeting which closely concerns this story. It occurred most unexpectedly, and probably the two stars of the drama were no more expectant of its happening a moment before it actually did take place than anybody else who was waiting to go in to dinner on the *Victoria and Albert* on the second night at Reval. The classic clash between the Dowager Empress and her daughter-in-law—the leap of the rival tigresses with claws extended—came at last. And now that it did come, it concerned not those deep-seated emotional issues of jealousy and mental incompatibility which had always divided them, but the most childish, unreasonable, irrelevant matter.

Alicky had not for some time attended any function with her mother-in-law at which the question of precedence arose, except at the opening of the Dumas, when the Dowager Empress had made no claims to precede her, and had seemed rather inclined to think those were occasions when the Emperor's consort should have the place of prominence.

But that evening on the *Victoria and Albert* Marie Fedorovna had decided that her brother-in-law the King of England would take her on his arm and lead her into the dining saloon when dinner was announced. She felt, perhaps, that on this night when they were celebrating the Anglo-Russian alliance on the British royal yacht, she, who had worked so hard to pave the way for it, had earned this honor. Unhappily, Alicky believed that King Edward would inevitably wish to lead with the Empress of Russia at such a solemn moment in the history of the two great empires.

As soon as the doors of the dining room had been thrown open and dinner announced, Queen Alexandra murmured to her husband, "Bertie, will you—," and the genial host, who happened to be chatting with the Dowager Empress and the Empress, braced himself, raised his left elbow slightly, and, mindful of the old

Russian rule of precedence, was beginning to smile courteously toward the Dowager Empress when suddenly the dawning smile faded from his face. An "atmosphere" had come in the cabin, and he was in the heart of the tempest. He saw two empresses facing one another, their cheeks suffused with scarlet. Two flashing dark eyes stared into two flashing blue eyes. Their lips trembled, he felt that their fists were clenched, and though neither spoke, both looked as if they might utter heaven knew what shocking words if he dared to approach one or the other. Never had "the arch-schemer of Europe—*le grand diplomate, l'homme d'état remarquable*," tackled so delicate a dilemma.

King Edward perceived that in selecting one empress he relegated the other to the mortification of third place in the procession, since Nicky and Queen Alexandra must come second, and that, he told himself, in the present crisis was simply unthinkable. If Alicky was rejected he would not put it past her to walk out to the deck and order the boat to take her back to the *Standart,* and if he did not act quickly two empresses might be actually jostling for him.

The King of England laughed politely. "Tonight I am going to enjoy the unique honor of taking two empresses in to dinner," he exclaimed. "It is I who shall have the privilege of taking your arms," and suiting the action to his words he gently caught both by the arm and brought an empress to each side of him, so that they all faced the open door of the dining saloon. "We must keep step together," he announced cheerfully.

The conductor of the Marine orchestra, peering through the saloon door, saw his cue and struck up with the Russian anthem, and the procession moved gravely to the table.

We do not find anything further of especial interest in the life of the Dowager Empress until early in 1909, when, hearing that a young governess, Sophie Troutcheff, who had been engaged by Alicky for the two youngest girls on her strong recommendation, had suddenly returned to her home in great distress, she sent for her to inquire the reason. She knew Sophie Troutcheff well, for she had long been a friend of her parents, and feeling that something had gone seriously amiss she felt she was in part responsible.

Marie Fedorovna had, of course, been aware that the *Staretz* Rasputin had been visiting the Empress at Tsarkoe Selo, and she had heard vague stories about him. Once she herself had seen the *Staretz* when on a visit to Tsarkoe Selo. That strange-looking individual had passed down a corridor with his ponderous yet catlike tread as she walked up it. He had bowed to her almost insolently, with a kind of familiarity, evidently aware of her identity, but till she inquired she had not known who the man was. It did not surprise her that such a person should have got round Alicky; and as for the *Staretz* being the savior of her grandson Alexis, she surmised that the child had probably turned the corner and been on the way to recovery before Rasputin performed his "miracle."

But now the truth was revealed to her by Sophie Troutcheff. Sophie was a young woman of character. She had been so outspoken to the Empress about her opinion of the holy *Staretz* and the harm his visits to the Palace were doing to the reputation of the sovereigns that she had been dismissed after a stormy scene. Sophie informed Marie Fedorovna that the Empress not only received Rasputin in her private apartments, and quoted his words and opinions as if these were divine law, but that she more frequently met him at the flat of a friend, Madame Vyrouboff, who entertained the *Staretz* for the benefit of the Empress, and who visited Tsarkoe Selo almost daily and carried messages between the Empress and Rasputin. Sophie further disclosed that when Rasputin visited fashionable houses he would frequently break off even in the middle of a prayer session, because he must "telephone to Tsarkoe Selo." He was always said to shout down the telephone so that everyone could overhear him, and people imagined that he was speaking to the Emperor or the Empress; but actually she thought he was calling up members of the palace staff who were his friends, and that it was done to impress his followers with his importance.

The Madame Vyrouboff who was the go-between for the Empress was a young widow, and a violent emotional friendship existed between them. Anna Vyrouboff was as much under the spell of Rasputin as the Empress, which made her all the more dangerous as a friend, because she would do anything to please the *Staretz*. It was the opinion of Sophie Troutcheff that, although the Empress was tied to Rasputin because she regarded him as the only person who could save the Tsarevitch in case of one of his attacks, the real secret of his power over her was that he had established a complete spiritual domination. She would listen hungrily to him, convinced of his inspired holiness and his oracular gifts, and she consulted him on matters which she knew worried the Emperor in his state duties. The Empress was, in fact, naïvely quoting the political ideas of the *Staretz* to her husband, who seemed either to value them or to hesitate to ignore his wife. All kinds of ambitious men, politicians and climbers in government posts, were supposed to be chasing Rasputin and making him presents in hopes of getting an introduction to the imperial family.

Sophie did not believe that the Empress was connected with Rasputin in the scandalous circumstances in which many married women and young girls of the highest families in Petersburg had entangled themselves.

How much the Dowager Empress then knew of Rasputin the Beast is not recorded; but doubtless Sophie Troutcheff's information caused her to make searching inquiries about this man of evil influence who had crept into her family.

Grigori Rasputin had, in fact, developed his theory of passionate repentence for great sin to satisfy his own libidinous desires. He was teaching it to his growing band of female disciples. Most of these had never committed horrible and degrading sin. Therefore they could never truly repent, and God could never "wash them white as snow." If they had to befoul themselves to achieve this wonderful state of holy immaculacy, who better was there to sin with than the *Staretz* himself—he who best understood their motives and who daily communed with the Almighty? The vilest orgies were alleged to be taking place behind locked doors in the best houses, even in some of the palaces of Petersburg, and aristocratic husbands were rushing dementedly about the capital, swearing to thrash Rasputin, and refraining only for fear of their bemused wives.

But horrible as it was to Marie Fedorovna that her daughter-in-law should be in any way concerned with this unclean and mysterious peasant, the most terrifying aspect to her must have been the realization that the insidious influence of Alicky over Nicky, which at first had only been that of a jealous, selfish and wrong-thinking wife, might now with ever-growing frequency take the form of a transmission of dangerous opinions planted in her by a third party, whose whole character appeared to be strange, sinister, unbalanced and totally unscrupulous.

In May 1909 the Dowager Empress is met in happier circumstances. She joined Bertie and Alix on the *Victoria and Albert* at Marseilles to accompany them on a Mediterranean cruise.

The royal yacht had not long left Marseilles when Marie Fedorovna was warned by her sister to steer clear of Bertie. A wireless message had reached the yacht which had caused the King of England to fall into one of his ungovernable rages. The Mediterranean Fleet, which was to have greeted him at Malta, had been suddenly ordered out on a "demonstration." An empty harbor would await the King. He was like a pricked balloon. He roared that the Prime Minister and the Foreign Secretary, who had ordered the "demonstration" for reasons of policy, had personally insulted him by sending no warning. Nobody could do anything with the King, and no Russian autocrat could have expressed himself more blisteringly.

King Edward made sure that nobody derived much enjoyment from the Malta visit, and the subsequent meeting with tiny King Victor Emanuel and his statuesque Queen on the royal Italian yacht in the Bay of Baiae was of no especial interest; but a rather more picturesque incident followed, to which Bertie's bad temper added color.

They had chartered a special train at Naples to take them for a picnic party on the slopes of Mount Vesuvius. When the train reached the little terminal station some way up the mountainside, a group of small donkeys awaited them. King Edward, who weighed 225 pounds and who valued his dignity, asked sarcastically what the donkeys were meant to be for. Queen Alexandra had ordered them without telling him to carry the party up to the crater.

"I have no intention of riding one, and I certainly shan't walk!" muttered the King sulkily.

Queen Alexandra shrugged her shoulders philosophically and the two sisters eyed each other eagerly. Then they seated themselves on donkeys. Nobody else seemed to fancy a donkey ride, but Major Ponsonby, King Edward's private secretary, thought it his duty to accompany them, and told the courier, Fehr, to do so as well. The picnic had to wait, and the King declared with resignation that he might as well fill in the time with a stroll.

Any idea that the sisters might indulge in a close-run donkey race up to the crater was quickly dispelled. Ponsonby, whose donkey, like the courier's, was no match for the other two, saw the Dowager Empress "romping away" ahead and Queen Alexandra in cheerful pursuit, although badly outclassed. Strung out in this way they labored up the mountainside. When this order had been followed for half an hour and miles of lava slope seemed still to rise before them, a long blast from the train whistle shrieked up into the silence.

Ponsonby knew what that meant. But neither sister looked around—Queen Alexandra was too deaf to hear it, and the Dowager Empress "was by this time quite a quarter of a mile ahead" and was too interested in reaching the summit to care. By tremendous efforts Ponsonby brought his donkey level with Queen Alexandra. "I shouted at her that the King was having the whistle blown to tell us to return, but she merely said that if we wanted to see the crater it was no use giving up only halfway." He could do no more; his donkey dropped back into its melancholy amble and the Queen went ahead.

Suddenly the train whistle started again. Shriek after shriek in rapid succession pursued them. It sounded as if someone were going demented. "I feared that the King had got hold of the string and was pulling it himself." Once again Ponsonby caught up with the Queen. This time she seemed to grasp the urgency of the situation. She turned down the mountain. The Dowager Empress "was a speck in the distance."

Ponsonby forced his donkey into a trot. Scrambling painfully up the jagged lava ascent, working like a jockey, using all his experience as a horseman, he reached the Dowager Empress in a state of exhaustion, and gasped out his message. "She was much disappointed, but consented to return." A moment later she had left Ponsonby and was proceeding downward at speed. In no time Marie Fedorovna had overtaken her sister and the courier and arrived at the royal train well ahead.

When Ponsonby came up to the train the courier had vanished, scenting trouble for which he might be held responsible, and King Edward stood glowering at his wife and sister-in-law, who returned his gaze with amiable indifference. Apparently the King had up to that time made no comment; but his secretary knew that he would have to make his feelings plainly understood before the air cleared. A ferocious royal blast struck the innocent Ponsonby as he dismounted. He was expecting it. "As I knew that his remarks were intended for the others, I didn't remonstrate."

Less than a year later, on May 6, 1910, King Edward VII was dead. Marie Fedorovna and Queen Alexandra had been staying with Queen Olga of Greece at her villa in Corfu when the first news came of the King's illness. The seriousness of the case was not fully explained in the message, and although Queen Alexandra had set out for home, she had planned to spend a few days in Venice with Charlotte Knollys en route. But her trunks had scarcely been unpacked in the hotel when she was overcome with deep foreboding. She ordered the luggage to be repacked and set out immediately for London. She barely arrived in time.

As soon as the news of King Edward's death reached Corfu, Marie Fedorovna hurried across Europe to join her sister at Buckingham Palace.

Bertie had not always been an easy husband for Alix, and she, by his precise standards, had often seemed an exasperating wife. But now that he was dead Alix simply could not imagine how her life could go on without him. Marie Fedorovna found her sister in a state of overwhelming desolation, and endeavored to give her the comfort which Alix had given her after the death of Sasha.

The Dowager Empress stayed for some time with her sister to help her adjust herself to the new life of a Queen Dowager. In doing this Marie Fedorovna cannot have helped reflecting on the great contrast between the tranquil life which lay ahead of Alix in her widowhood and her own troubled career since Sasha had left her, which seemed to grow sadder and more frightening year by year.

On September 18, 1911, there befell the Dowager Empress another of those grim experiences which would recur again and again in her mind.

She was staying at Lividia with Nicky and Alicky, and together with the five children she accompanied them on their official visit to Kiev. It was the occasion of great celebrations, and on the night of the eighteenth the Emperor, the Dowager Empress, the three eldest girls and young Grand Duke Dmitri, the Emperor's ward, who lived with them, attended the gala performance at the Kiev Opera House. The Empress was unwell and had stayed at home.

A prominent figure in the front row of the stalls was the tall, bearded Prime Minister Stolypin, who was himself a native of Kiev. Among the friends and admirers of Stolypin was the Dowager Empress, for although like many "old Russians" she disapproved of some of his advanced ideas, she well understood how much easier Nicky's lot in Russia had become since this great and courageous man had administered his Empire for him. The tragedy which she was forced to witness that night, and the extraordinary rumors which followed it, were therefore all the more terrible and shocking to her.

In the box next to the imperial box sat some men in evening dress, who were presumably secret-police agents, and among them was a noticeable little man of Jewish appearance.

When the curtain dropped for the interval, the Prime Minister was seen to be standing up. Rising head and shoulders above those around, in his white uniform, he caught the eye of anyone looking toward the stage. The little man in the box quite unexpectedly vaulted over the front of it and alighted among the crowd; but his action had been so smooth and confident that its oddness did not occur to anybody till he had almost reached Stolypin.

Two shots were heard above the din of voices. Few in the busy throng even turned their heads, but a circle suddenly opened round Stolypin. The shrill scream of a woman brought a swift silence, and heads turned toward the sound. The tall form of Stolypin now stood out plainly, and the occupants of the imperial box watched amazed as a red blotch spread over the front of his white tunic. Stolypin swayed, then his eyes turned toward the Emperor. His lips parted, his arm rose and he made a gesture, which some have called a blessing. The Prime Minister tumbled to the floor. Yet even so, he tried to pull himself up and repeat his gesture. He did not die, but he was carried away mortally wounded.

None will ever know what thoughts were passing through Stolypin's mind as he struggled to gesture to the Emperor; but at that moment the wounded man was aware of what others learned only later. Bagroff, the assailant, who stood defiantly watching his agony, was not only a member of the Ochrana, the trusted imperial bodyguard, but he was one of those detailed to guard the life of Stolypin himself at Kiev. Stolypin knew that the Emperor disliked him, resenting his power and firmness, and that the Empress hated him and headed the jealous court party which had been intriguing to overthrow him. The cause of the antagonism of the Empress was solely that he had urged the Emperor to expel Rasputin, his sworn enemy, from the capital for lowering the dignity of the throne.

Count Vassili and also Prince Felix Youssoupoff have revealed some strange facts about the shooting of Stolypin, the man who might have saved the imperial Romanoffs from destruction. Vassili has stressed the astonishing calm and apparent indifference of Nicholas II at the sight of the stricken Stolypin, when all others in the imperial box were stunned with horror.

Prince Youssoupoff, who married the Dowager Empress's

granddaughter Irina and was an intimate of the Emperor's ward
Dmitri, goes farther than Vassili. He clearly believes that Rasputin was at the bottom of the affair. "Stolypin's death," he declares, "was a triumph for the enemies of Russia." Youssoupoff
had also heard from his friend Dmitri about the Emperor's "indifference"—but, more astonishing, he supplies a truly sinister
fact. Dmitri had told him that the Empress, after hearing of the
Stolypin attack, had said to him (Dmitri): "Those who have
offended against *our friend* [Rasputin] may no longer count on
divine protection. Only the prayers of the *Staretz,* which go
straight to Heaven, have power to protect them."

As for Bagroff, the assassin, an inquiry soon caused the facts
about him to be noised through Russia, with the added suggestion that he was in league with terrorists. He never appeared
for public trial. He simply disappeared. This was not the only
instance in Russia of a political murder being hushed up.

At the end of September 1912 the Dowager Empress was
suddenly called to Spala, the great imperial shooting lodge in
Poland. Her grandson, the nine-year-old Tsarevitch, had tumbled
down while climbing out of a rowboat. His injury brought on
the most severe attack of internal bleeding which had yet beset
him. A huge tumor had risen on the groin, he was in high fever
and suffered agonizing pain down the lower left side of his body
and in his left leg. The doctors, who dared not operate, seemed
to be helpless. The attack developed swiftly, and official bulletins
had begun to be published about the dangerous condition of the
Tsarevitch before his grandmother reached Spala.

When Marie Fedorovna arrived at the imperial shooting lodge,
she was asked to go straight upstairs to her grandson. Terrible
screams of childish pain sounded from above as she ascended
the stairs. Alicky, pale and frantic, met her on the landing. Nicky,
pacing to and fro below, wincing as the sharp cries of his son
rent the silence of the house, had murmured to his mother:
"There is no hope. He will die of exhaustion. The doctors have
given him up."

In the bedroom Deverenko, the gigantic and awkward-looking
sailor servant and guardian of the Tsarevitch, was bending over

the bed, putting the little boy into a dressing gown with infinite care. Then the sailor picked him out of bed and settling his master in his arms walked with him toward the mother and the grandmother at the door. Alexis scarcely moaned now that the huge sailor held him, and the man paused by them while the shrunken, haggard child feebly greeted his grandmother. Deverenko strode through the open door. A wooden expression covered his big coarse face, but he clutched the Tsarevitch with a kind of passion and yet with the gentleness of a mother. He slowly carried the Tsarevitch down the stairs and out into the sunlit gardens.

Seeing the look of surprise on the face of the Dowager Empress, the mother explained: "When Alexie can't bear lying flat any longer, Deverenko takes him and walks to and fro with him for hours. It lessens the cramp. Only this works. . . ."

No atmosphere of restraint hovered over Marie Fedorovna and her daughter-in-law that afternoon. For the first and perhaps the last time they were at one in their fear and pity for the tortured child. Nevertheless, while the heart of Alicky cried out for comfort, while she grasped at her mother-in-law's hand in her frenzy of terror, she was withholding one secret from Marie Fedorovna, knowing instinctively that even in that hour of crisis the disclosure would disturb and alienate her.

Alexis was no better the next morning. His cries had filled the house during the night. He was only nine, but he had shrieked out, "Why can't I die—let me die!"

In the middle of the morning they were gathered in the Empress' room when a telegram was handed to Alicky. She tore open the envelope and read it with feverish intensity. Then she looked up at them, and her face had filled with joy.

"The *Staretz* says, '*I have prayed for him. He will live. To-morrow he will start to recover.*'"

On the previous afternoon, just before the arrival of the Dowager Empress, Alicky, without even telling her husband, had telegraphed to Rasputin asking for his prayers.

In the evening the temperature of the Tsarevitch was found to have fallen. The pain had eased and he was quiet. He slept peacefully through the night. The doctors declared next morning that the tumor on the groin was subsiding, and by the evening they believed Alexis out of danger.

As Nicky remarked to his mother on an occasion when his wife was absent during the days that followed, "it was difficult entirely to disbelieve in the *Staretz*." She was aware that he was not as convinced as Alicky about Rasputin; but there were moments now when even she herself began to wonder as, indeed, all the enemies of the *Staretz* would do at one time or another. She also recalled what Grand Duke Alexander had confided to her after a visit to Nicky, when he had remonstrated with him about the harm Rasputin was doing him. In answering, Nicky had embroidered on an old theme.

"I would rather stand Rasputin," he muttered plaintively, "than Alicky in hysterics."

But what did it matter if Rasputin was a crazy prophet, or an inspired rogue! One thing was certain: after the Spala telegram, nothing in the world would turn Alicky from the *Staretz*. Marie Fedorovna could see days ahead when Holy Russia would virtually lie in the hands of a mysterious and unpredictable human monster.

Hardly had they returned to Russia when a scandal of international proportions broke around Rasputin.

A friend of Rasputin's, a drunken and renegade monk named Iliodor, had quarreled with the *Staretz* in a public resort. The police were called in. The details are vague, but the result was sensational. Shortly afterward Continental newspapers began talking of the monk Iliodor, who had fled from Russia and who proposed to publish a number of compromising letters in his possession, which the Empress of Russia had written to Rasputin.

Baroness Buxhoeveden, who was then serving the Empress, admits that Iliodor probably had acquired some "notes" penned by Alexandra Fedorovna, and believes these to have been harmless if indiscreet; but Iliodor, beyond the frontiers, was free to make what he pleased of them. Some spurious publications with these alleged letters do actually seem to have appeared abroad, but the books have now long vanished.

This was too much. Rasputin, who had been the whisper at every European court even before the scandal of the Empress' letters, had now become a national problem, and the ministers came to complain to the Emperor, requesting him to get rid of the *Staretz*.

Marie Fedorovna, also, seized the opportunity to tackle her son.

"The *Staretz* will have to go—for all your sakes!"

The reply was unexpected.

"I agree. The *Staretz* has agreed to return to his native village. He will become a pilgrim. He understands our position."

"If he has only *agreed* to go—what is to stop his returning later on?"

"The *Staretz* is not a criminal. Many will one day want him to come back. Alicky says that, as to his return, God will guide him in this decision."

On March 5, 1913, the Dowager Empress was seen for the last time at a great official function in Russia, and who can better portray her on that day of grim skies and pelting rain than old Count Vassili? He never saw his idol again, for he himself was very near to death.

The occasion was the third centenary celebration of the Romanoff dynasty, and for the first time since the massacre of 1905, the sovereigns had returned to the Winter Palace.

The Ball of the Nobility given to the imperial family had been of unsurpassed splendor—worthy of Old Russia—and the aristocracy had done their best to revive the ancient spirit of pageantry and festival; but Vassili, who had watched for so long, perceived sorrowfully that the heart was not in it.

The people showed little enthusiasm. The only Romanoff who could draw their cheers was the Dowager Empress, and she herself was melancholy: it was a celebration of mockery and futility to her.

It might have been thought that at such a centenary even the rain would not have kept the crowds off the streets as the brilliant ceremonial State Drive passed along to the Kazan Cathedral for the thanksgiving. It was not so; the streets were almost empty but for the troops and the police.

It was in the glory of the draped cathedral, among floating clouds of incense, beneath the crimson imperial canopy opposite the altar, that Count Vassili found himself near "sweet Empress Marie" for the last time. "—On the right side of Nicholas II, his mother, tears filling her beautiful soft eyes, the only pathetic figure in the vast assemblage save the child [Alexis]—white, pinched, carried by a Cossack to a chair beside his mother—on whom so many hopes were centered, and who, by an irony perhaps realized by few among the spectators, appeared to have been brought there to show into what weak and frail hands was entrusted the future of the proud Romanoff dynasty."

Had old Vassili, or indeed Marie Fedorovna herself, as they sadly contemplated the glittering scene from their different stations, heard of the rumor in high life that the *Staretz*, writing from Jerusalem to one of his female disciples, had declared that he would be back in the capital within a twelvemonth? And this, indeed, was to happen.

The year 1913 was a bad one for Marie Fedorovna. On March 19 news reached her that her brother, King George of Greece, had been shot dead by a madman in Salonika on the previous day.

With the autumn came further cause for grief. It was a different kind of distress which beset her this time: that of a mother over the misdemeanors of a child. Mischa—her youngest son, the Grand Duke Michael, who had for some time filled to a great extent the place of Nicky in his mother's affections—declared that, come what might, he was going to marry a twice-divorced commoner, Madame Woulfert. Michael was heir to the throne after the Tsarevitch, and with the life of Alexis such an uncertain quantity, his reckless and selfish action seemed in the eyes of many to be almost that of a criminal. Once again the name of the imperial Romanoffs was trailed in the international mire, and scandal and sensation raged around them. In Russia people were asking one another if the whole imperial family had become completely decadent. As for the Empress, who was nearly always said to be confined to her room when she was expected to appear in public and who was naturally identified with the most lurid stories told about Rasputin, some people were beginning to declare that she was mad.

At Tsarkoe Selo Nicky and Mischa, both weak men, both hysterically obstinate, stormed at one another. The rage of the brothers soon involved their mother. Bitterly and miserably she found herself siding with Nicky against Mischa. Such conduct by the Heir Presumptive could not be tolerated by the Emperor.

Mischa had to leave the country; but at least she had been able to save him from the degradations inflicted upon Grand Duke Cyril. And, ironically, Cyril, who had been allowed to return home and had been reinstated in his honors, was now declared Heir Presumptive in the place of his cousin Mischa.

Mischa settled on the Riviera, and his wife became known as the Countess Brusoff. But the exile of Grand Duke Michael was destined to be short-lived, for war lay around the corner.

Olga's marriage had collapsed. She and her husband had separated and there was to be a divorce. Olga had returned to the Anitchkoff, where her companionship was a joy to her mother; but it would be difficult to believe that Marie Fedorovna, with her old enthusiasms and impetuosities behind her, was not blaming herself for the unhappy years she had in part been responsible for inflicting on her youngest daughter.

Prince Felix Youssoupoff records an interesting encounter with the Dowager Empress in the winter of 1913 when she was staying in Copenhagen with her brother King Frederick. Youssoupoff had just returned from being an undergraduate at Oxford and had become engaged to Irina, the only daughter of the Grand Duke Alexander and Grand Duchess Zenia.

Felix Youssoupoff himself admits in his memoirs that he had earned a lurid reputation in the Russian capital and shocked many people. As a result the parents, who had consented to the marriage because he belonged to one of the first families of Russia, always closely identified with the imperial family, had on reflection decided to forbid a matrimonial union with this particular member of it. The young couple were dismayed by this

stern parental veto, which descended on them most unexpectedly; but they were not beaten.

Eventually Youssoupoff was given to understand that the final
arbiter was the Dowager Empress, who always spoke of Irina as
her favorite granddaughter. It seemed that it was she who had
heard something and had put a spoke in the wheel. Youssoupoff
was informed that if he cared to go to Denmark the Dowager
Empress would be willing to interview him, and on this his fate
would hang. At that moment his ex-fiancée and her mother
were also in Copenhagen, and he felt this fact must be in his
favor, for although he was out of touch with Irina, he surmised
that she would become aware of his approaching visit and do
her best to soften the ground with her doting grandmother before
his arrival.

Nevertheless, Felix Youssoupoff was in a state of perturbation
as he set out. To the younger generation of Russian nobility the
Dowager Empress was a legendary figure, regarded with venera-
tion and awe, a splendid survival of Old Russia, and Youssoupoff's mood as he traveled grew more full of dread with every
mile he advanced toward "one of the most striking personalities
of our time."

Arrived at Copenhagen, Youssoupoff telephoned the palace.
He was told to come to luncheon. In the drawing room he found
Irina and her mother. Their attitude did not leave the nervous
young suitor without hope. He was introduced to the Dowager
Empress, who was majestic and yet kind to him at the same time,
and at the table he found himself opposite to her.

"Several times during lunch I felt the Dowager Empress's
observant eyes on me. She afterward expressed the wish to see
me alone. During the conversation that followed I had the impression that, little by little, I was winning her over to my side.
At the end she rose and said kindly, 'Do not worry, I will do
what I can for your happiness.'" Prince Youssoupoff had judged
rightly that the matter was settled in his favor. His worries were
at an end.

At the beginning of February 1914 the Dowager Empress gave
a great ball at the Anitchkoff for her granddaughters Olga and

Tatiana, the two eldest imperial grand duchesses, who were aged eighteen and sixteen. The public had seen little of these attractive daughters of the Emperor and Empress, but soon their beauty and their simple charm would be the talk of hundreds of admiring wounded soldiers.

One subject of comment at the Anitchkoff ball, the last fashionable function at which Marie Fedorovna was seen, was the astonishing appearance of youth which still lingered with the Dowager Empress, who took a childish pride in assuring her friends that she was sixty-eight!

In Britain, Ascot Week in 1914 was a special occasion, for Queen Alexandra was to make her first appearance driving down the Royal Mile since the death of King Edward. The crowds were enormous, and people wept in the frenzy of acclamation as the "Beloved Lady" appeared in her open landau with the Dowager Empress of Russia and the Grand Duchess Zenia.

Prince Youssoupoff has an amusing and quite unusual tale to tell of the sister queens during that summer of 1914. In spite of their ages we see that Queen Alexandra and the Dowager Empress were still as excitable as ever when together.

Felix Youssoupoff had married Irina, and at the end of their honeymoon trip they came to London, where the bridegroom had retained a flat since his Oxford days. In Palestine the Prince had engaged a young Lebanese servant, attentive, obedient, jealous of his high status, but somewhat simple-minded.

One night when Felix and his bride returned very late to the flat he told his Arab servant that they were not to be disturbed on any account on the following morning.

When morning came, however, they were awakened by the noise of shrill, indignant voices, shouts of protest and scuffling from the hall. The Prince judged that the disturbance might be more than his raw Arab footman could cope with, and slipped on his dressing gown.

When he appeared in the hall, Queen Alexandra and the Dowager Empress were standing outside his open front door in a state of great agitation. All efforts to dart past his servant had failed. The Dowager Empress, "run short of words—was threatening him with her umbrella."

A few days after this episode the newspapers of Europe reported the murder of Archduke Franz Ferdinand at Sarajevo, and many with behind-the-scenes knowledge of international politics began to hold their breath. Yet, as the hot summer days passed and mobilization orders were posted up in one country after another on the continent, the "best informed" people in England declared that there was going to be no war. Such optimists moved in the circle of Marlborough House, and their ready confidence impressed the Dowager Empress and her daughter. When Grand Duke Alexander, who was in Paris, hurried over to urge them to come home with him, they laughed at his fears and assured him that they knew things would soon quiet down. They were not going to spoil their holiday. He had to return to Russia, for since leaving the Navy he had become Commander of the Russian Flying Corps, a body which he had, in fact, created himself by his own initiative in the face of widespread mockery.

Telegram after telegram from anxious relatives in Russia came to Marlborough House advising a quick return. Marie Fedorovna and Zenia persisted in calling the senders alarmists. At last things grew so threatening that their mood changed. They packed up in haste and the sisters parted with tears.

When the imperial train carrying the Dowager Empress drew into Berlin on August 1 on its way to Russia, the city was in a state of excitement and chaos. The big station was an armed camp, and the platforms were packed with departing troops, accompanied by their wives and relations. Two days before Russia had called a general mobilization. It was the last straw, and now that this had happened no German doubted what was coming. To the infuriated Berliners every Russian was a "dirty pig." Hundreds of Russians were seeking desperately to get home. Many had already been detained by the authorities, and among these, at the Continental Hotel, were Prince Youssoupoff, his parents and Irina, together with the enormous staff which highborn Russians invariably took abroad with them.

Their exact position was uncertain, and when the Dowager Empress was informed of their whereabouts by a member of the Russian Embassy staff at the station she declared her intention of waiting in Berlin until a message could be taken to them, telling them to leave everything and hurry to join her on the imperial train. She was unaware as her message left the station that the Kaiser himself had ordered their detention, and that he meant to hold them as prisoners.

These arrangements had not taken long, but in the meanwhile the appearance of the imperial train began to attract the curiosity of the platform crowds. The Russian insignia was quickly recognized, and faces grew ugly. Soldiers and civilians began to peer into the train. Inquiry elicited the identity of the occupants. If there was one land in which the Dowager Empress of Russia was unpopular it was Germany, for she had never hidden her dislike of Germans. And now all these Germans who had to go to war, because Russia had mobilized, could plainly see her sitting in the glass-sided saloon and haughtily refusing to look at them.

Angry growls swelled into hoots, jeers and finally a roar of curses. The Dowager Empress herself pulled down the blinds near her and ordered all the windows to be covered. There was a crash of splintering glass. The blinds were ripped away. Fists were shaken. Rifle butts battered the shining paint off the side of the train. Stones and missiles rattled against it and dropped into the gaping window spaces. The crowd were hitting each other and growing more infuriated. Marie Fedorovna was always calm in a crisis, and her patience had its effect on those with her. They knew they were helpless, at the mercy of the growing mob.

Police and station guards thrust through the crowd. A semblance of order was restored. But the demeanor of their deliverers was scarcely more friendly than that of their assailants. The shouting continued, while officials stood arguing as to whether they should hold the imperial train or let the Dowager pass through to Russia. Somebody had warned the Kaiser by telephone that the Dowager Empress was detained in Berlin. His first impulse was to intern her. On second thought, foreseeing awkward repercussions, he refused to give passage to the Imperial train, ordering it to leave German soil by the shortest route—to be diverted to the Danish frontier.

As soon as the instructions of the All Highest reached the station staff the imperial train was moved out to a siding until the diversion could be arranged, and as it slid away from the platforms in its battered splendor with guards and policemen running beside it, fierce execrations and a shower of stones sped its passage. But nobody was hurt, and they had their liberty.

In Copenhagen, where the King and Queen of Denmark welcomed them, they were joined next day by Prince Youssoupoff and his party, who, owing to a slip in the orders about their detention, had succeeded in leaving the Continental Hotel unchallenged, and had got aboard the special train evacuating the staff of the Russian Embassy.

They were a bewildered and rather subdued party as they crossed in the passenger ferry to Sweden, and Youssoupoff observed the Dowager Empress as she bleakly gazed back from the stern of the boat toward the land of her birth, with the look of one who expects a long separation.

CHAPTER XV

Meeting on a Train

THE FIERCE ONRUSH of the Russian armies into East Prussia in those sweltering August days of 1914 ended at the beginning of September with the crushing defeat of Tannenberg. Mass surrenders, retreat, stalemate followed, and these were but the prelude to further defeats, disasters and retirements.

It was the old story: bad leadership, lack of everything—faulty supplies, swindling contractors, dishonest and indolent staff officers, chaos behind the lines. Rasputin had returned and all the old crowd had gathered around him. His following was growing. He bore himself in all circles with an insolent confidence he did not have before. He saw himself as something higher than the tame prophet of the Empress, with whom he was known to be in constant communication. To the masses the nature of his hold over the Empress was a mystery. Some said that from time to time he cast an evil spell over the Tsarevitch.

One of the great surprises of the war had been the emergence of the Empress before the nation. Alicky, the erstwhile invalid, was seen everywhere. She had apparently forgotten about her ailments. She no longer rested with her feet up for the best part of every day. After the first few months of the war she was almost acquiring popularity. She was seen more than the Dowager

Empress, who had, in fact, suffered a profound shock after her brutal reception in Berlin, and was, it seems, at last beginning to feel her age.

The greater part of Tsarkoe Selo Palace had been turned into a military hospital for officers and men. When in residence the Empress with Olga and Tatiana attended daily in the wards in nurses' uniform, and the Empress was addressed as "Head Sister." She sat for hours by the bedside of dying or desperately wounded officers and went at night to pray over their graves.

By early 1915 the Empress had overexerted herself, and real heart trouble took the place of her previous hysterical ailments. The doctors forbade her to walk upstairs, and for a long time she was always carried up in a chair at the hospital, even to the operating theater. This was a sight which caused certain of her ill-wishers to declare that either she was playing for effect or she derived ecstatic pleasure from the sight of blood and horror.

General P. N. Krassnoff, after describing the hospital activities of the Empress at Tsarkoe during the black months of 1915, reveals that already "she was conscious that to continue the war meant ruin to Russia. She pictured to herself an immediate separate peace with Germany; a peace which, very lucrative for Russia, would mean the possession of Constantinople, the Dardanelles and part of Asia Minor, and the triumph of the Monarchy."

This idea emanated from the party of Rasputin, who, rightly or wrongly, would soon be accused by his enemies of being a German agent.

The views of the "peace party" were as yet merely theoretical. The Empress at that moment held less power over her husband than before the war. She did not see him so much, and when she did he was always tired out. Every member of the imperial family saw the "peace plan" as an outrageous piece of treachery toward Britain and France. It is doubtful if Alicky had even ventured to suggest it to Nicky as a practical solution of Russia's ills. In one thing the weak Nickolas II was very strong to the end: his absolute loyalty to his allies. In any case, Krassnoff opines that in 1915 "the influence of his mother stood in the way" of such a dastardly project.

Since the war the influence of Marie Fedorovna with her eldest son had increased. He rarely saw her, but they constantly communicated by telephone, by telegram and by brief notes. He seems to have rediscovered an inspiration in her strength, wisdom and common sense, which was lacking elsewhere. But the march of events was about to overthrow the balance in a most unexpected way.

The Dowager Empress was still head of the Russian Red Cross, but her work was confined more to that of a supreme authority to settle complicated questions that arose than to the administrative activities and the constant visitations in which she had employed herself in the previous war. Her prestige was enormous, and a word from her could generally smooth out the difficulties of anybody who could gain her ear.

Military disaster stared Russia in the face in the summer of 1915. People recalled the landslide of the Japanese War. Even those who were themselves contributing to the causes of chaos cried out indignantly that Russia still had all the old faults. On the home front despair and disappointment created ready listeners to revolutionary propaganda. On the battlefronts the morale of the neglected and ever retreating troops grew daily more uncertain. Soldiers returning on leave told of newly arrived regiments advancing into counter-attacks against machine guns with sharpened stakes, because the rifles promised them at the advance depots had disappeared.

But honest Russians who were in posts of authority knew that the real danger was in the rear. In the late summer of 1915 the ministers advised the Emperor that decisive action must be taken; a change in the Supreme Command of the armies, which was held by the Grand Duke Nicholas, was suggested as a first step, and the necessity of this was also urged in the imperial study by several of the grand dukes.

Nobody believed that Nicholas II would be brought to agree to this without the greatest difficulty: he would cast about frantically to save himself from the task of dismissing his terrifying cousin Nicholas.

But the news spread that the Emperor had at once agreed that the dismissal of Grand Duke Nicholas was the right course to take. He seemed to have been expecting this advice.

Yet, only a few hours after the projected change of command became known, fresh news spread. Dismay and incredulity stunned all who heard it. The Emperor, with his humble lieutenant colonel's epaulets, had announced that henceforth he himself assumed supreme command of the armies and would live at G.H.Q. at Mohilev.

It was not the military ignorance of Nicholas II which dismayed them—a good chief of staff could supply that want. But if this mad decision was really carried out, then an Emperor whose reputation was already in rags would personally make himself responsible for every minor disaster at the front, for every local shortage of supplies, for every scandal in administration. Not a thing which went amiss in the battle against Germany and Austria but could be blamed squarely on him.

The imperial plan was suicidal, and those with the welfare of the Romanoffs at heart rose up in vehement protest. The shrewdest among them were foreseeing something else: a sinister consequence following upon the departure of the Emperor to the seat of war. Nicholas II could not conceivably command both his huge armies and the home front. Someone would have to deal with the ministers in the capital, to make quick on-the-spot decisions, to carry out a hundred and one tasks normally undertaken by the monarch. In his absence that person would be the Empress.

Nothing would shake Nicholas II. He flew into a hysterical rage with all who tried to remonstrate with him. He was deaf to their arguments. Who had brought him to adopt this fatal idea? He said he was acting for the sake of Russia—nothing but the inspiration given by the personal leadership of the Emperor could save Russia now! It was the duty of an emperor to lead at such a moment, no matter what consequences came to himself.

Soon the identity of the mind behind Nicholas II was becoming sufficiently obvious. The Empress, moved by some mysterious mystical urge, had decided that the salvation of Russia and of the dynasty depended on the actions of the Emperor himself. All saw in this the mark of Rasputin. If members of the family came to her, stressing the dangers of the project, suggesting she should speak to Nicky, she flushed and answered with a lifeless expression in her blue eyes: "It is Nicky who has to make this decision. He is the Emperor. Go to him."

As for Nicky, he had taken to screaming at all who came to argue with him, "I will perish, but I will save Russia!" From the first Nicky had been left in no doubt as to his mother's opinions about what he was going to do. Now, since all else had failed, she proposed to go to him as a suppliant.

None knew what passed between the mother and the son about whom Vassili had once said "he would not go against her in anything she wanted." But after the interview she was crushed and shaking, and she left the palace in tears.

A few days later the Dowager Empress announced her intention of closing the Anitchkoff Palace for the war and retiring to Kiev, where her daughter Olga supervised a military hospital. The shallow rift which had cracked the ground between mother and son after the birth of the Tsarevitch had split into a chasm. For the first time Nicky had rebuffed her with harsh words.

When his Imperial Majesty the Commander in Chief called upon his mother before her departure, the coldness of his manner pained those who loved the Dowager Empress. Some asserted that he was actually rude to her in the presence of a number of people.

For the first time since Marie Fedorovna had traversed Germany on the eve of war her magnificent imperial train, glistening and newly painted over the bruises inflicted in Berlin, glided arrogantly from the railway sheds. And as the Dowager Empress walked across the station platform, leading the smallest staff which had ever followed her, and the lofty station roof rang with the clatter of thousands of morose, ambling soldiers who ignored her advance, she must have seen the gallant train she had so loved as yet another monstrous mockery in her life. She would never give up Nicky in her heart. But at last she was abandoning him in the flesh. She left without hope, obsessed with the conviction that she had looked on her beloved Anitch-koff for the last time and that some fearful catastrophe lay ahead, from which it was beyond her power to save either Nicky or Russia.

Holy Russia was indeed a prey to strange powers in the closing months of 1915. Even while the Dowager Empress was settling into the small palace at Kiev with Olga, Alicky was writing to Nicky at G.H.Q., Mohilev: "All my trust lies in our Friend [Rasputin], who thinks only of you, and Baby [the Tsarevitch] and Russia. Guided by him we shall win through." That December the *Staretz* with the flaming eyes was able to bring the Empress even more firmly under his thrall. The Emperor had taken the Tsarevitch with him to Mohilev, since it was thought that frequent photographs of the little boy in uniform among the generals would further inspire the withering armies. But just before Christmas Alexis broke a blood vessel in his nose after a violent fit of sneezing. Two days later the Emperor appeared at Tsarkoe Selo with "Baby," paper-white and still bleeding, held upright in a chair. The *Staretz* came, he prayed, he touched the nose of the frightened little boy and the bleeding stopped.

But for every fresh disciple made by Rasputin, now that he was growing into the national ghoul—the Bad Man of Russia at last embodied in the flesh of one being—he created a thousand bitter enemies; not only against himself but against the powerful Empress whom he controlled. Among those enemies, already beginning to watch the activities of Rasputin with cold hatred, was young Prince Youssoupoff, who, originally exempted from military service as an only son, was about to join the Imperial Pages Corps to train for a Guard commission. His military duties would hold him in the capital for another year, during which space he would see and learn enough to bring a rather gentle nature to a grim and terrible decision.

At Kiev the Dowager Empress lived quietly in her little palace beside the river. Hers was the most honored name in Russia, and the news of her forthcoming arrival had given immense satisfaction to the citizens of Kiev. They had gathered to give her a stirring welcome at the station. She was not much seen during the winter, but when the spring came she drove out every afternoon in an open carriage through the city streets into the countryside. Everybody had a wave and a smile for her, including the groups of crippled soldiers who filled the streets. Olga spent most of her time at her hospital, but she returned to her mother for meals. They were out of things at Kiev; but whenever Marie Fedorovna heard that anybody had arrived from Petrograd (Petersburg was renamed Petrograd in 1914) she sent to them to come to the palace and she cross-questioned them eagerly. Her household were aware that she did not often hear from the Emperor now, and that when she did she never opened his letters before others but retired to her bedroom. Afterward, she was always sad for some time. The handwriting of the Empress was seldom seen, but Alexis, who was back at Mohilev among the generals, wrote often to his grandmother.

In the late spring of 1916 Grand Duke Alexander moved his Air H.Q. to Kiev, and she was delighted to see Sandro again— more especially because he was able to give her much news from the west. He frequently had to visit Mohilev, and often went on to Petrograd. His time was fully occupied, but he always came to lunch with his mother-in-law on Sundays. After lunch they adjourned to Marie Fedorovna's sitting room and discussed the developments of the week. Olga often had her contribution, too, for she heard much at the hospital. If Sandro had been to Mohilev the Dowager Empress would listen with tense anxiety while he told her all he knew of Nicky.

Even in 1916, when the Dowager Empress was in virtual retirement, she was a figure of national significance, and when the Crown Prince of Japan visited Russia in the late summer he found that he was expected to depart to a distant province of the Empire solely to call upon her. Prince Nicholas of Greece, when he came to Petrograd on an important political mission for his brother King Constantine, likewise journeyed to Kiev to pay his respects to her. Nicky did not visit his mother at Kiev until November. His stay was brief, and their relations together

were subdued but affectionate. It was the last time she saw him
as Emperor.

There was at that time a growing body of opinion among patriotic Russians, especially in the services and not excluding
some members of the imperial family, that Nicholas II ought to
be deposed and another put in his place, if the war was to be
carried on to victory. And it is now known that the British Government of the day, frightened by the power of the Empress and
the "peace party," believed that only by this means could Russia
be kept in the war on the Allied side, and had given instructions
to the British Ambassador to feel his way toward this.

Hate for Rasputin had become a mania in Russia in the latter
months of 1916. Soldiers in the trenches talked of this mysterious
phantom figure as if he were a fiend with supernatural powers
sent by the Evil One to overthrow Russia. In Petrograd his flat
was guarded night and day by secret-police agents, and the Empress had implored the *Staretz* not to venture abroad without his
guards. But he himself was fearless in this respect, believing
perhaps that he was immortal, and it frequently suited him to
evade his shadows, which was to be his undoing.

All over the fashionable parts of Petrograd Rasputin, dressed
now like a rich peasant in embroidered blue silk shirt and baggy
velvet trousers over shining top boots, mingled his prayer ses-
sions with boastings and braggings about his high position, his
powerful connections, his resolve to save Russia with God's
guidance. His enemies declared that he was in direct communication with German agents in Sweden and possibly in the capital, and that he received German pay.

The Germans were, in fact, at that moment working toward
one of two objects in Russia. Either Russia was to be taken out
of the war by her "peace party," or an internal revolution was
to destroy her in the rear, and to this end exiled Russian revolutionaries supplied with German funds were being smuggled back
into the country.

Grand Duke Alexander returning from Petrograd and Mohilev
in December had gloomy news to tell the Dowager Empress.
All kinds of wild rumors had reached Kiev about the Emperor,

and she questioned him about these. Was it true that Nicky was drinking himself to death? Was it true that a Mongolian medicine-man was keeping him alive with strange Tibetan drugs? Sandro admitted that Nicky was taking drugs. He seemed to be "drifting—gazing out of windows." Sandro had remonstrated with him, explaining the gravity of the situation, urging him to take action, complaining that he no longer seemed to listen to his "real friends."

"I believe in no one but my wife!" he had snapped suddenly, growing pale; but later he had let slip words which hinted that he had no faith in her either.

In Petrograd the male factory workers had been called to the colors. Dirty, unbuttoned recruits with caps on the backs of their heads slouched about the pavements, refusing to salute officers and pushing generals into the road. The authorities were so frightened of the factory soldiers that they dared not send them among the troops at the front and were keeping them as the garrison of Petrograd. Peculiar sentimental films of foreign origin with blatant revolutionary themes were exhibited in cinemas all over the capital, and officers returning from the front were staggered to see general officers and their ladies lazily watching these childish screen plays, while the cheaper seats cheered the working-class heroes and heroines and hissed the villains, who were always aristocrats, generals, factory managers.

It was not the least of the ironies in the last days of Imperial Russia that, while confusion reigned at home, the armies at the front had been brought into good fettle, well supplied, well led, and in busy preparation for the major offensive which had been promised them.

We must return to Kiev, where one moonlit night with the snow shining on the ground a little party came to a small and aged chapel on the city outskirts to celebrate a wedding. It consisted of Grand Duchess Olga in her white hospital uniform, Colonel Koulikovsky of the Akhtyrsky Hussars, the man who was to be her second husband, the Dowager Empress, Grand Duke Alexander, two hospital nurses and four fellow-officers of the bridegroom. No imperial grand duchess in Russian history had ever enjoyed so peaceful a wedding as did Olga in the dim candlelight of that shabby chapel, and probably none ever loved the memory of her wedding day so well. There had been much melancholy in Olga's life, for all her cheerfulness and unfailing good-nature to others, and her mother and her cousin Sandro were glad to see her happy at last.

On the morning of December 18, 1916, an item in the morning newspapers caused a sensation throughout Russia. *Rasputin the Staretz had vanished.* On the night of the 16th he had not slept in his bed, though his guards had imagined he was in his flat. He had not returned. *It was believed he had been murdered and that members of the imperial family were involved.*

The rumor of Rasputin's murder had flown from mouth to mouth in Petrograd on the previous day, and the story went further than the newspapers. The police were said to know the murderers—Prince Felix Youssoupoff and the Grand Duke Dmitri, the Emperor's ward.

Some traveler brought the Petrograd story to Kiev. Hearing shouting, cheering, clapping in the streets, Grand Duke Alexander sent to inquire the reason. Apparently he instantly accepted the rumor as the truth, including the names of the alleged murderers. He rushed off to the Dowager Empress.

For a moment Marie Fedorovna seemed scarcely to understand his words. Then she gasped, *"No—no—no!"* in horror, a frequent expression of hers in moments of stress. Felix Youssoupoff was the husband of her adored granddaughter, and Dmitri was almost a grandson to her.

Nevertheless, a kind of horrible, shameful exultation began to spread in the Dowager Empress because of this terrible deed. It was heroic, tremendous, it might be the salvation of Nicky, of Alicky, of the Romanoffs, of Russia. It was a glory of self-sacrifice on the part of Felix and Dmitri.

On the evening of December 16 one of the weirdest and most macabre events in the last days of Imperial Russia had been enacted in the Moika palace.

Felix Youssoupoff had lured Rasputin to a basement room in his palace on the pretext of meeting a certain lady. Upstairs waited Dmitri and two confederates. Youssoupoff, alone in the dim basement with the *Staretz*, had sung and played his guitar while his guest sat awaiting the lady and greedily feasting on little Russian cakes stuffed with strychnine, washed down with poisoned Crimean wine. Time passed, but the *Staretz* showed no signs of distress.

At last Youssoupoff, panic-stricken lest he was truly faced by the supernatural, drew a revolver and fired at the heart of the *Staretz*. Rasputin crumpled backward and lay motionless.

Felix had fled upstairs, but later, while his friends went for a car, he returned to the basement and bent over the corpse. Rasputin rose up at him with a bestial howl. "The reincarnation of Satan himself held me in his clutches!" wrote Youssopoff many years later.

Then followed the escape of the dying Rasputin, staggering, crawling, growling like a wolf, through the courtyard door in the spiral staircase, which Felix knew he had locked.

The others had returned and at the noise rushed down to the basement. Across the snow ran the terrified assassins, scouring the dark courtyard, shooting frantically at their floundering victim when they saw him, till he died at last behind a mound of snow.

An inquisitive policeman had approached them. One of them hysterically boasted of what they had done. The others were only half-hearted in offering excuses for the shooting. The policeman left them. He had not seen the corpse. Felix collapsed and fainted. The others had taken Rasputin and dropped him over a bridge into a hole in the frozen Neva.

The body of the *Staretz* came up from the ice into a patch of open water on New Year's Day. In the darkness of the following morning the Emperor, who had returned from Mohilev for Christmas, the Empress and Madame Vyrouboff attended the secret burial of Rasputin on a lonely plot of ground in Tsarkoe Selo park, where it was later intended to build a chapel in his memory.

It was from that hour that Empress Alicky ceased being a self-obsessed neurotic and became a heroine until her grim death in the cellar at Ekaterinberg eighteen months later. The blow inflicted by the death of "our dear martyr," as she ever afterward called Grigori Rasputin, was crushing, devastating. Firstly it seemed to her a death sentence to "Baby." Secondly, she firmly believed that the prophecy of the *Staretz* would come true— *"If I go, all of you will perish with me."*

The murderers were never brought to justice, although the Empress in her first cold rage had demanded their execution. Indeed, so popular were they that Prince Youssoupoff was actually offered the crown of Russia in the first days of the Revolution, when Russia lacked an Emperor. Banishment from the capital, the only penalty inflicted, was a farce in the disturbed conditions of the time. Their patriotic action had come too late: far from saving Russia they had paved the way for revolution.

The hour of revolution struck quite unexpectedly. It came on March 12, 1917, when the striking factory workers poured across the Neva bridges. The garrison of Petrograd and the Cossacks called out to meet them joined with the mob, striking down their officers and murdering every policeman who resisted. Shops were looted. Houses went up in flames all over the wealthy quarter. Epaulets were ripped from the shoulders of every officer who did not wear a red bow. A mass of mutinous troops and armed factory workers set off for Tsarkoe Selo Palace.

Suddenly, for the first time since Empress Alicky had come to Russia, she appeared to those around her as a calm, courageous figure. Many at Tsarkoe Selo were plainly losing their heads as news of the approaching rebels was brought in. After darkness had fallen the Empress, wrapped in a cloak, passed along the lines of fortified posts at the courtyard wall of the Palace, calling upon the guardsmen not to open fire first on the mutineers, whose drunken shouts sounded from all directions outside.

The distant sky glowed with the fires of Petrograd, and soon the night skies of the whole of western Russia would be alight. Where were the troops hurrying to relieve Petrograd? Three quarters had vanished on the way. The other quarter appeared and joined the rebels. The Cossacks of the Household were disloyal. The Imperial Guard regiments were shooting their officers and electing others in their place. The Empress, ignorant of the fate of her husband, was placed under arrest at Tsarkoe Selo.

Around G.H.Q. at Mohilev the troops were orderly. Only rumors disturbed the calm. The Emperor set out by train for Petrograd. With every mile the signs of revolution grew plainer. At Dno the imperial train was stopped and diverted to Pskov. There the line was closed, and representatives of Kerensky's Provisional Socialist Government, formed by the Soviet of Workmen's and Soldiers' Representatives, met him.

Nicholas II abdicated the same day. The pressure put upon him that day was not heavy. It was almost half-hearted. Everything was in a state of confusion. The abdication was the feeble act of a feeble man. His father would probably have refused, and mastered the situation. But Nicky was worn out; he had suffered enough.

—Not wishing to be parted from Our beloved son, we bequeath Our heritage to Our brother, the Grand Duke Michael Alexandrovitch, and we give him Our blessing on His accession to the Throne. We urge Him to govern Russia in close communion with the Representatives of the Nation, and to swear inviolable allegiance to them in Our beloved country's name.

In crude but expressive modern slang Nicholas II had "tossed the buck." Mischa, the bravest of the brave among his Don Cossacks, was not bold enough for this. To his brother's honest amazement he refused the crown. In the hour of that refusal modern Russia was born, for nobody but Michael possessed sufficient Romanoff prestige to be an effective rallying-point for the powerful forces of Old Russia. Michael created the political vacuum, the Socialists struggled to fill it, and Lenin arrived from Germany to turn the Bad Man of Russia into a bloodthirsty Bolshevik.

What was to happen to the Emperor? That was a headache for the Provisional Government. Themselves moderate intellectuals for the most part, they wished him no harm, but there were plenty of others who, remembering the past, did so. The Emperor had expressed the embarrassing resolve to stay on his native soil, to live among the people to whom he had been the Autocrat for twenty-three years. It was an indication of how falsely Nicholas II had assessed himself, for even among foreigners his record was so black that when King George V offered refuge to the exiled Emperor and his family, the Labor Party leaders declared unhesitatingly that the workers of Britain would not tolerate in their midst "the blood-stained Russian tyrant"—an action toward an exiled ruler unique in British history.

For the moment the Emperor was to join the Empress in arrest at Tsarkoe Selo, but first he was given permission to return to Mohilev to collect his possessions and bid farewell to his staff officers and the military representatives of the Allies, for at G.H.Q. Nicholas had made many good friends.

A telegram came to the palace by the river at Kiev. Could the Dowager Empress meet the Emperor at Mohilev as soon as possible?

That same afternoon she set off in her train for Mohilev, accompanied by Grand Duke Alexander. They were shocked, stunned, and they glared at one another in speechless dismay. Marie Fedorovna did not really understand what had happened. She had heard of the Emperor's Manifesto of Abdication. But she could not believe that Nicky, with millions of loyal troops at the front, could have done so weak and cowardly a thing. She had been told, also, that Mischa had refused to take Nicky's place as Emperor. If the abdication was a fact, and Mischa had actually done this, then it seemed to her that her youngest son, whom she believed a hero, had acted treacherously to them all, like a mean wretch, worse than Nicky.

The imperial train of the Dowager Empress chugged into Mohilev station. The "Emperor's Platform" was empty but for a few guards and officials. Groups of soldiers on the other platforms smoked and watched the ornate train with curiosity. A car drew up outside the station. The Emperor appeared, walking toward his mother's train. His uniform was always waisted, he had a good military figure, he liked the cap at an angle. His pace was almost jaunty. But his face was pale and drawn as he answered the soldierly greeting of the Cossacks in the doorway. The troops were watching, sitting and lolling; few had stiffened or saluted.

Nicky went in to his mother. They were alone. Two hours passed. Sandro was sent for. "When I was invited to join them, she [the Dowager Empress] sat in a chair sobbing aloud, while he stood motionless, looking at his feet and, of course, smoking. We embraced. I did not know what to say."

There was a big luncheon on the train. Generals and staff officers attended. It was a nightmare, and the Dowager Empress wept all the time. Like Sandro, nobody knew what to say.

Two days of painful farewell ceremonies passed at Mohilev. There were generals who wept, adjutants who wept, H.Q. clerks who wept, and were studiedly polite and kind to the Emperor. But none begged him to rescind his decision. It would be better without him. Each night lights blazed from the uncurtained windows of the Dowager Empress's train. There were electric bulbs on the outside, too. The illumination stood out in the darkness over Mohilev with the challenging color of a fairground, and a sniper's shot from the alleyways of that morose, bewildered town might well have shattered the glowing glass, for revolutionary agents were becoming obvious among the soldiers. Were those unflinching imperial lights a last pathetic gesture by the Dowager Empress to those who were witnessing the shame of Nicholas II?

The third, the last, day at Mohilev dawned bleakly. The last strained military farewells had been muttered. The bowings, salutings, the chanted greetings were over for ever. Nicky had done with Empire. It was even possible to detect a kind of boyish holiday look in his eyes as he lunched with his mother in the train. And yet—where was he going from there? Where, indeed, were any of them going? Marie Fedorovna could scarcely speak. Sandro, as during the whole of that Mohilev visit, did not know what to say. Nicky was "trying to cheer up his mother—he was expecting to see her 'soon.'" She begged him to go to England. He shook his head uncertainly. Naturally, neither gave a thought to the feelings of the British workers.

Opposite stood the train waiting to carry the Emperor to Petrograd and captivity, to his wife and children. They came to tell him it was time to depart, and Nicky rose with fleeting smile, a tiny shrug. He kissed his mother desperately, "covering her face with kisses." Then, briskly and with well-tilted cap, the Emperor crossed to his own train, from which the imperial double-eagle insignia had been ripped.

The Emperor's train whistled, gliding slowly from the platform. A forlorn figure, feebly waving a cap, gazed from the big window of the imperial saloon toward his mother, "his expression infinitely sad." The platform was empty.

The thunder of belching steam gave way to the sound of rising grief in the Dowager Empress's saloon, and Sandro stood helplessly watching as Marie Fedorovna cried unrestrainedly. Yet even now there was the ghost of a girl in that collapsed and trembling elderly form.

She would never see Nicky again.

CHAPTER XVI

Revolution—Terror, Defiance and Tragedy in the Crimea

IN MAY an imperial party had collected at Ay Todor, a big white sugar-cake villa smothered in roses and wistaria, with gardens running down to the shores of the Black Sea. Among those who had reached the Crimea were the Dowager Empress, Grand Duke Alexander and Grand Duchess Zenia, their six sons, Prince Felix Youssoupoff, his father and mother and his wife Irina, Grand Duchess Olga and her husband Colonel Koulikovsky. The party, with a few faithful members of their suites and old servants, made a full household.

It had only been with difficulty that Marie Fedorovna had been persuaded to abandon Kiev. There, as in all the big towns, even on the shores of the Crimea, trouble was brewing; but she had lingered stubbornly, believing that one day Nicky might send for her and that she could reach him more easily from Kiev.

Nicky and Alicky and their family were still close prisoners at Tsarkoe Selo. We know from Baroness Buxhoeveden, who was with them, that they daily underwent every kind of cruel insult, humiliation and pointless restriction which their dirty and undisciplined guards could devise. If the Empress opened an upper window for air the sentry, lolling in his cushioned armchair below, swore at her and, raising his rifle off his knees, threatened to shoot if he saw her again. If the imperial family were escorted down to the park for exercise, the off-duty guard slouched out to watch them, making loud, ribald remarks about the Empress and the young Grand Duchesses.

All this they were bearing with extraordinary courage, patience and dignity. So much was this the case that in time their brutal-looking guards were impressed. They rudely hailed them as "Comrades of the Revolution" and brusquely ordered them about, but little attempts at kindness became perceptible.

Only one letter ever came out of Tsarkoe Selo and reached Ay Todor. It was from Nicky to his mother. It had been written at the direction of Minister Kerensky himself, who apparently had always been an intense admirer of the Dowager Empress. It was hoped at Ay Todor that Nicky's letter was the first of many, and joy prevailed; but after that came eternal silence.

Peace reigned around Ay Todor as the hot days of summer began, and at first as they took their meals in the beautiful shady gardens and wandered by the sea, it was difficult to believe that they were not enjoying one of the old Crimean holidays. Outside the grounds the peasants had not changed, but reports began to reach them of the butchery of "enemies of the Revolution," which had started under the terrible commissars in many of the provincial towns. As yet the insatiable greed for human slaughter had not gripped these commissars, and killings were hot-blooded and casual. It was still a matter of luck in Russia whether you lived or died. You might travel quite freely dressed in a good suit on the railways, packed in suffocating proximity to the filthiest *komrad* soldiers and sailors, and nobody would notice you in the stinking throng. But there was always the chance that some fanatic might take a dislike to you, and your corpse might be dropped out of the carriage window. Even a general's uniform, minus epaulets or with red bows, did not condemn you.

The men of the Ay Todor party traveled several times to Petrograd on family business, and none molested or questioned them. In the capital, sentries had been set over the chief imperial palaces, but these were not averse to a tip from a friendly grand duke who wished to enter. In the lesser palaces you might join the casual treasure-seekers and collect such of your possessions as remained.

In many of the palaces members of the imperial family had hidden jewels and money. Sometimes they triumphantly returned after a visit with these. Sometimes, having satisfied themselves that their caches were still undiscovered, they preferred to leave them undisturbed in hopes that better times would return.

One day Felix Youssoupoff arrived back at Ay Todor from Petrograd and handed the Dowager Empress a parcel. She opened it, and there, folded small, was a large painted canvas of Alexander III. He had walked into the Anitchkoff and cut it from the frame. It was her favorite portrait of Sasha. Her unbounded joy at the sight of it made it easier for him to break the news that the hiding-place where many of her jewels had been placed was empty. But he had at least discovered their whereabouts. Marauders had not taken them. Agents of the Provisional Government had found the jewels, and they had been stored in Moscow.

Nobody around Ay Todor looked askance when the big imperial cars slipped through the countryside, bearing the old flags with a crown and the Romanoff two-headed eagles on the doors. A kind of imperial twilight seemed to exist there. But one summer night they awoke at Ay Todor as heavily armed sailors trod into the bedrooms. A commissar led the invaders into the room occupied by the Dowager Empress.

Ignoring the figure in the bed, the sailors started immediately to pull out drawers and tear open cupboards, tossing the contents on the floor and kicking things apart with their boots to examine the items. The commissar stood regarding the Dowager Empress, who had pulled the bedclothes tight about her.

"Out of bed with you, old lady!" he growled roughly. "I'm going to search your bed. You're hiding something, aren't you?"

Above the sheets those eyes, those wonderful eyes of Marie

Fedorovna, which pierced into the souls of men, regarded the chief intruder witheringly.

"I shall not get up. Kindly take your men out of my bedroom."

The man laughed, but nervously, and looked down at the revolver in his hand as if to give himself confidence.

"Who is she?" he snapped at a member of the Ay Todor party who had entered the room.

"Her Majesty the Dowager Empress Marie Fedorovna."

"Well, out of bed, Comrade Marie Fedorovna. D'you hear?"

"I refuse—whatever your authority."

"Get her out of bed," he ordered the sailors. The men were all regarding her with surprise, and nobody moved toward the bed. "You can sit behind the screen while we search, if you like, Comrade Marie Fedorovna," the commissar added more gently.

"Very well, I will get out of bed if you all leave the room."

"Out of the room!" shouted the commissar at his men. "Hurry up, Comrade Marie Fedorovna. You're a bad comrade, I see. You may be sorry for it."

When they returned the Dowager was seated behind the screen. They pulled off the bedclothes, ripped the mattress and the pillows, tore up floorboards and beat the walls for hollow sounds. A sailor who was trying to read letters and papers upside down tossed every document into a sack. On the bedside table was an old Danish bible. This had always had a place beside Marie Fedorovna since she first came to Russia to marry Sasha. It was her most treasured relic of the past. For some reason, the commissar put the bible in his pocket as he walked from the room.

All through the next morning the house was turned upside down from cellar to attic, and many personal possessions disappeared. Alarm clocks were especially favored by the sailors. Everybody in Ay Todor was questioned separately by the commissar and ordered to sign a statement.

The Dowager Empress, who had been at a disadvantage in her nightdress, entered the interrogation room in a mood of scornful recalcitrance. Her examination, which all expected to be the longest, was one of the shortest. She reappeared with a look of triumph. She thought she had got the best of the commissar till the very end. When he had put the statement before her and told her to sign "ex-Empress Marie," she had nodded, taken the pen from him and written *"the widow of Emperor Alexander III,"* before he could stop her. "I left him speechless with rage," she informed them.

When the examinations had ended the commissar approached General Youssoupoff, the father of Felix.

"You people can stay as you are for the present," he said, "all except Marie Fedorovna. She is under arrest and will come along with me. Get her things ready. She has insulted the Provisional Government."

"Don't you think you should make some allowance for her age?" urged General Youssoupoff. "Elderly ladies don't expect armed sailors to burst into their bedrooms in the middle of the night and order them out of bed. She was very much disturbed and excited. Can you blame her? Suppose it had happened to your mother?"

The man shrugged. "Very well," he muttered in the end, "but Comrade Marie Fedorovna had better be careful. Another time she may find that she hasn't insulted such a soft-hearted comrade as I am."

In Petrograd the Bolsheviks were wresting the power from the weak Kerensky Government. Truckloads of shouting soldiers and sailors with banners raced through the streets, knocking down all in their way, while men squatting on the running-boards sniped any passer-by they fancied. Lenin, the magnetic, had appeared out of Germany, haranguing his mass meetings in Petrograd, where few understood a word he said and all cheered him madly. Denikin was taking the field with his White Russians. The bewildered armies at the front were still holding the line against the Germans, who did not trouble to attack them. Across the hills from Ay Todor, at Yalta, the Black Sea Fleet had mutinied, murdering hundreds of officers. Sailors stormed through the port, looting, raping, burning and killing with demented ferocity.

News came to Ay Todor during August that the Emperor and Empress with the family had been taken across Russia to Tobolsk, in far Siberia. Up to then Marie Fedorovna had lived in the hope that one day she would be allowed to see them. Even to her, the prospect seemed less likely now. To some at Ay Todor the report of this news had a sinister ring. It was as if the imperial family were being spirited away. Others suggested that they were safer in Siberia than in the chaos of western Russia, where anything could happen at any moment. It was the latter viewpoint which was stressed to the Dowager Empress to keep her mind at rest.

One day—it was after the Fleet Mutiny—they watched cavalry coming over the hills from the direction of Yalta. They could see the red slogan banners fluttering in the wind, and they nerved themselves against the worst.

The troop, jogging on shaggy horses, which eventually clattered into the Ay Todor courtyard, were the horsemen of nightmare. Sailors' caps and blouses topped cavalry boots and breeches. All bristled with weapons, and several were small boys. Necklaces, brooches, earrings and bangles glittered all over them. Half of them had faces grotesquely powdered and rouged. Hand grenades dangled round their belts. Their white blouses were thick with bloodstains. They announced with brutal guffaws that they were the "naval cavalry." Officially they were a patrol from Yalta; but the deeds of these brigands were a dread legend throughout the district.

It was the presence of Felix Youssoupoff which saved the situation. He went out to them, and the two leaders demanded food and wine for the troop, and ordered him to give them particulars of all persons in the villa. He brought the two men inside, expecting at any moment to be threatened with death if he did not reveal the whereabouts of all valuables on the premises.

One of them asked Youssoupoff his name.

"Did you kill Rasputin?"

He assured them that he was the man. They solemnly drank

his health, exclaiming that nobody need have any fear in this house, whoever they were.

Astonishment reigned in the upper rooms at Ay Todor as Felix Youssoupoff was heard singing to his guitar. The horses were tied up outside, and the whole blood-stained band had trooped into Ay Todor. The songs of Felix soon gave way to wild choruses. Several hours of uproar followed before the naval cavalry staggered out to their horses. Their host shook hands all round, the banners were raised aloft and the weird troop trotted away from Ay Todor.

With the autumn the Bolsheviks were in power, and for the first time a mixed guard of soldiers and sailors came as a permanent part of the imperial establishment at Ay Todor. The family lived dully from day to day, trying as far as possible to avoid offending their surly and disheveled guards, who evidently regarded them, especially the Dowager Empress, with great curiosity. In their chief jailer they were lucky. Commissar Zadorozny was a huge sailor. His face was as rough and cruel as his speech when his men were around, but alone with any of his prisoners Zadorozny's expression grew more kindly and he did what he could for them.

Senior Commissar Spiro arrived one morning with his squad and sharply demanded a roll-call assembly of the household in the hall. The party lined up. Only the Dowager Empress was missing. "Fetch her," growled Spiro at one of the servants. Everybody stood in the silent hall while Spiro scowled at them and tapped his heel impatiently.

The Dowager Empress appeared at the top of the stairs. She did not descend. She fixed Spiro with an angry glare and waited till he looked up. Then she turned her back and walked off to her room. For a moment it seemed that Commissar Spiro would explode. He shot toward the foot of the stairs as if a powerful spring had impelled him, and his hand even went to the open holster of his revolver.

They trembled for Marie Fedorovna—trembled, indeed, lest the commissar might avenge the insult upon them all. The guards were watching Spiro expectantly with grins on their faces. He wheeled round, strode to the middle of the hall and brusquely called the roll. He moved down the line and spat out a few questions. Then he shouted at his men and walked out of Ay Todor.

In February 1918 the Ay Todor party was broken up. The Dowager Empress, Grand Duke Alexander and Zenia, Grand Duke Nicholas and his wife were to go into detention at Dulber, a large nearby villa. There were reasons for this. Ay Todor lay roughly halfway between Sebastopol and Yalta, and the district soviets of both places claimed jurisdiction over the imperial party. A motion had been passed at Yalta for the immediate execution of the Dowager Empress and those who were to go with her to Dulber. The move was ordered by the Sebastopol Soviet, which up to that time had provided the Ay Todor guard. It had been agreed by the Sebastopol Soviet that the prisoners should not be killed unless Lenin himself sent an order for their extermination. Dulber, unlike Ay Todor, was encircled by a high, thick wall, and could easily be defended from all points of the compass by machine-gun nests. The Yalta men were not to be allowed to have them.

Those who remained at Ay Todor were practically free and were able to move in the district; but none of them was to be allowed to visit Dulber. An original plan, however, was soon invented for daily communication with the inmates of Dulber.

The guards at Dulber had no objection to Irina, the two-year-old daughter of Prince Youssoupoff, visiting the fortress villa. Irina could call upon her great-grandmother the Dowager Empress whenever she liked. Each morning the nursemaid wheeled Irina in her pram to the sandbagged gates of Dulber. The two-year-old was lifted down, and thanked the guard politely when the gate was swung open. She passed through and walked alone up to the villa, with a letter pinned inside her coat. She returned bearing the reply in the same manner, bid the sentries good-bye at the gate and resumed her place in the pram.

The gigantic sailor Zadorozny and his men had moved to Dulber with the prisoners, and in March 1918 he was undoubtedly responsible for saving their lives. On March 18 the Bolshevist

Government signed the Treaty of Brest Litovsk. This ended the war with Germany and among other things gave the Germans the right to occupy the Crimea.

The Yalta Soviet, frantic to get possession of the imperial prisoners before the Germans arrived and rescued them, sent a strong company of sailors to Dulber, bearing what appeared to be a genuine warrant from the central government entitling them to custody.

Zadorozny refused to recognize this warrant, believing it a forgery, and declared he would have to consult the Sebastopol Soviet. The parley had taken place with the Dulber gates closed, and the angry Yalta party threatened to smash them down. Zadorozny brought his machine guns to bear. The Yalta company exposed before the gates would be torn to pieces in a few minutes if the guns opened fire. They had no doubt that Zadorozny really intended to do so.

The Yalta sailors jumped into their trucks and, shouting, "We'll be back tomorrow. Look out for yourselves!" they roared away toward Yalta.

Their meaning was plain enough to Zadorozny: tomorrow an overwhelming force, probably with artillery, would assault Dulber.

Zadorozny must get reinforcements quickly, and he would have to go personally to Sebastopol to explain things to the Soviet. Even so, he did not know what force they could scrape together by the following morning. Yalta was better off: they had crowds of sailors. Moreover, the Yalta road was much straighter and easier than the long, twisting Sebastopol road. The chances were that the Yalta attackers could reach Dulber and secure their prisoners before he arrived back with Sebastopol reinforcements.

At Dulber the prisoners were but vaguely aware how their fate hung in the balance, and Zadorozny, who was by this time on friendly terms with them, did not reveal the truth. They knew that something was amiss, and that Zadorozny had to hurry to Sebastopol, leaving them in charge of his ruffians, who were similarly well disposed toward them.

It was an anxious time at Ay Todor; for there they had learned from the Dulber guards how desperate things were, and from dawn on the following morning they stood on the high turrets of Ay Todor. From there they scanned the white roads to Yalta and Sebastopol, waiting for the sight of distant dust clouds. For every one minute they hopefully watched the empty Sebastopol road, they nervously peered for three down the Yalta road. In their hearts they were sure that dust would rise first on the Yalta road. There was nothing they could do. They knew that the Dulber garrison could not withstand a mass attack, and could only pray that at worst the Sebastopol party would catch the Yalta men while still at Dulber, or on the way back to Yalta; but that would mean a dangerous pitched battle and anything might happen to the captives.

The time drew on, and the sun shone brightly on the two bare ribbons of road. A speck was moving on the Sebastopol road. It turned into a long dust cloud, whirling upward, sliding swiftly toward them. A big column of armored trucks bristling with troops swept past the gardens of Ay Todor toward Dulber. There was something strange, orderly-looking, about the passing vehicles which puzzled them.

Dulber was saved—but it was not the Sebastopol men who had saved it. It was the advance party of German troops, who were occupying the Crimea.

The Germans treated the Dowager Empress—indeed, all the imperial Russians—with great courtesy. They were set free and might come and go as they pleased. When the giant Zadorozny returned he was arrested, and it was the German intention to hang him and his unkempt-looking squad. With astonishment they listened to the released captives speaking of these desperadoes in the highest terms and begging for their freedom. Zadorozny and his men were released and took a tearful departure —nor, according to Prince Youssoupoff, were the tears all on the side of the liberated guards.

That summer the Dowager Empress and the Dulber party moved to Harrax, another of those sugar-cake imperial villas, belonging to one of Grand Duke Alexander's brothers. Harrax was nearer Sebastopol, and as it turned out it was just as well that this was the case.

Meanwhile in April 1918 the Emperor and Empress had been forced to make another journey. Their meager but more or less comfortable life at Tobolsk was broken up abruptly by an order for the imperial family to depart for an unknown destination.

But Tsarevitch Alexis was too sick to be moved. Even the Bolsheviks agreed about that. The Empress might stay or go, as she pleased. The Emperor must leave immediately.

It was a nightmare decision for Alicky. Should she allow Nicky to go alone? Should she abandon the weakling son for whom she had suffered so bitterly and striven so recklessly? Her heart troubled her. She fell into a state of collapse. She rallied and grew frantic. Perhaps all of them, even the rough guards and she herself, were astonished when she declared that she would accompany her husband. It was agreed that Marie should leave with her parents. Olga, Tatiana and Anastasia were to stay with Alexis till he recovered.

The mystery of this hasty move, which was to take them only to another place in the Urals, has never been explained. They went by orders from Petrograd, brought by a mounted courier with a large escort. Their journey, which carried them over many circuitous miles in a seatless and jolting peasant cart, ended at Ekaterinburg. Some say that their intended destination had been Moscow, but that a suspected attempt at rescue on the road by loyal army officers caused their frightened guards to stop at Ekaterinburg.

At Ekaterinburg they were lodged in a low white house in the Russian style, requisitioned from a wealthy engineer called Ipatieff. A high, close-set wooden stockade hid the new inmates from the curious townspeople. With the Emperor, the Empress and Marie were the physician Dr. Botkin, the maid Anna Demidovna and two menservants. From the outset the commissars and soldiers treated them with a cold harshness which had not been used at Tobolsk.

By June the whole imperial family was together at Ekaterinburg. Alexis was still weak. Several faithful members of the suite had been allowed to travel by train from Tobolsk; but they never entered the house of Ipatieff. Either they were arrested at Ekaterinburg station and disappeared forever, or, as in the case of Baroness Buxhoeveden, they were permitted to find lodgings in the town in the hope of one day seeing the imperial family. Alicky and her daughters had at this time a look almost of destitution, being clad in odd second-hand garments sent in by wellwishers.

It was on June 4 that the commissar and ten soldiers of the interior guard were dismissed for softness and lack of vigilance. Commissar Yiourovsky, tall, dark and sinister, with eight factory soldiers arrived to take their place. The atmosphere in Ipatieff's house changed within the hour. Shouting, sneers and snarls replaced the curt orders of the former guardians. The new interior guards were militant and ferocious Bolsheviks. Such men as they now controlled Russia.

Every door was removed from the house of Ipatieff. The men watched the Empress and her daughters even in the bathroom. A lounging soldier observed the imperial ladies in the bedroom, where all slept together with the Emperor and Alexis. Cruel jests and barbarous and filthy insults were so incessant that the ladies ceased to hear them. Eyes constantly glared and leered at them. In the dining room the guard picked food off their plates with dirty fingers. The rooms stank of dirty feet and dirty bodies and the fumes of vodka.

The family faced their daily ordeal with courage and patience, even with cheerfulness. This is known not only from the many penciled scribbles sent out by the Empress to those who lingered in Ekaterinburg, which, strangely enough, the servants were allowed to deliver uncensored, but also from her diary, which was found afterward. The diary entries show a serenity and calmness of spirit quite foreign to Empress Alicky of earlier days. Clearly Alicky had found herself at last and was deriving true solace from the religion which had pursued and harried her.

Many details are known of the grim drama enacted within that house screened off from the world up to the moment when the imperial corpses sprawled in the dark cellar soon after midnight of July 16, with those mysterious messages scrawled above them on the bullet-torn wall. *That same night Belshazzar was murdered by his servants,* ran the top one in German, and below in Hebrew another declared, *Here was slain the Head of the Church and State. The order has been obeyed.*

Who gave the "order"? It must have been a macabre scene, indeed, as one who had obeyed the "order" stood over the human welter below and wrote on that wall. The Bolshevist Government appears to have been ignorant of the killings till they were accomplished. In the middle of July Kolchak's White Army was advancing rapidly on Ekaterinburg, and the guards at Ipatieff's house must have been terrified of being caught with the imperial prisoners.

Nicholas Sokoloff, the examining official appointed after Kolchak's occupation of Ekaterinburg, elicited many details of the murders from several of the assassins who were brought before him, and the facts were later transmitted from Harbin to Paris. But it was General P. N. Krassnoff, himself in the White Army, who gave the world the most vivid and terrible description of the night of July 16 at the house of Ipatieff in his monumental four-volume work *From the Two-Headed Eagle to the Red Flag,* which in 1923 caused a continental sensation.

On the night of July 16 the hot summer air was still and stifling. The Empress, sitting in her bed, penciled the last words in her diary, "Played bezique with N. 10:30 to bed."

There seems to have been a vague idea among the imperial prisoners that Ekaterinburg was only a passing phase and that at any time they might be moved to some better place. Thus it was not a total surprise when they all awoke at midnight to see Commissar Yiourovsky standing in the bedroom.

"Dress! Hurry!" he shouted. "You leave Ekaterinburg immediately."

They tossed back the bedclothes and washed and dressed almost in a mood of gaiety, especially the grand duchesses and Alexis. The commissar was drunk every night and his flaming eyes never left them, but they talked among themselves as if he were not there. They bundled up their tattered possessions and each grand duchess took a pillow for the cart. There was no hope of a carriage.

Botkin, Anna Demidovna and the two men joined them. A curt order came from Yiourovsky. None of them gave a glance at the room they were abandoning. Glad to see the last of it, they groped down the dark stairs as briskly as possible. The Empress stumbled, turning her ankle, and moaned.

The Imperial party paused at the foot of the stairs, peering at the closed front door.

"Down to the basement. Hurry! Follow me," shouted Yiourovsky, taking the lead. The cart evidently had not arrived, and they descended obediently behind him into an air of dank, musty stench, where one lamp burned dimly in a bare room "dirty and uncanny."

The Emperor asked for chairs. Yiourovsky shouted, and a soldier brought down three from above and reascended. The Empress sat down in a chair against the far wall, with Alexis, who was beginning to look exhausted, beside her. Tatiana stood by them, watching her mother and brother anxiously. The third chair was left for the Emperor, but he stood in the middle of the room with Dr. Botkin, staring at the dark door aperture. Olga, Marie and Anastasia leaned against the wall near the door with the silent menservants beside them. Anna Demidovna waited patiently, holding the pillows. Whispers gave way to silence. Yiourovsky was watching them.

Perhaps they had all ceased to expect the arrival of the cart before uproar broke out above and heavy boots started trampling down the basement stairs. Disheveled figures burst out of the darkness. The men of the interior guard were glaring at them. Each man gripped a revolver.

Yiourovsky roared out— "Those who belonged to you wanted to save you. But they did not succeed! We must shoot you—"

He fired and the Emperor dropped on his back, his face a mask of blood. All the guns were firing, with the soldiers shouting and screaming. It was bedlam. Splinters, boarding, dust, chips of stone filled the room. The victims lay in a black pool that shimmered dully. "Only the Tsarevitch and Anastasia moved and moaned horribly," says Krassnoff. "Yiourovsky finished the Tsarevitch." Yakimov, an assassin who was later caught, confessed to unshouldering his rifle and bashing the head of Anastasia. By the state of the floor Sokoloff believed the others had attacked the corpses with bayonets.

After that comes mystery and contradiction. Krassnoff believed in 1923 that the bodies had been dragged out, cut up and burned in benzine. He had heard also of a story that the remains of the imperial family had been thrown down a lonely mine in the forest. Mr. W. Studdart, a Yorkshireman, late of the English Hampshire Regiment, who served with a British military mission at Ekaterinburg in 1920, was given a photograph showing corpses lying in the mud of a drained forest pool, which local peasants declared were those of the imperial family. Studdart states that at that time there was a strong belief in Ekaterinburg that one of the imperial grand duchesses had survived the massacre in the house of Ipatieff. This legend or theory, which is thus established as having existed prior to the first appearance of the alleged Anastasia in the United States, need not be regarded in any way as a confirmation of her story. It might equally well have been the seed from which grew an elaborate imposture.

Perhaps Grand Duke Alexander offered as sane an argument as any upon the problem of the resurrected Anastasia when interviewed by journalists in New York in the 'twenties: "It is not conclusive that no surviving member of the imperial family can recognize this girl, who has undoubtedly suffered. Maybe shock could have obliterated the knowledge of French and English, which once Anastasia spoke so fluently. But I can tell you that the greatest shock in the world could not give a true Russian *a strong Polish accent!*"

The tragic news spread down into the Crimea in September. But the first terrible story concerned not the imperial family but Mischa. This said that Mischa, who had vanished earlier in the year, had been shot in a wood near Perm. It was the truth. The Dowager Empress refused to believe it. "It's nonsense," she cried. "Bolshevist lies!" She really did not believe it and was not in the least distressed. Nor would she ever believe it.

Then the household at Harrax heard of the Soviet communiqué announcing that the bodies of the imperial family had been burned at Ekaterinburg. All shrank from breaking the news to Marie Fedorovna. Perhaps she guessed the truth from the terrified demeanor of the servants and wrested the facts from them. At all events, she startled everybody when she had heard the story. "I don't believe it," she declared. "Those people always lie. Nicky's friends have rescued him. Probably they have all escaped from Russia and the Bolsheviks are trying to hide it."

Few Romanoffs outside the Crimea survived the summer of 1918. In July Grand Duchess Elizabeth, with six other Romanoffs and several of her nuns, was hurled down a mine shaft at Alapaevsk, and it was said that for a time the sound of chanted hymns floated up from the depths. The Grand Dukes George and Nicholas, brothers of Alexander, died violently in the Fortress of Peter and Paul. A third brother, Serge, was murdered elsewhere. The Grand Duke Paul, youngest brother of Alexander III, was so ill that they shot him on a stretcher. Dmitri Constantinovitch, a brother of Queen Olga of Greece, died praying for his executioners. The story was told of Nicholas Michaelovitch that he had been shot hugging his prized Persian cat. Even distant relations of the imperial family were destroyed that summer, whenever they could be discovered, and more than seventy suffered death for their Romanoff blood.

Dmitri, the Emperor's ward, the companion of Felix Youssoupoff at the murder of Rasputin, survived and joined the British troops in Persia. Grand Duke Cyril and his wife Victoria Melita escaped to safety through Finland. Somewhere in the wild Caucasus the once redoubtable Marie Pavlovna, the Grand Duchess Vladimir, lurked in peasant disguise, depending for her life on the kindness of poor Caucasians.

In the summer of 1920 Marie Pavlovna managed to escape from Russia in a steamer packed with ragged and destitute refugees to Venice, and eventually joined her daughter Helen and her son-in-law Nicholas of Greece in their Swiss exile, for the

Greek royal family, too, had been forced into their first exile in 1917 by the Venizilists. Among the little party who greeted Marie Pavlovna beside Lake Constance was eleven-year-old Marina, now Duchess of Kent. The tall and once proud beauty whose court had rivaled that of Marie Fedorovna appeared as she stepped from the train to be a terrible peasant crone, a bent and yellowed skeleton with dull and sunken eyes, carrying a dirty bundle of rags. A few weeks later they buried her at Lausanne.

The sad year reached November and, for many, November 1918 was a month of rejoicing—the Armistice, the end of World War I. There was no jubilation at the imperial villas in the Crimea. The Germans were beginning to evacuate the region and in their place would come the Red Army.

The Allied Fleet steamed into Sebastopol. For the moment the presence of this large fleet made the Romanoffs safe, for the Bolsheviks were not yet ready to give their attention to this area, which was full of refugees from the wholesale exterminations of the Russian bourgeoisie and the landowning classes.

The Crimea remained undisturbed for a few months, and the Romanoffs lived on in a kind of numbness. Then in March 1919 the terrible and victorious Red troops began to move down on the Crimea. All the Romanoffs were now collected at Harrax, and few of them doubted what would happen when the Reds reached them.

On April 7 the Commander of the British fleet, having received instructions from Whitehall, arrived at Harrax. The British royal family offered the Dowager Empress asylum in England. All the imperial Romanoffs were advised to go aboard the British fleet that evening.

"I shall not go," exclaimed the Dowager Empress firmly; "my sons may still be in Russia. I cannot leave until I know. If I go there will be nobody to help them."

Dismay prevailed at Harrax. Sandro, whose word probably had more weight with his mother-in-law than anybody else's, was already abroad, engaged on a fruitless mission to the Allied governments, endeavoring to persuade them that if they did not send large forces to defeat the Red Army before it was too late a terrible thing would appear in Russia which would menace the world.

The position of those with Marie Fedorovna was perplexing and desperate. They understood the emotions which swayed her and they shrank from brutally attacking her illusions. None of them would go without her; yet if they stayed all would perish. The Dowager Empress was, after all, the head of the imperial family. It was she who gave orders, and at present she was adamant that they—or rather she—should remain on Russian soil. Thus things hung in the balance at Harrax on that day.

The situation did not go unappreciated by the polite but impatient Briton who waited upon them. It was he, acting from the impartial standpoint of a foreigner, who in several feverish hours persuaded the Dowager Empress that she must go, if not for her own sake then for that of the others at Harrax. He hinted that if she refused he might be sorely tempted to take her aboard by force since she could only achieve her death by staying. Among the persuasions used—and not the least effective—was the reminder that the day was Grand Duchess Zenia's birthday, and that a death warrant would be a sad birthday present.

Early the following morning they all boarded H.M.S. *Marlborough*. No sooner had they embarked than the news began to spread through the district that the imperial family were leaving Russia. Panic broke out at Yalta, where a large body of refugees had hopefully collected, believing that when danger approached the fleet would evacuate them. Now it appeared that the fleet was abandoning them to their doom.

Thousands of terrified people with their belongings crowded the waterfront at Yalta, pleading with tears to any British officer they saw to save them from the Red troops. But no orders or instructions had envisaged a mass evacuation of this kind. The refugees were regretfully ignored. None who witnessed the horrible scene of terror, with men, women and children wandering about in dazed despair, could ever forget it.

It was the Dowager Empress's granddaughter Irina, Princess Youssoupoff, who came and told her what was said to be taking place at Yalta. Marie Fedorovna sent for the Admiral. She asked him if the report was true. He admitted that it was; but he was without orders.

"You have plenty of room on your ships for these poor Yalta refugees," she said. "Do you understand that if you leave them they will be massacred by the Red soldiers? Either you embark them—or you put me ashore now!"

The Admiral used his discretion. A signal went out, and a number of warships immediately got up steam and left the roads. The feelings of the refugees can be imagined when, having given themselves up for lost, they saw the British warships glide into Yalta and start lowering boats.

As H.M.S. *Marlborough* started on her voyage for England she passed close alongside a steamer packed to the rails with young officer volunteers from the Crimea on their way to join the forlorn hope—the reeling and sorely battered White Army. A little old woman in black, very slender and upright, stood before a group in the bow of the British warship. She was waving a handkerchief, while the tears streamed down her cheeks. Suddenly the men who were going to almost certain death in the cause of Old Russia recognized the Dowager Empress. They stiffened, they saluted, and the silence, which was broken only by the wash of the passing vessels, burst into a roar of the traditional imperial greeting. Then they began to wave madly as to an old friend. There, symbolized by that one small figure, was all that had been best in Imperial Russia. For her it was the last scene—the end of fifty-three years of imperial glory.

$\widehat{G}wo$ $\mathcal{A}ged$ $Sisters$ — $\widehat{G}tvidore,$ the Last $\widehat{G}aded$ Glory

FROM THE SPRING of 1919 onward for several years, the two
aged sisters lived together, and divided the months between
Marlborough House and Sandringham.

Perceptive visitors to either of these royal homes when the
sisters were in residence soon realized on passing the threshold
that they had entered a world of fantasy. They were standing in
a home of ghosts.

Both Queen Alexandra and Dowager Empress Marie Fedorovna of Russia, who had become her guest, were occupied for
much of the time in living in their own pasts. The manner in
which the sisters pursued this end differed: the Dowager Empress, for the most part, journeyed down the years in silence—
that is to say, her mind was frequently on a journey while she
herself was chattering quite brightly about some everyday topic;
but Queen Alexandra really was in the past, and quite often
when talking to a guest addressed him or her by the name of
somebody who had been dead for fifty years. It sometimes appeared that the Dowager Empress was so much aware of her
elder sister's eccentricities as to be irritated, pitying, apologetic,
a little superior in her attitude toward her.

There were still moments when a trick of the light, a chance angle of vision, revealed both sisters with that extraordinary look of youth which until well into their sixties they really had seemed to possess. The Dowager Empress now appeared to have abandoned any conscious effort to achieve this. The youthfulness was simply inherent in her being. Her elder sister was less content to admit the ravages of the years. Queen Alexandra wore a striking auburn wig, which was either not of such a quality as might be expected for the head of a queen, or suffered from lack of care. Yet even Queen Alexandra sometimes laughed when she saw her wig in a mirror. It had a way of going crooked in moments of stress, which was funny, and which clearly annoyed her neat sister. "Is it straight, dear?" the Queen would ask cheerfully, shifting it about on her head.

The sisters had been celebrated for their generosity for many years. They could not bear to send away a visitor to whom they had taken a liking without some gift, which they imagined would be pleasing to them. The Dowager Empress, to whom money had meant nothing since she was nineteen, had been in the habit in Russia of giving parting gifts which were choice and costly by any but Romanoff standards, to recipients who were often astonished and overwhelmed by her generosity. Queen Alexandra, with a more modest purse, had usually given her own prized souvenirs, of which she had many hundreds, good and very bad, in her overburdened rooms, and her gift was as likely to be rubbish as a genuine antique. With Queen Alexandra the gift-giving urge, once used with discrimination, had turned into a mania with old age. The Queen would almost chase embarrassed people with her offerings; no visitor must be allowed to go without something. Nor did any cunning beggar who came to the door at Sandringham go unrewarded if the Queen could escape her aged attendants and reach him undetected.

Both Charlotte Knollys and white-bearded Sir Dighton Probyn did their best to control the generosities of their mistress, and in this the Dowager Empress was often their ally. She sometimes scolded her elder sister severely. It was not that Marie Fedorovna was shocked and scandalized by such wanton giving, as were the two faithful old courtiers. Marie Fedorovna was jealous. She wanted to be a gift-giver too. But, alas, the Dowager Empress had nothing to give. Except for an extremely valuable sealed box of jewels, which her nephew, King George V, held in trust for her—he was a very prudent man—she was destitute, and dependent on the hospitality of her British relations.

In November 1919 the Bolshevist Government, after considerable negotiations with the British Foreign Office, had agreed to send a large consignment of the movable possessions of the Dowager Empress from the Anitchkoff to London. During the worst days of the Revolution the Anitchkoff had been under guard, and a surprising number of valuables were known to have survived at the time when the negotiations were opened.

The advent of the packing cases from Petrograd, so eagerly looked forward to by Marie Fedorovna, turned out to be a tragic fiasco. Eight huge wooden cases, roped and sealed by the Bolshevist governmental seal, were handed over at the Anitchkoff to a British naval officer and, upon arrival in London, were brought for unpacking and checking of contents to the Throne Room at Buckingham Palace. A large party of men had labored up the great staircase under the big boxes, and there could be no doubt that Lenin's officials had packed the goods of the Dowager Empress into the cases with conscientious generosity.

The imposing rank of sealed packing cases, each about 8 ft. by 4 ft., and bruised and grimy from their journey, were probably the most crude and incongruous objects which had ever decorated the magnificent red and gold chamber, and the empty throne, gleaming from under the tall emblazoned canopy, presided over the opening ceremony like some stern and impassive supervisor.

The Dowager Empress was at Sandringham at the time, and—mercifully as it turned out—it had not been thought necessary to bring her to London for the official check. The King had delegated Sir Frederick Ponsonby to take charge of the opening and to draw up a detailed report of the contents for her, and Ponsonby in his turn had thought it prudent in case anything might be amiss to request the presence of the only Bolshevist repre-

sentative then in London to witness the breaking of his government's seals and the unpacking. This individual hovered in a
corner of the Throne Room with an air of surly reluctance.

The elaborate seals were examined, and there could be no
doubt that these had not been tampered with since leaving the
Anitchkoff. The workmen cut the cords and attacked the lid of
the first case. Underneath a covering of sacking was pulled away.
The case was full to the top with rusty fire irons, common pokers,
shovels and tongs, which must have been collected from the
servants' quarters, cellars and workrooms of the palace.

Even then nobody fully anticipated what was to come; seven
great cases remained. They opened the second case. Inside was
harness and saddlery, old, moldy and perished; broken straps
without buckles, burst and torn saddles, scarcely salable even in
the junk market. The third case bore the label, "Books from the
Empress' Library." Marie Fedorovna had been fond of books,
and she had collected many in fine bindings, which she was delighted at the thought of seeing again. The case was tightly
packed with old Russian railway guides, packages of soiled
paper-backed novels and tattered children's books.

Every case held rubbish, not one valuable object among them,
nearly all useless to the Dowager Empress, mostly lacking in
even sentimental appeal. No wonder the Bolshevist official appeared to be on the point of slipping out of the Throne Room
when Ponsonby called him to come and sign the inventory. The
matter would have to be taken up with the Bolshevist Government, and the wretched man visibly shuddered as he glared at
his signature on the document which revealed their perfidy.

When they broke the news to Marie Fedorovna she seemed
stunned at first, scarcely understanding; then she smiled wryly
and said that it was just what she had expected from all she had
heard of the tricks of the Bolsheviks. She went to her room and
was not seen for a long time. She never mentioned her packing
cases from the Anitchkoff again. Some of the goods were sold
for her, but these fetched almost nothing. Strenuous diplomatic
efforts were made to the Bolsheviks to get some redress. All
kinds of excuses and promises of investigation were offered; but

nobody expected any results and their pessimism was justified.

In July 1922 Queen Alexandra gave a garden party for children at Marlborough House, and for the last time she and the Dowager Empress were seen at a function in London. This was Queen Alexandra's farewell to Marlborough House. She was retiring to Sandringham for good, and was already packed up for departure. Only two people present at that last party, old Sir Dighton Probyn and Charlotte Knollys, had attended those celebrated Marlborough House occasions of 1873 when the two lovely sisters, dressed alike, had ravished London. Now the "Beloved Lady tottered about, comically vague and a little strange and disturbing to small children; while Marie Fedorovna, though still quite nimble, had such a sad, tired and haunted look in her glorious eyes that it seemed as if she was always looking round for somebody who might be standing among any group of strangers she saw. And it was quite true: she was searching for people. She was looking for Nicky, for Mischa, Alicky, Olga, Tatiana, Marie, Anastasia, or for a handsome, delicate young man, Tsarevitch Alexis. She knew they had escaped from Russia—possibly to South America or China. They would all turn up one day.

Perhaps the prospect of life in the Sandringham wilds, unrelieved by the annual sojourn in London, frightened the Dowager Empress. Since she was physically in good fettle her spirit, no doubt, had by that time revived from the blows inflicted by the Revolution. Perhaps she was beginning to find that the foibles and eccentricities of her elder sister were growing more tiring to her patience. The companionship of Alix, which she had so constantly longed for in the days when they were parted, was now an uncertain and sometimes a discomforting quantity. The tranquillity of Sandringham was disturbed by bouts of elderly disagreement of a lively character, which fluttered the time-worn inhabitants of the royal home, and which they found themselves listening to with increasing frequency.

The British royal family became aware that the Dowager Empress had begun to talk wistfully of an establishment of her own. Her box of jewels was mentioned longingly in this connection, as well as the name of Hvidore—where, in fact, a fully furnished home, together with many of those cherished mementos and family portraits and groups which Marie Fedorovna loved, had existed empty since before the war. She wanted to go back to Denmark. Perhaps, in a way, Queen Alexandra, who at times was extremely coherent, had decided that it would be better if she and Minnie parted company.

Aunt Minnie had always been loved by members of the British royal family, and a secret family council met and agreed to provide a life pension for the Dowager Empress, which would enable her to live in a fitting manner at Hvidore. Among them King George, Queen Mary, Queen Alexandra and the Princess Victoria arranged to subscribe for her an income of £10,000 a year, out of their own private means. They did not want her to break into her jewel box.

When Marie Fedorovna heard of this decision her delight was unbounded. She brimmed over with excitement. She almost tripped about like a girl, and her eyes glowed as they used to do when she was arranging some grand imperial entertainment. Not only would she be able to have a little court of her own, but she could employ real Russian servants, whom on great occasions she could put into uniforms like the old imperial liveries. In Denmark the exiles would flock to her court from all over the place, which they had not been able to do while she was at Sandringham and Marlborough House. She would be able to entertain them—to hold her Court—to wear her beautiful jewels sometimes and some lovely dresses. Hvidore would be the headquarters—the spiritual home—of exiled Russians.

All this had also been foreseen by her prudent nephew King George V. Even £10,000 would not stretch far enough to cover such a project—certainly not if it was administered by the generous hands of the Dowager Empress. He was very willing to make Aunt Minnie happy and contented in her last days, but he did not want his money to go into the pockets of all the White Russians who called at Hvidore with a good story. He knew that the Continent abounded with Russian exiles who were rascals and impostors, and that these would be the first to reach the doorstep of Hvidore. Even more dangerous, perhaps, would be once decent Russians of high position, known to Marie Fedorovna, whom the burden of misfortune had turned into crafty, greedy and unscrupulous beggars. Free meals, loans and gifts would all be in demand at Hvidore. If the Dowager Empress saw some of her old friends in shabby suits and dresses she would probably buy them new clothes, and as the news spread the shabby brigade would gather.

The whole thing was tragic, pitiful; but Marie Fedorovna could not be allowed to go too far. Left to herself she would be bankrupt in no time, and then she would cheerfully ask what she was to do—how could she help herself? It was because of the poor Russians.

Somebody would have to look after the Dowager Empress's accounts at Hvidore and keep her in order. It would have to be somebody who would be stern and not too sympathetic, somebody of whom she could be a little frightened. King George's first idea was that the ubiquitous Sir Frederick Ponsonby should do this. He would be ideal. Everybody liked him, but you could not get round him.

Sir Frederick felt, when the matter was put to him, that to supervise the household accounts and disbursements of a totally irresponsible lady living in Denmark was beyond his power. But he would arrange things, and keep a watchful eye upon affairs at Hvidore for the King.

As a result Marie Fedorovna's nephew, Prince Axel of Denmark, was asked to nominate a Dane of suitable character who would become Comptroller of the Purse at Hvidore. The Prince chose Captain Andrup, a retired officer of the Danish Navy, with whom he was personally acquainted.

The Dowager Empress was perfectly satisfied with this arrangement. She never had worried about money, and she did not want to begin doing so in her old age.

Captain Andrup soon proved himself well chosen. He managed to inspire in the old Empress just that feeling of awe, of anxiety not to incur his precise disapproval, which was desirable. The system devised between Ponsonby and Andrup for keeping the court at Hvidøre solvent soon began to work with perfect success.

The establishment opened in the autumn of 1923 and, as had been anticipated, with a great gathering of the exiles and entertaining on a somewhat princely scale. Not only were deserving friends rewarded; many old servants of the imperial palaces presented themselves in hopes of a job, and the household staff and the payroll grew top-heavy.

Some months had to elapse before the balance could be adjusted and the Dowager Empress could be gently tutored to an attitude of mind in which she co-operated with the "system."

The "system" was simple. Andrup divided the £10,000 into equal monthly portions, so that Marie Fedorovna was perfectly aware how much money was available to her for all purposes each month. At the end of the month Andrup paid all salaries and household bills, which were greater or lesser in accordance with the scale of the Dowager Empress's entertainments. All that remained of the month's portion he handed over to her. She could do what she pleased with it. Thus the Dowager Empress discovered that the more economical her monthly bill for entertainment and household items, the more she had in hand for charitable purposes. She learned quickly, and serene contentment reigned at Hvidøre under unclouded financial skies.

It was in the bitterly cold and snowy days at the end of November 1925 that Queen Alexandra died peacefully at Sandringham. In the intervening period she had not been strong enough to visit her sister at Hvidøre; nor, because of the cruel weather, was it now considered feasible for the Dowager Empress to attend her last rites.

Another link had gone in the chain of Marie Fedorovna's life. The death of the sister to whom she had been so devoted and who had always come to her in trouble was a bitter blow from which she never quite revived; yet it was much less devastating than it would have been if she had been at her sister's deathbed, and if all her interests had still centered upon Sandringham and their life together there. At Hvidøre there were many other things to occupy her mind.

The Dowager Empress lived on for another three years, and gradually the tempo at Hvidore grew slower. She never ceased to talk of Nicky, Mischa, Alicky and the children as if they were somewhere around in the world and would one day arrive on the doorstep at Hvidore, perhaps in a state of destitution. She was always alert for the vague reports which sometimes in those years occurred in foreign newspapers that a mysterious person remarkably like the late Emperor of Russia had been seen in some distant place or that a drunken hobo in the United States had declared that he once ruled Russia.

She grew rather feeble and childish toward the end, sitting still for hours in her favorite chair, with her favorite family pictures hanging around her. She watched everybody with that wonderful smile in her eyes; but the look was rather puzzled now and it did not pierce to the soul. Perhaps she had never been happier and more content in her life than she was at Hvidore. Had she lived through 1928 she would have attained her eighty-second birthday, and looking back on that tremendous chronicle of triumph and bitterness, horror and tragedy which had been her life, it must have surely seemed to her a much longer span than fourscore years. She died on October 13 as peacefully as her sister Alix, and the exiles of Imperial Russia gathered at Hvidore to honor her body.

There may have been some among those who crowded her graveside, wearing old medals and orders on shabby, obsolete uniforms, who still believed that a new Imperial Russia would rise in their lifetime, but none doubted that with her passing went the last splendid figure of Old Russia.

Index